CW00650104

AUTHOR: Matthew Watson-Broughton
Born in Newcastle upon Tyne
Football journalist and translator
Lifelong Newcastle United fan

EDITOR: Tony Boullemier
Contemporary local journalist with The Journal
Successful newspaper publisher and author
Lifelong Newcastle United fan

EXECUTIVE ADVISOR: John Gibson
Award-winning Evening Chronicle journalist for more than 50 years
Author of 16 sports books
Lifelong Newcastle United fan

GRAPHIC DESIGNER: Áron Hujbert

First published in Great Britain in 2019 by
TechtoSports LTD
Clavering House, Clavering Place,
Newcastle Upon Tyne NE1 3NG

ISBN 978-1-5272-3891-6

A catalogue record for this book is available from the British Library

The book's layout and file preparation for the printing house is the work of Rézbong Bt and Áron Hujbert.

Printed in the UK by TJ International, Padstow, Cornwall.

CONTENTS

For my parents, my wife and my children.
If you're proud of my work, it's been worthwhile.

PREFACE

Thank you for picking up this book. You may have been lucky enough to have watched Newcastle United's famous Fairs Cup matches, or you may just want to learn more about how this unfancied but remarkable team conquered Europe.

I've always felt there should be something to read which really conveys all those thrills and devotes itself to reliving how Newcastle, against all the odds, won the European Inter-Cities Fairs Cup in 1969. I'd like that book to be this one.

I didn't want to come out with something predictable either. Instead, I wanted to be ambitious and creative, so I've set it back in 1969, as if the reader is a fly on the wall listening to conversations between the people who made it all happen: the players, managers, fans and journalists.

The Fairs Cup dialogue is based on accurate, authentic quotes from many interviews with the protagonists as well as from contemporary sources. To create a whole book of dialogue though, I've sometimes had to use sentences which were only ever supposed to be read, for example from the journalists.

Therefore, please be patient with certain conversations where it might be difficult to imagine a person saying those words out loud – when that happens, you can be sure it was originally written down.

Still, it's worth including this content because it gives us more insight into what happened. Similarly, I've had to ensure dialogue runs smoothly by imagining some greetings and 'link' phrases. Furthermore, some of the foreign conversations take place in settings created just to provide a plausible backdrop. The essence and real value of this book is in what the key personalities really thought, wrote and said.

I hope you enjoy this work. As well as to inform and to entertain, it's here to pay tribute to the finalists and to our heroes, Bob Moncur's winners.

TELEPHONE
NEWCASTLE [illegible]

TELEGRAMS.
"FOOTBALL NEWCASTLE"

NEWCASTLE UNITED FOOTBALL CO. LTD.

WINNERS, F.A. CUP, 1910 - 1924 - 1932 - 1951 - 1952
1955
LEAGUE CHAMPIONS, 1904-5 1906-7 1908-9 1926-27
F.A. CUP FINALISTS, 1905 - 1906 - 1908 - 1911.

J. D. BARKER,
SECRETARY

Registered Office,
ST. JAMES PARK,
NEWCASTLE-ON-TYNE, 1.

P. Arentoft, Esq.,

20th June, 1969.

Dear Ben,

EUROPEAN FAIRS CUP 1969 - CELEBRATION

The Directors take great pleasure in inviting you and partner to attend a Celebration Dinner and Dance on Tuesday, 15th July, 1969, at Michael's Club, Northumberland Street, 7.15 p.m. for 7.45 p.m.

It would be most appreciated if you could kindly complete the tear-off slip below to confirm your acceptance in order that catering arrangements may be completed.

Yours sincerely,

J.D. BARKER

Secretary

Newcastle United's official letter inviting players to the celebration banquet at Michael's Club on 15th July (letter courtesy of Benny Arentoft)

INTRODUCTION

It is the summer of 1969 and Newcastle United's Welsh international centre forward Wyn Davies is finally out of hospital.

He'd fractured his cheekbone in the first leg of the Fairs Cup final and soldiered on with it throughout the epic return match in Budapest.

Now his club has decided to give him and everyone else another chance to celebrate that sensational victory. The Newcastle United family is heading for one of the city's most popular and upmarket nightspots, Michael's Club on Northumberland Street, for a celebratory banquet, some dancing and no doubt many nostalgic drinks.

Here, we recreate this unique event and, using extensive quotes from the club's playing heroes, tell the inside story of how the trophy was won. Further contributions from journalists, fans, local celebrities and even the police help us paint a definitive picture of what happened 50 years ago. We'll also join similar social gatherings around Europe and hear detailed analysis from players of all six opponents who tried – and failed – to stop the Newcastle United juggernaut.

Serving the drinks are the previously uninformed – but now curious – bar manager and his keen young barmen. They already know much of the Fairs Cup story, having attended many of the games and meticulously kept scrapbooks of the local and international media coverage, which they've brought in to show to everyone.

Crucially, John Gibson, the erstwhile Evening Chronicle journalist, who was at every match in this Fairs Cup campaign and without whose valuable help this definitive account could not have been written, is cast as the omnipresent hack with his finger on the pulse. He holds court at the journalists' table with a glass of wine, sharing stories with his Press pals and always ready to tell us how he and others reported on the campaign.

We start with 'Gibbo' – the first to arrive in Michael's Club that balmy summer evening at around 7pm. He gets a drink for a colleague from Fleet Street and they hark back to where it all began...

Trio write about the North-East's Big Two

STRICTLY NEUTRAL by Geoff Whitten

Europe? It's 3-1 against United

...a toss-up which is ...more unlikely—a ...in the First Divi- ...for Sunderland next ...n or a place in ...pe for Newcastle ...d next season.

...even if Sunderland ...lost at Wolverhampton ...afternoon I shall still ...their chances rather than Newcastle's which ...ld rate as at least 3-1 ...t.

...pessimistic am I, United ... Well, let's have a long, ...ook at the facts.

...that Leeds United have ...he Football League Cup ...possible that the club ...ng in fifth position in ...rst Division will get one ...three places in the Inter-Fairs Cup.

...assumes that the F.A. ...won by one of the clubs ...higher than fifth in the ...e and that Leeds also ...win the F.A. Cup or finish in the first four of the League.

If any of those conditions do not apply, then no club below fourth in the First Division would have a chance of a Fairs Cup place. In my view, that would almost certainly rule out Newcastle.

Top four

Let us assume, then, that fifth place will be good enough. Having studied the prospects carefully and in detail, it seems very probable to me that the top four places will be filled by Manchester United, Leeds, Liverpool and Manchester City, though not necessarily in that order.

That, in my view, would leave four clubs—Newcastle Tottenham, Everton and West Bromwich—to fight it out for the remaining European spot.

I have tabulated here the programmes facing these four clubs up to the end of the season and what they indicate to me is that the other three all look likely to be more productive of points then United's run-in programme.

The question is, though, whether they will prove productive enough to close the present gap between these three and Newcastle, West Bromwich being five points behind, Everton four behind and Tottenham three behind.

The odds must surely be that at least one of them will draw level on points—and if it should be either Everton or West Brom. that would be enough, since both have decidedly better goal ratios than United.

A closer look at the matches to come reveals that, of these four clubs, only Newcastle still have to meet each of the others at least once.

There are in fact, five key matches that might well decide the whole issue—and United figure in four of them. Here they are:

March 16: West Brom. v. Everton.

March 23: Everton v Newcastle.

April 12: Newcastle v West Brom.

April 15: West Brom. v Newcastle.

April 27: Newcastle v Tottenham.

So it can be truly said that, to a greater extent than might be expected, Newcastle's future is in their own hands. But to achieve what is necessary they will, in my estimation, need to win more than four points from the four key matches in which they are concerned, and that will not be easy.

The two Easter games against West Bromwich are obviously particularly vital and it will be surprising if the issue is very much in doubt by the evening of Monday April 15.

As I said at the start, I do not think it is being unduly pessimistic to say the odds are against United making it.

They might, indeed, do well to finish higher than eighth in the final table—which will still be a good deal better performance than almost anybody expected from them seven months ago.

MATCHES TO COME FOR UNITED AND THEIR RIVALS

Newcastle		Tottenham		Everton		West Brom.	
HOME	AWAY	HOME	AWAY	HOME	AWAY	HOME	AWAY
Leeds	Everton	Stoke	Nottgm. For.	Newcastle	West Brom.	Everton	Leicester
Leicester	West Ham	Southampton	Liverpool	Arsenal	Man. City	Sunderland	Burnley
West Brom.	West Brom.	Leeds	Chelsea	Sheff. Wed.	Sheff. Utd.	West Ham	Newcastle
Burnley	Fulham	Coventry	Leeds	Chelsea	Sheff. Wed.	Sheff. Wed.	Leeds
Tottenham	Man. Utd.	Man. City	Newcastle	Stoke	Nottgm. For.	Newcastle	Sunderland
Man. City.		Burnley	Wolves	Leicester	West Ham	Man. Utd.	Arsenal
				Fulham		Stoke	

NEWCASTLE by John Gibson

UNITED RESULTS,

Geoff Whitten's article raising the possibility of European qualification (credit: Chronicle Live)

Ifs and buts

IS it not possible for the top six in the First Division to enter Europe? If a club no lower than fifth win the F.A. Cup and Manchester United win the European Cup but don't win the championship, the position then might be:

1—European Cup (Division I winners); 2—European Cup (holders); 3—European Cup-winners' Cup (F.A. Cup winners); 4, 5 and 6—Inter-Cities Fairs Cup.

Also, if Manchester United should win both the European Cup and the League championship, do not the First Division runners-up qualify for the European Cup?—**R. BRANCH, Wallsend.**

We think all your suppositions are correct, but the possible combinations of "ifs and buts" are so numerous that there is little point in further speculation at the moment. — SPORTS EDITOR.

The letter in The Pink which alerted The Daily Mail's Doug Weatherall to unlikely prospect of Newcastle United reaching the Fairs Cup (credit: Chronicle Live)

INTRODUCTION

THE CLUB CELEBRATION DINNER, 15TH JULY 1969

BAR MANAGER: Good Evening, gentlemen. What can I get you?
GIBBO: Two house white wines please, young man. **(to Doug Weatherall of the Daily Mail)** It's good to hear Wyn's out of hospital, isn't it? I tell you what, this promises to be a cracking evening. Do you remember where this all started?
DOUG WEATHERALL: Well, of course, the Chronicle first mentioned the possibility of qualifying for Europe and I then pinched the idea as I thought it would make a good article...
BARMAN 1: I remember that! Is this it?
DOUG WEATHERALL: No, Geoff Whitten's article from the week before (pictured opposite at the top) wasn't what alerted me... this letter in the Pink (also pictured opposite) was though:
That's quite some scrapbook you've got there, young man.
BARMAN 1 (beaming): Thank you, I kept all the match reports and asked people to bring me back newspapers from the away games. And this is your original article, Mr Weatherall. From that moment on, me and my mates debated our chances after every First Division result, but we thought the game was up after one win in 12 and five straight losses at the end of the 1967/68 season...
GIBBO: We all did!
TONY BOULLEMIER of the Newcastle Journal: Did you know that the Inter-Cities Fairs Cup was first dreamt up as a competition for cities holding international trade fairs? One club from each city could take part, so after taking out the teams that had qualified for the other two European competitions, you looked down the table to find England's representatives.
In 1968, Manchester City were English league champions so they were in the European Cup along with Manchester United, who'd just won that competition so qualified as holders.

NEWCASTLE UNITED
CELEBRATION DINNER
on the occasion of their
success in the
INTER CITIES FAIRS CUP
1969

MICHAEL'S CLUB · NEWCASTLE UPON TYNE · JULY 15th · 1969 · 7-30 P.M.

A black and white copy of the official club celebration banquet at Michael's Club on 15th July 1969 (menu courtesy of Benny Arentoft)

Manchester United were also First Division runners-up, so third-placed Liverpool got the *first* Fairs Cup place and Leeds behind them got the *second* one. Fifth-placed Everton couldn't qualify because city rivals Liverpool were already in, so that let in sixth-placed Chelsea for the *third* Fairs Cup spot.

It looked like the Fairs Cup committee might expand the competition from 48 to 64 teams so that would leave one extra place. As West Brom had won the FA Cup, they were going to play in the Cup Winners Cup. Spurs and Arsenal were ruled out because Chelsea were already in the Fairs Cup as London's representative.

So everyone looked down to see who'd finished 10th... and there was Newcastle United. That's how we got in.

GIBBO: Even then, it came as a tremendous surprise after Sir Stanley Rous, who was Fairs Cup chairman and FIFA president, voiced his disapproval at expanding the tournament. He went out on a limb in saying only three English clubs would be admitted – probably Leeds, Liverpool and Chelsea. Newcastle United's name was conspicuous by its absence.

It was hardly surprising that while Leeds and other clubs sent out deputations to Copenhagen for the meeting of the Fairs Cup committee, United didn't bother. Instead, they relied on me to find out their fate! The indication of whether United had been accepted would come with the actual draw. If United's name didn't appear, they were out.

Then came that wonderful fax from Copenhagen. In Group 13, Newcastle United were to play Feyenoord from Rotterdam; evidently, the Fairs Cup Executive had decided to increase the number of entries from 48 to 64. That meant we'd be the North-East's first representatives in Europe and we'd meet this crack Dutch team home and away in the first round.

At this point, a few of the players and club officials start to arrive, amongst them captain Bob Moncur, Tommy Gibb and Bryan 'Pop'

Robson with their wives. They see Tony Boullemier and, amidst smiles and chuckles, start in unison to sing the opening bars of the famous hit song by Newcastle group The Animals:

'There is a house
in New Orleans
they call the
Ri-sing Sun!'

GIBBO (smiling): Hey now, hold your horses – stories from Budapest are for later! Nice to see you **(handshakes all round)**. Bob, we're just talking about when we heard we'd made it into Europe. When did you hear?

BOB MONCUR: I was away. We'd finished 10th in the league and Manchester City had won the title on the last day when they beat us 4-3 at St James' Park. So I was away on holiday when I got a call saying *'Just to let you know, we're in Europe'*. I said: '*You're kidding! How's that happened?*' But that's how it had worked out.

I've got to say that at the time I thought: 'Ah, that's fine. It's a bonus experience to be playing in Europe but we'll not last long.' The thing that gave it momentum was that the first game was against one of the best sides in the world; Feyenoord are a great team.

GIBBO: Too right they are! Pop, not many people know that your nickname since childhood comes from the phrase 'snap, crackle and pop' but tell us another secret, would you? How did you suddenly go from the fringes of the squad to being one of our most crucial players?

BRYAN POP ROBSON: Yeah, I was in and out of the team, but I was still only 23. I was also a really keen golfer. We get 12 weeks off at the end of a season and we don't go on tours like other teams do, so in previous years that'd be my golf season when I'd be down the golf course at 9am, playing in the afternoon, then playing with my mates in the evening after they'd finished work.

I got down to a 2 or 3 handicap through playing every day. I became club champion at Prudhoe and won events on Tyneside. Then I played in the Professional Footballers' Championship. We had to go down to Sand Moor Golf Club in Leeds for qualifying and then to Coventry for the main tournament. And I won it.

I starting thinking: 'This is great, like; you're on your own, you can play when you want.' However, I then started going out with Maureen. Before we got married, my future father-in-law Lennie Hepple said to me: *'So you're going to play golf but you're on 45 quid a week now – where are you going to get that sort of money in golf?'* I said: '*Well, I'll work in a shop.*' To which he replied: '*Why don't you have a real good go at your football instead of playing golf?'*

So last summer I didn't play any golf at all and trained two or three times a day instead. It wasn't about pounding the roads, although I would stick a run in now and then. It was balance training and speed training because Lennie was a dancer, so we practised getting my balance position right, my body ready, being on the balls of my feet and ready to receive the ball and turn. I had to walk around like that all the time. Also, making contact with players, getting involved, pushing and shoving. When people like George Best were dribbling, their arms would be out, which would have a screening effect. So we worked on that.

Maureen's a top table tennis player – she was England junior number 1 and then number 3 in the seniors – so I started playing table tennis really well too.

At one point, I went on holiday to Majorca with Frank Clark. He'd picked up a newspaper and found out we'd qualified for Europe, which was fantastic news but I wasn't a regular in the team. In Majorca, we'd play a little 1 v 1 game involving dribbling and tackling on a bit of ground outside the hotel – not even on grass but on a kind of shale car park area.

Well, soon, Frank started complaining about my tackling. I did do a little bit of dodgy block tackling at one point – which was good because Lennie had said: *'I want players to complain about you pushing and shoving and getting involved because right now you're just running around. You're not involved, you're not having physical contact, but you need this in your arms and your balance to dribble with the ball.'*

He had me dribbling with the ball in and out of cones, using the outside of my right foot. But he said I needed physical contact so it started with Frank on that holiday. From then on, players started complaining and telling me to keep my arms down but it was what I needed to do.

That was the idea of trying to screen the ball and it meant I obviously had more touches and became a more popular player by scoring goals and retaining the ball and dribbling. I could always pass it and I'm a good striker of the ball but before, I never stayed in games much or had enough confidence.

Lennie would watch me play; not the game, just me all the time and how I was moving. Sometimes I'd get slagged off if I missed a chance. I'd read *'Robson misses a sitter'* in the papers but Lennie would say: *'Yes... but you played really well. You had loads of touches, your footwork was really sharp, you made some good passes.'* It kind of gave me confidence, instead of being slagged off by a headline in the Press.

Little did I know that Stan Anderson had been in touch with the club about buying me. He'd become player-manager at Middlesborough and I'd played with him at Newcastle where he'd been a massive influence on Joe Harvey and assistant coach Jimmy Greenhaugh in terms of getting young players into the team. He could have bought me for £15,000 but he said it was too much.

So those were the two early influences in that season and obviously qualifying for Europe from 10th position. Hearing that Stan Anderson wouldn't even pay £15,000 for me made me think: 'Better start sticking in at my football now, like, and seeing just where it takes me.'

I was really flying in pre-season and people were surprised how fit I was. I was at the front of all the running exercises and this work I'd put in was allowing me to be sharp in the box and be quick in front of defenders because I was well balanced.

The first game in the 1968/69 season was West Ham and I was sub, but I came on and scored in a 1-1 draw. Then I scored in the next game at Sheffield Wednesday and twice at home against Chelsea. More goals followed, which gave me the confidence to carry on and have a fantastic season. That's how I got into the team for the Fairs Cup.

TOMMY GIBB: Well, the season started on the Saturday and I'd been doon since the Monday – I'd signed from Partick Thistle the previous Friday and went home for the weekend before heading down to Newcastle at the start of the week. Dave Elliott had been injured in the first game at home to West Ham, so I played all the games after that, wearing the number 4 shirt.

At this moment, manager Joe Harvey passes the group on the way to his table. After overhearing Tommy and greeting everyone, he adds his thoughts:

JOE HARVEY: Actually I viewed Tommy as a valuable member of our pool who could be brought into the team any time we suffered an injury. I never expected him to come in so soon and stay in but he's done such a good job that I can't drop him. He's a real worker – a 90-minute man who doesn't need a breather.

Just then, a glass is tapped.

ANNOUNCEMENT: Would the ladies and gentlemen like to make their way to their seats please. Dinner is due to be served.

The bar runs down one side of the big room with the tables in the middle; they'll be removed from the dance floor which will host the cabaret and dancing later on.

LORD WESTWOOD (to everyone): Dear Ladies and Gentlemen, just a few weeks ago Newcastle United carved out a fresh chapter in their already illustrious history with a never-to-be-forgotten rally in Budapest to win the Inter-Cities Fairs Cup. It was a night which will stay with me for ever **(cheers all around the room).**
As celebrations went on and on in our hotel on Margaret Island, I felt proud to be associated with a great bunch of lads who had done so much to restore Newcastle's image in the eyes of the soccer world. Winning the Fairs Cup is a moment which will figure prominently in United's history.
I'd like us all to bask tonight in this victory and look back at our favourite memories of a long, exhaustive but glorious season. As we can see on these wonderful menus in front of us, first up on the menu is our appetiser 'Prawn Cocktail Feyenoord' and this is where we shall start.

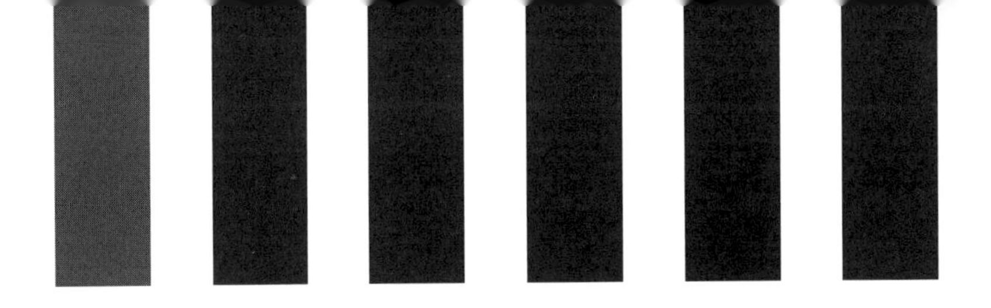

FAIRS CUP 1ST ROUND

NEWCASTLE UNITED
v
FEYENOORD

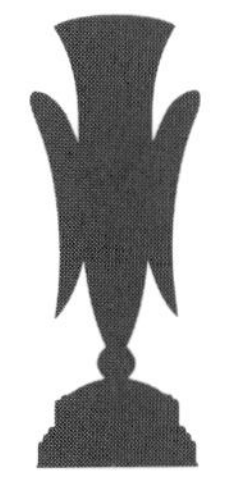

FEYENOORD AT HOME...

INTER-CITIES FAIRS CUP 1ST ROUND 1ST LEG

NEWCASTLE UNITED 4

FEYENOORD 0

Kick-off: 19:30, Wednesday 11th September 1968
Referee: Hans Carlsson (Sweden)
Venue: St James' Park, Newcastle upon Tyne, England
Attendance: 46,348

Newcastle United: Willie McFaul; David Craig, John McNamee. Ollie Burton, Frank Clark (c); Dave Elliott, Tommy Gibb; Jim Scott, Wyn Davies, Bryan Robson, Geoff Allen
Substitutes not used: Gordon Marshall (GK), Jim Iley, Jackie Sinclair

Feyenoord: Eddy Pieters Graafland; Frans van der Heide, Rinus Israël, Theo Laseroms, Cor Veldhoen (c); Jan Boskamp, Wim Jansen, Willem van Hanegem (Ruud Geels 67); Henk Wery, Ove Kindvall, Coen Moulijn
Substitutes not used: Eddy Treijtel (GK), Pieter Romeijn

Goalscorers:
1-0 Scott (7)
2-0 Robson (35)
3-0 Gibb (42)
4-0 Davies (70)

MICHAEL'S CLUB ON NORTHUMBERLAND STREET, NEWCASTLE UNITED'S CELEBRATORY FAIRS CUP VICTORY GALA BANQUET

The starter course has been served. The three bar staff are together at the bar which is a few metres from the dining area and dance floor.

BAR MANAGER (to his two barmen): So alright, Newcastle and Feyenoord were in it, but which other teams were in the draw for the first round?
Any I might have heard of? Or was it not quite the creme de la creme?
BARMAN 1: Boss… it was packed with top teams – that's what makes winning it so special.
BARMAN 2: So from here, we had Shankly's Liverpool, Don Revie's Leeds and Chelsea from down south. From Scotland, there were the likes of Rangers, who'd already been in two European finals. From abroad, how about Juventus? Or Athletico Madrid?
BAR MANAGER: Really? Get away!
BARMAN 1: Or try Marseille or Valencia. Or Sporting Lisbon. Or Napoli.
BAR MANAGER: Are you having me on? These famous clubs were in there too?
BARMAN 2: And what would you say if the top teams now in Italy, England, Holland, Poland, Hungary and Greece were going for the Fairs Cup last season while winning their championships?
BAR MANAGER: Now I know you're winding me up. Go away and take some drinks orders!

The two young lads walk off indignantly towards the tables

BARMAN 2: Why doesn't he believe me? Fiorentina, Feyenoord, Legia Warsaw, Újpest Dózsa and Panathinaikos – they were there too.
BARMAN 1: And we didn't even get to Hamburg, Dinamo Zagreb, Athletic Bilbao, Lyon or Leipzig – or tell him that a third of our

rivals in the competition had already experienced a European semi-final. He must realise now though that this was a top tournament.

In fact, Jackie Charlton wrote something I really agreed with when he said the Fairs Cup is so tough because teams that finish second or third in one season often go one better the following year and win their championships, so these champions are in the Fairs Cup at the same time. Anyway, you go and serve the directors, I'll go to the first players' table. Have you got the layout there?

BARMAN 2: Yes, I've quickly written a table plan now that everyone's sat down so we know where to deliver drinks. Here it is:

Table 1, the top table, is Lord Westwood, the rest of the club directors, Joe Harvey and partners;

Table 2 is Bob Moncur, David Craig, Willie McFaul, Bryan Pop Robson, Jim Scott, Frank Clark;

Table 3 is Wyn the Leap, Dave Elliott, Tommy Gibb, Ollie Burton, Big John McNamee and Jackie Sinclair;

Table 4 is a bit bigger: Benny Arentoft is sitting next to Ron Guthrie with Alan Foggon, Keith Dyson, Geoff Allen, Tot Winstanley, John Craggs, Dave Clarke and John Hope there too, plus Jim Iley, Arthur Horsfield, Albert Bennett and Gordon Marshall, who've come along despite having transferred to other clubs since they played for us in Europe – it's nice to see them again.

Table 5 is where the backroom staff are: First-team coach Dave Smith, reserve-team coach Keith Burkinshaw, juniors coach Benny Craig, physiotherapist Alec Mutch, Joe Richardson, plus others from behind the scenes.

On the journalists' table we can see Gibbo (John Gibson), Doug Weatherall, Tony Boullemier, Ivor Broadis, Jackie Milburn, Tony Hardisty and others.

All the other tables are for the reserves and juniors.

BARMAN 1: OK, see you back at the bar in a few minutes.

On the journalists' table:

GIBBO: Well, it seems a lifetime ago now, but the build up to United's adventure into the unknown was depressing to say the least.
If we're going into specifics, Bob Moncur, our defensive rock, was carried off in Edinburgh during the first half of a pre-season friendly with Hibernian and very soon we all knew it meant a cartilage operation on his right knee.
Added to this was Albert Bennett, who, in the opening First Division match of the season at home to West Ham, didn't see half-time either. Do you remember, he'd been playing his first league game for seven months following an identical operation to Bob's, but badly twisted the same knee? That was two key men out before the 1968/69 season was a day old. No wonder Joe winced!
TONY BOULLEMIER: And the team was going through a transitional period, wasn't it?
GIBBO: You're bloomin' right it was. Experienced campaigners such as Gordon Marshall, Jim Iley and Tommy Robson were fading rapidly, so it meant that half the team that had got them into Europe were viewing things from a distance.
In came Willie McFaul in goal, the Irishman whose future had seemed as bright as a coalmine at midnight; Geoff Allen, whom I called a shy, ruddy-faced 21-year-old winger with 11 senior appearances scattered over five years; Bryan 'Pop' Robson, discarded the previous season but dusted down and brought back with devastating effect; and Tommy Gibb, a lanky midfielder who, as our only major signing last summer, arrived on the eve of the season from Partick Thistle for £25,000 plus £10,000 in add-ons.
Mind, these men, together with Ollie Burton, the permanent stand-in who took over Moncur's sweeper job against Feyenoord, achieved a standard of personal success few of us really expected.

▌1ST ROUND 1ST LEG▐

TONY BOULLEMIER: When Willie heard Newcastle were in the cup draw and were playing Feyenoord, his first reaction was that he'd be on the bench again in case regular keeper Gordon Marshall was injured. In the event, though, he got the nod.
GIBBO: And McFaul surprised everyone with some great displays early on. There were problems elsewhere though – Jim Scott had only played 20 minutes of football in the first six league games of last season and I remember he told me:
'I've spoken with the chief and he's agreed to help me get a new club – I've made it plain that at my age reserve-team football is no good to me. How can I prove myself in these circumstances? I'm working like a beaver every day in training and then never kicking a ball.'
Jackie Sinclair was also unhappy at being unable to hold down a starting place. Wyn was the subject of interest from Coventry City. Ollie Burton was battling a groin injury, Pop Robson and David Craig had hamstring and thigh niggles respectively and the team had only scored 10 goals in the first nine games!
You can't fault Jim Scott's predictions though… he also told me:
'I'll get into this team sometime… and when I do, I won't be shifted easily.'
If we take a look at the lineups for the first leg versus Feyenoord at home in that young man's scrapbook…
Excuse me, son **(as the barman passes the journalists)**, could we borrow that scrapbook of yours? I'll give it back in a moment. **(receives it)** Thank you.
… we can see Scottie forced his way in on the right wing in a 4-2-4 formation. McFaul was in goal behind a back four of Clark on the left, Craig on the right, McNamee and Burton as the centre-backs with the latter sweeping; Gibb and Elliott in central midfield behind Wyn and Pop upfront, Allen on the left and Scott on the right. A decent enough eleven, eh?
As for the opposition, well, Joe and some of us hacks here went to see Feyenoord in their first home match of the league season, a routine 3-0

win over DWS, managed by Englishman Leslie Talbot and featuring their young star Robbie Rensenbrink, after which Joe said:
'*It was a good win and Feyenoord are technically a good side; the best players were outside-left Moulijn and right-half Jan Boskamp. It was too easy for Feyenoord against DWS but the two games between Newcastle United and Feyenoord will be very interesting because of the differing styles of English and Dutch football.*'

THE SCENE MOVES TO THE DUTCH CITY OF ROTTERDAM ON THE SAME EVENING, 15TH JULY 1969

Young sports journalist Mark Meijer has been tasked by his newspaper to interview some key players for a review of Feyenoord's outstandingly successful domestic season in 1968/69. To do this, he's been allowed to join a farewell dinner for their likeable utility player Frans van der Heide, who is moving to another top-flight club, Holland Sport, in search of more first-team football.

MARK: Mr Van der Heide, thank you so much for letting me join you here.
FRANS: You're very welcome, young man. Call me Frans. I hear you're looking for some information on last season? Well, I'm here now and first-choice goalkeeper Eddy Pieters Graafland and central defender Rinus Israël are already here too, so maybe now is a good time for your questions before more people arrive...
MARK: That's great, thank you. Nice to meet you too **(shakes Eddy's and Rinus's hands)**. Thank you for agreeing to talk to me. The Eredivisie season had started well with four wins from four league matches, but then came that Fairs Cup first round tie against Newcastle United. How was the build-up to that first leg in England?

▌1ST ROUND 1ST LEG ▌

FRANS: Well, last summer, Feyenoord signed a group of us from a club called Xerxes, including myself, Willem van Hanegem and second goalkeeper Eddy Treijtel. Earlier, we'd actually beaten Feyenoord 1-0 in the Eredivisie, so that may have helped the move happen. At Xerxes, I'd always been a midfielder but I've always been played as a right-back at Feyenoord, ever since I'd come through the youth setup here. Pieter Romeijn was my competitor for the right-back position but I started in the first match in Newcastle because I was holding the jersey at the time.

Life as a footballer is different for me, mind, because throughout my career I've only been a semi-professional, even at Feyenoord. I work from 6am in the morning until 1pm before I go to football training. I have a job to supplement my income and I work in the family painting and decorating business, like my father and grandfather. There's a responsibility to carry on the line there.

EDDY PIETERS-GRAAFLAND: We're really talking about Feyenoord's golden period, this period of the 1960s and now. When I came here from Ajax in 1958 – where I'd already played in the European Cup against Vasas of Budapest – Feyenoord were already good and had just been lacking a reliable goalkeeper. With that solved, we embarked on a run of several league titles and now two league and cup doubles, so these have been great years with some very strong lineups.

FRANS: Of course, for me, European football had been a big attraction to coming back to Feyenoord, who, you'll remember, had finished runners-up to champions Ajax the previous season. Prior to the Newcastle tie, we'd narrowly lost to Belgian champions Anderlecht and comfortably beaten French title-holders St. Etienne in friendlies and I'd received lots of compliments for my displays.

RINUS ISRAËL: Since we're discussing backgrounds, I'd actually come to Feyenoord from DWS Amsterdam where we'd been champions in 1963-64. In the following season's European Cup, we were knocked out in the quarter-finals by RÁBA ETO Győr, managed by the great Hungarian forward Nándor Hidegkuti. Prior to 1968, hardly any of us had any experience of playing English clubs in European competition.

MARK: Did the players really take the Fairs Cup seriously at the start?

RINUS: No. That was our mistake. We treated the game in Newcastle like we would a friendly match and we never expected them to be so strong. There was a very tall striker called Davies whom we tried to stop by heading the ball and kicking him, but he was too strong for us. Even when I was climbing on the shoulders of our other central defender, Theo Laseroms, and jumping, I would still lose the heading duels. He was unbelievable, but the most important thing was that we just weren't concentrating in this game.

FRANS: I also feel we were complacent. The staff exuded this feeling and the players picked it up from them. It was a big mistake from them. Our coach Ben Peeters wouldn't make this mistake again.

EDDY: Well, I don't believe we didn't take it seriously because for me, all games were serious. Sometimes the opponent's name wasn't as familiar to us as that of others, so that might have been the difference... By the way, a word on Ben Peeters. In 1967, all the players wanted him as our next manager so we went to the board to ask for him to be appointed. We all liked the way he trained us so we supported him off the pitch. For example, he had a very small, old car and no suit to wear, so we bought him a new radio, a suit and things like that. We really liked him as coach and particularly that he was focused on conditioning. We already knew we could play football, so what we really wanted was someone to help us with the physical side instead. That's why the board accepted our request.

RINUS: Peeters wasn't a strong personality though. OK, with him, we won the league and cup in 1968/69 but it wasn't enough – now he's gone and Austrian Ernst Happel has come in. Peeters had no experience of coaching a first team, having moved up from the club's youth setup.

▌1ST ROUND 1ST LEG ▌

EDDY: It's true, we'd been getting better but there came a point when it felt like 'the stretch had gone from the elastic', that, you know, he'd taken us as far as he could. That's why I think the board took the decision to bring in Happel, who'll lead us in the European Cup next season.

FRANS: Yes, Peeters was able to bring us success on the domestic front but we need something more on the international stage. There are plenty of experienced players together there and they decide how we play; there's a lot of player power. The team is close-knit though so we often decide things together, not in small cliques or groups.

If we go back to the Fairs Cup first match, the day we arrived in Newcastle we rested, then the day before the match we trained. I remember the hotel was a nice hotel – the Gosforth Park. The day before the match – my birthday actually – we trained in St James' Park where it was raining and the grass was slippy.

On matchday, we didn't wake up too early. We went for a walk in the hotel grounds before heading to the stadium for the match. That evening, the players decided how we'd play – we made our own decisions. For example, the coach told us to play with three midfielders spread out across the pitch but we decided that we'd be more compact and squeeze inside rather than cover their wingers. This was a tactical misjudgement.

MARK: The team used a 4-3-3 formation that evening. Having read the match report in my newspaper, Frans, it sounds like you were given a tough task in stopping their left winger Geoff Allen…

FRANS: You know… head coach Ben Peeters, his boss Guus Brox and scout Fred Blankemeijer all told me that Newcastle's left-winger wasn't very good and that I didn't need to worry about him! They'd seen recent matches of his and concluded I'd take care of him without a problem. Now I wish they'd told me it would be tough so that I'd have played better against him.

In truth, Geoff Allen was very quick and tricky. The pitch was wet and slippy so it didn't help me, but he was small so he had an advantage. My first tackle was good but after that he kept getting away. On that heavy pitch, he was simply too fast – he was much lighter and could move quicker than me. He would knock it past me and run on to it, but it was also about his tricks.

The right-sided of the three central midfielders, Jan Boskamp, wasn't doing great either – he wasn't coming over to help but rather he'd stay more central and then wonder what to do when he'd been caught between two opponents; a central midfielder and Allen on the wing.

He would regularly let Allen go – the whole concentration, the focus, was missing so there were often moments when he'd burst through and I'd be faced by two men, which caused difficulties. The connection between midfielder and defender was missing.

EDDY: Frans playing for us at right-back was OK without being ideal. He's a more technical player who would try to play football when under pressure, rather than be the big, robust defender who would simply clear the ball into the stands.

RINUS: We weren't worried about a midfielder playing at right-back though – our team was confident enough not to be worried about anything.

MICHAEL'S CLUB, NEWCASTLE UPON TYNE

We are a fly on the wall, listening to conversations between players, officials and their partners at various tables on the first match against Feyenoord at home...

GIBBO: Feyenoord had only lost one out of 16 home matches in Europe before this season, so everyone on Tyneside knew Harvey's men had to aim for a good lead to take to Rotterdam. And my, didn't they do that in style!

BRYAN POP ROBSON: Everybody was so excited. No one knew what was going to happen. People were after tickets… you sensed there would be an atmosphere. Feyenoord were a well-respected European team but we knew nothing about them and didn't realise how good their players were. For their part, they were probably shaken up a little bit by the atmosphere at St James'.

Geoff Allen had a really blinding game and surprised everyone. He was taking the ball all the time and was so confident, which was surprising because he hadn't played many games. His crosses were coming in though, so they had to try to stop him. They didn't manage to stop him in the first half though, so when his crosses came in, we were on top of them and we took an early lead. We were pressing all the time in that atmosphere, but it wasn't organised... it was just raw enthusiasm. It wasn't something we'd done in training, it was just that the atmosphere and the adrenalin took a hold of us really.

JOHN CRAGGS: I didn't play in this one but I remember in the lead-up to the home leg, the Press were advising us to just go out there and defend; keep it tight. However, we went out there, played our normal game and won 4-0. They said you're not supposed to play like that.

GEOFF ALLEN: Well, it was the start, wasn't, it? I was determined to make it my season. I knew I had to do something. I'd been in the shadows for far too long. Joe Harvey just said to us: *'Get yourselves out there and just show them what you can do'* and everybody did. It was like a tsunami hitting Feyenoord; they just didn't know what to do! We just went at them at the start.

Our first European night, the floodlights, the crowd... it was electric. They couldn't get their breath – it was a rampage, an onslaught. The first time I got the ball, their right-back, Van der Heide, came a bit too close and I went by him so I thought: 'OK, let's see what happens now', and it just got better and better.

It didn't matter where he was, I just seemed to go by him at will. Then they sent another player across so I thought: 'Well, that's another one out of the game'... and I went past him as well. Others kept winning the ball and giving it to me and they just didn't have an answer to it.

After about seven minutes, Wyn nodded the ball down to Pop who sent it out wide, I crossed the ball low and hard for Jim Scott and he scored our very first goal in European football. What a great feeling that was!

JIM SCOTT: You had the right-back on toast, Geoff. The ball came across the goal about six yards out and I side-footed it in, having come in off the right wing. I'm not saying it was a great goal but we'd scored and we were up and running. My older brother came up from Bury and my mum and dad came down too so they saw me score.

GEOFF ALLEN: Then it got worse for them. They just didn't know what had hit them. We were making runs, they weren't winning the ball in midfield and their forwards, I mean, they might as well not have been there. They never got a kick.

GIBBO: Joe's men pushed for a second and Tommy Gibb saw a piledriver punched away by bewildered goalkeeper Graafland. Dave Elliott blazed inches wide after Geoff Allen had run two defenders ragged, Geoff himself hit the crossbar and Laseroms cracked the ball against his own post with Graafland at full stretch.

GEOFF ALLEN: So everything just went fantastic. They didn't know where it was coming from – it was unbelievable. And the crowd... as a local lad, to hear 46,000 Geordies shouting... it makes the hairs on your neck stand up and if you can't get up for it after that... but nobody had any nerves. No nerves at all. We were just eager to get out there.

FRANK CLARK: We played with no fear really.
DAVID CRAIG: And Geoff just had one of those games, didn't he? He just tore the right-back to pieces, so he did. Tore him to pieces. I'd played against Geoff quite a lot in training and he was a good player – he was quick, had a nice turn of pace and he was clever. He just had one of those nights where everything went right for him. He just kept taking them on, getting past them and knocking it in and somebody was getting on the end of it.
Bob, you missed the Feyenoord games because you'd had your cartilage out, hadn't you? Mind, it should have taken you six weeks to recover and you played in the reserves after only a fortnight, isn't that so?
BOB MONCUR: Aye, that's right. When we played them here, I was actually in the Paddock watching the game with the punters.

DAVE ELLIOTT: For my part, I'd moved to left of central midfield and was playing behind Geoff Allen that night. Geoff played out of his skin and was superb – it was a typical left winger's performance, taking the ball up to the full-back and beating him for pace and skill on the outside.

GEOFF ALLEN: I remember Israël, the big centre-half who's a Dutch international, going up for a header with John McNamee when they clashed in the air. One of the players asked him if he was alright, to which he replied: '*I think he's broken my head!*'

DOUG WEATHERALL: After 35 minutes, Wyn's shot from 20 yards rebounded from a post to Bryan Robson, who dived forward to head in. Then there was Tommy Gibb. His shot glanced in off defender Israël for the third goal on 42 minutes after another clever Scott dribble. I remember the Dutch journalists saying at half-time: *'They'll never believe this score in Holland...'*

BACK IN ROTTERDAM, FRANS, RINUS AND EDDY ARE EXPLAINING HOW THEY FELT AS THE FIRST HALF CAME TO AN END.

FRANS: No one was angry at half-time – we were just surprised and shocked. It had rarely, if ever, happened to any of the players that they'd be 3-0 down after 45 minutes.

EDDY: It's true. I don't remember ever having being 3-0 down at half-time.

FRANS: The coach was of no use at this point though. He didn't say anything and the players didn't know what to do. I've experienced coaches who shout and throw cups around the dressing room but this coach didn't do anything or tell us to do anything differently. We needed a push from the backroom staff, some motivating words like 'C'mon! We need to go for it!' but we didn't get any of

that and we missed it. Ben Peeters hardly ever talked about tactics so there was nothing different for the second half.
Our substitution in the second half in Newcastle wasn't about tactics either. It happened because Van Hanegem didn't want to continue playing; he just walked off the pitch. The rest of the players just accepted it because he was usually so good.
RUUD GEELS (the substitute who came on for Van Hanegem in Newcastle): This is what you can expect from 'De Kromme', eh? 'The Curve' is his nickname because of the curved passes he gives with the outside of that famous left foot of his. You can only act the way he does if you have his quality and character.
FRANS: That's how he is as a person. We weren't angry afterwards. He and Rinus run the team basically – they decide what's going on and what happens and Van Hanegem was already a big star by this point. He's a forthright person – he says how he feels. We're all a bit like this but Van Hanegem is a bit more special in this sense.
MARK: Is this because he has such high personal standards?
FRANS: It's just his personality. He doesn't necessarily think he's better than the others… it's just how he behaves. Van Hanegem was a central-left midfielder and Ruud here is a forward, but there wasn't a special plan at that point – it was just a random selection from the bench.
Everyone played badly that day – Van der Heide, Israël, Laseroms, Cor Veldhoen, Jan Boskamp, Wim Jansen, Willem van Hanegem... everyone was outplayed. It was a bad birthday for me and I played badly, but I'm not even sure I was the worst player. Jan Boskamp, Van Hanegem, Wim Jansen... nobody was in their best form. I'll always remember that the St James' Park crowd was huge and seemed to be making a loud, rhythmic noise together.
RINUS: In the end, we weren't concentrated enough or good enough that day. If we'd shown the right concentration in both

games, maybe we'd have had the chance to go on, but it wasn't to be. Nevertheless, our board were actually angry because they thought Newcastle had been training much more than us, a conclusion they'd come to because our opponent had been stronger and had won all the 50/50 duels. This was also very bad for Peeters because he was not strong enough. In this instance, a good coach says to the board: '*This is not your job – I am the coach*', but he was easily influenced.

It hadn't been down to our training though – it was our mentality in that game. One week later, we played like Newcastle United had at home with their crowd behind them. We'd been aware of the huge crowd cheering them on but we're used to it. Whenever we'd play friendly matches against foreign teams, the De Kuip would be sold out with 63,000 fans.

MARK: It's true. Even after that 4-0 defeat, 41,000 came to watch the 2nd leg…

RINUS: At this point though, we also made a change in our tactics. We'd played 4-3-3 in Newcastle but then we made an important change in defence. Previously, I'd played as one of two central defenders, but after this game we employed a different system. Now, I play as the libero, the sweeper, and Laseroms has become the man who challenges for the ball first and handles the striker. I'm never far away from them – maybe a little to the right, a little to the left. This position, for me, is ideal.

We continue to play four at the back with full-backs and two central defenders but when I drop behind them, they become three central defenders. This became the basic tactic for Feyenoord's double-winning team of 1968/69 and it'll stay like this for the European Cup campaign.

The match in Newcastle made us realise the need for this tactic because once the main opponent striker has headed the ball on, the libero is the one who can intercept it and avert the danger.

MARK: So their big centre-forward Wyn Davies was the inspiration for this *'big development'*?

RINUS: Theo and I – we weren't good enough to stop him in that first game. He was big, he was jumping so high. We had no chance.

EDDY: Theo really didn't like to lose. It wasn't something he dealt with well and he was really unhappy with this defeat. He's very hard. Rinus too but he's also sportsmanlike. Theo is... achhh **(sighs)**. He isn't very flexible so he plays as a traditional centre-back with Rinus now always playing slightly behind him.

Rinus and I have always had an optimal central defender-goalkeeper connection on the pitch – whether he turns left or right, I always know what he's going to do and it's become even better since he started playing as a libero.

RINUS: Of course, we didn't invent this libero tactic but for us it became clear it's the right way to go. I'd been a part of it at my previous team DWS and the Dutch national team, but in those cases I had been the 'marker' and someone else, often Daan Schrijvers, had been the sweeper. Now, it's different.

If we'd won in Newcastle, maybe this change would never have happened and this was the birth of these good times for Feyenoord, so **(smiling wryly)** we're very thankful to Newcastle United that we lost 4-0...

MARK: Thank you, that's great. Were there any repercussions to this defeat then?

FRANS: Ha, yes. On landing at Rotterdam airport, we were told by Guus Brox to head over to the De Kuip stadium for immediate extra training as a punishment and to improve our fitness. From then on, we did more stamina training to try to eliminate any risk of physical struggles. We were obviously unhappy about the defeat but the punishment training focused our minds and we began looking towards the next match.

MICHAEL'S CLUB, NEWCASTLE UPON TYNE

GIBBO: Though the second half didn't bubble so much, it still had its moments. Frank Clark hammered a shot against Graafland's left-hand post following a short corner and Gibb had a goal disallowed before United struck a fourth in the 70th minute.
And what a cheer it brought as Wyn Davies ended his seven-month, 21-game famine with a goal from that golden head of his. Scott floated over a free-kick from the right and Wyn was there to flash home a header at the far post. The way he leapt in the cold night air in celebration made me wonder if I'd just seen the Cup final winner at Wembley!

GEOFF ALLEN: Van der Heide played the game the right way, no matter how he must have been feeling. He was having a torrid time but we shook hands at the end. They were a good side but we just caught them and I can't for one moment think they ever expected what we hit them with – they were shellshocked – they couldn't get any rhythm going. The thing was, what we did to them at St James', they did to us in Holland...

THE BRIDGE HOTEL, NEWCASTLE UPON TYNE, 15TH JULY 1969

Members of the Newcastle United Supporters' Club are arriving at the club's headquarters, The Bridge Hotel on Castle Square near the Central Station. They're there to renew their subscriptions for the new season and be first to sign up for a place on the official trips to two upcoming pre-season friendlies, away at Hull City and Hibernian in early August.

▌1ST ROUND 1ST LEG ▌

18-year-old Bill Gibbs and his pal Harry Watson call in at around 8pm and immediately head for a table with a couple of spaces. Sitting there already are several people including their friends Arthur Spowart, known as Spow, and Tony and Mick Rodgers, two brothers who are Newcastle United fans up from London to visit family.

BILL GIBBS AND HARRY WATSON: Evening, lads.
SPOW: Evening, how are you? Ready for a repeat of last season?
BILL GIBBS: Whey aye. Can't wait!
HARRY WATSON: At least we know what to expect this time.
TONY RODGERS: Same again will do me. I don't think our next Fairs Cup opponents Dundee United will be quite as good as Feyenoord either.
HARRY WATSON: Well, I wasn't scared of them anyway. Actually I was supremely confident that we'd do well. I don't know why, not having been in Europe before and playing a foreign team with a certain mystique, with players we'd never heard of before.
They were basically an unknown quantity. For some reason, I remember thinking: 'Ah, we'll tank this lot no problem, 'cos we're Newcastle United...' as if we'd have this God-given right. It's the wrong thing to say but I think a lot of people thought that and, as it happened, we did alright.
BILL GIBBS: I went there on the bus that evening with a few pals. I don't think it was all-ticket – it couldn't have been with 46,000 – and we were sat just on the corner along the line that Geoff Allen was on in the first half – we couldn't get in the centre of the Leazes End that day because it was chocca.
And Geoff Allen... God, you'll never see that again. It's one of the defining moments for me. His performance that night was totally unbelievable. He was skinning their right-back all the time and constantly supplying Wyn and the lads – they didn't need to do

anything, just wait and in would come the cross from this ruddy-faced little lad on the left wing.

HARRY WATSON: It was definitely his night, wasn't it? In those conditions, if you're playing on the wing, as long as the ball's fed to you, you can skin a full-back, no bother. He knew where Wyn was going to be so it was just a case of getting down the line and 'bang!'

SPOW: It was just absolutely brilliant - the noise was deafening. The first European game and all that... it was some game... and Geoff Allen was on top of the world!

FEYENOORD AWAY...

INTER-CITIES FAIRS CUP 1ST ROUND 2ND LEG

FEYENOORD 2
NEWCASTLE UNITED 0

Kick-off: 20:15, Tuesday 17th September 1968
Referee: Helmut Fritz (West Germany)
Venue: de Kuip Stadion, Rotterdam, Netherlands
Attendance: 41,000

Feyenoord: Eddy Pieters Graafland; Pieter Romeijn, Rinus Israël, Theo Laseroms (Frans van der Heide 13), Cor Veldhoen (c); Jan Boskamp, Wim Jansen, Willem van Hanegem; Henk Wery, Ove Kindvall, Coen Moulijn
Substitutes not used: Eddy Treijtel (GK), Ruud Geels

Newcastle United: Willie McFaul; David Craig, John McNamee, Ollie Burton, Frank Clark (c) (Jim Iley, 85); Dave Elliott, Tommy Gibb; Jim Scott, Wyn Davies, Bryan Robson, Geoff Allen
Substitutes not used: Gordon Marshall (GK), Jackie Sinclair

Goalscorers:
1-0 Kindvall (28)
2-0 Van der Heide (54)

Newcastle United win 4-2 on aggregate.

AT FEYENOORD RIGHT-BACK FRANS VAN DER HEIDE'S FAREWELL PARTY, ATTENTIONS TURN TO THE RATHER HAPPIER EXPERIENCE OF THE 2ND LEG IN ROTTERDAM.

EDDY: We weren't used to a defeat like that in the first match so it's possible that we took Newcastle too lightly at the start of the first leg, but we tried to make up for it in the home game.
RINUS: Already that far behind, we didn't really expect to recover, but we at least tried to erase the shame in Newcastle of the 4-0 and to show to ourselves and to our fans that we weren't as bad as we'd played over there.
FRANS: In the first leg, Davies' heading ability and his flick-ons for teammates caused our flat, four-man defence so many problems that Rinus Israël and Wim van Hanegem decided that Rinus would step back into a sweeper role and the team would play more of a 1-3-3-3 formation. This is how it was in the 2nd leg in Rotterdam, where we played very well, and for the rest of the season when we only lost one more match in doing the league and cup double.
EDDY: This was a tougher, more physical game though, especially as we were good enough to compete and go close to recovering the deficit from the first leg.
We really believed we could do it at 1-0 and 2-0 up and our supporters really got behind us.
However, I remember feeling that we had a lot of bad luck. I don't remember having much to do in goal but I don't know that we were so dominant that I could ever switch off. We were the much better team in that game but we needed the third goal to keep up the momentum.
And I remember the toughness of their defence – they became harder and harder as the match went on and there were some really serious tackles, so it depends how you look at that – whether you see it as good defending or too tough, but that's how they kept us at bay; by using that tougher approach.

▌1ST ROUND 2ND LEG ▌

FRANS: We really wanted to regain our pride. I didn't start because of my poor game in Newcastle but I came on as an early substitute for Laseroms who had a head injury after a heavy collision with Davies, who was playing in white boots.

Davies had hurt Laseroms. He was knocked out for a little while and after he left the pitch, he couldn't say anything; he was very groggy in the dressing room afterwards. Pieter Romeijn moved to centre-back and I slotted in at right-back.

This time I attacked a lot more from my position than I had in Newcastle, where I hadn't had the opportunity. Geoff Allen played again and I had him in my pocket this time, but it was too late.

The Newcastle defenders were very tough and the referee let a lot go. Kindvall had five or six chances, real ones in front of goal too.

RINUS: Kindvall was the kind of striker who didn't have a really, really powerful shot but he was very fast. He wasn't the kind of striker to score a lot from outside the box, but he was nearly always scoring.

MARK: He did score one in that first half though, didn't he? A low finish from your clipped free-kick over the wall, Mr Israël, just before the half-hour mark?

RINUS: He did, yes. It's always me or Willem van Hanegem who take the free-kicks.

FRANS: At half-time, even though we'd dominated the game and created many chances, it was still only 1-0, but we were still telling each other: *'OK, we can do it... it is possible.'* The feeling was there.

In the second half, we were even better. The keeper and defence were tough to beat and we simply missed easy opportunities. Kindvall was our top scorer so it wasn't normal for him to miss, but he simply had an off day, whereas everyone else played well this time.

Then, in the 54th minute, I scored our second goal which I was so happy about. I regained possession from the Newcastle left-back Frank Clark, surged into the penalty area and absolutely smashed the ball past the goalkeeper with my right foot, high inside the near post. I had a hard shot in any case but this was a strong connection even by my standards.

Now, we were even more convinced we were going to do it. We had plenty of chances to score more but we couldn't put them in the net – it was bad luck. You have to take your chances and if we'd got that third goal, I think we'd have flooded the attack and overrun them. Rinus had a free header in front of goal which flew just off-target and Kindvall had several more opportunities, but we couldn't get another.

We were so disappointed after the final whistle – a different type of disappointment to that we'd felt after the first leg in Newcastle though.

We went for a drink in the players' lounge after the match. The Newcastle players were there as well and it was all very friendly. We talked a bit with some of them but they left quite quickly by bus.

One thing I can say we learnt was that different tactic – a different way of playing with more force and more strength. After we'd taken note of this, we hardly lost another game all season on our way to becoming champions. We knew we needed to do something different after the match in Newcastle, so this new way of thinking about our game helped us move forward.

But we'd thought we'd go far in the Fairs Cup, so that loss was a setback, a surprise.

RINUS: And for sure, if we'd won this tie, we'd have started to concentrate more on the competition, but we lost, so it was over. It was probably an 8 out of 10 performance against Newcastle in Rotterdam, but the problem was we'd played a 3 out of 10 in England.

MARK: I understand. Were you surprised Newcastle went on to win the competition?

RINUS: Newcastle had a very good team. Our mentality was not OK but even if it had been OK, it's not for sure that we'd have done

much better. If they win, they are the best. Even if we had been concentrating more, who knows? Maybe we would still have lost 2-0 or 3-0 in Newcastle.
And against Davies, the striker... there was no way of playing against him. We tried because Laseroms and I were tough and strong and kicking, but we had no chance. He was still walking and he still scored a goal in the first game.
FRANS: I don't think we thought Newcastle would go all the way but it turns out we were knocked out by the champions.
It's always stayed on my mind that we lost that one – I think I know more about the game now because of the impression it's had on me. It was such a big disappointment, especially personally since I had shown such good form in the build-up, but naturally, learning from defeat has helped us get better.

MICHAEL'S CLUB, NEWCASTLE UPON TYNE

The dinner guests are nearing the end of their starters

BRYAN POP ROBSON: After the 4-0 at home to Feyenoord, you're thinking: 'Well, what's everyone been going on about? Feyenoord... they're not as good as people have been saying they are and they're supposed to be international players,' but then we found out when we went away from home.
They started pushing it and moving the ball around and we were under real pressure – that was certainly one game when we were lucky to get a result and go through. It was really amazing. But we had flights going out there with whole families on, your mates were going out to watch the games and there was just such excitement.
BOB MONCUR: I didn't actually travel with the team because I was injured. The only way I saw this game was by travelling with the

fans. Captain of Newcastle United and I was sat in the stands with the punters! To be fair, I didn't mind much either and anyway, I'd been invited by the Supporters' Club to go on their plane, go there, get the bus to the ground... I was just an ordinary punter that day.

JIM ILEY: Feyenoord had overtaken Ajax as the best team in Holland but they'd got a surprise in Newcastle. It was a good thing we scored four because, over there, it was touch and go, almost to the last kick, as to whether there'd be extra time.

Frankie Clark injured his ankle so he came off and I replaced him with five minutes left. I shouted to the lads: '*We have to get the ball to Wyn Davies and into the corners so we can keep the ball up there and stop it coming straight back.*'

We were taught a lesson over there. That it isn't always as easy as it had been at home.

DAVID CRAIG: They absolutely murdered us in Rotterdam. They played like a different team. The left winger, who'd given me no trouble at all here, was a different player out there. We managed to keep them down to to two and we scraped through.

I remember saying afterwards that we're daft enough to go and win the competition. After all, over there, it could quite easily have been a reversal of the first-leg score. Wyn was battered and bruised – he was defending and we just defended for our lives.

You do two things in football as far as I'm concerned – when you've got the ball you attack and when they've got the ball you defend, so every time we got the ball we'd try to attack, but sometimes your opponent just doesn't let you.

▌1ST ROUND 2ND LEG ▌

JOE HARVEY: Few people realised how badly hurt Davies was and I considered bringing him off at half-time, but we decided his presence was too valuable to the team.

GIBBO: Wyn's right leg was badly hacked actually. I saw him immediately after the game and it was black and blue from knee to ankle – one of the worst injuries I've seen – and he spent more than a week in hospital before making a grand recovery.

DAVID CRAIG: We could only play one way really – we'd hit Wyn and play from thereon. We'd knock the ball up to him and we didn't play pretty football or try to have a hundred touches before the ball would get to him. We didn't play that type of football – we got the ball out wide, got crosses in or we knocked it up to Wyn who held it up for us and we played from there. It isn't great football, I suppose, when I think about it – it's probably a bit bish-bash but I tell you what, it's exciting and the fans love it.

BRYAN POP ROBSON: Mind, when we went over there, we realised how many good players they had too. Van Hanegem was one of their Dutch internationals.

WILLIE McFAUL: Who was the centre-forward for Feyenoord?

FRANK CLARK: Kindvall – I thought he was their best player.

WILLIE McFAUL: Kindvall! That's him! He was some player.

The expectations from our point of view were… well, we were in the Fairs Cup. We never thought we'd get to the final – I'm talking at the start of it. As it went on of course...

WYN DAVIES: We were the underdogs – we weren't supposed to win this competition. John McNamee had a good game in Rotterdam when you consider the pressure we were under and Willie in goal played well too.

TONY BOULLEMIER: I remember vividly the bravery of McFaul coming out to the feet of Kindvall as Newcastle were hanging on by their fingernails.
DOUG WEATHERALL: Well, September 17th is my birthday, yet I spent most of that 90 minutes worrying whether United could hold out against fantastic Feyenoord pressure. United didn't play well. Instead of playing the ball out thoughtfully, they thumped aimless clearances which presented the initiative to the home team.
TONY BOULLEMIER: For me, Jim Scott really arrived that night. With the defence treating the ball like a live hand grenade, the situation cried out for a player to put his foot on the ball. Jim held it, beat a man or two, did some lively running down the right and a midfield stint in an attempt to establish control. From his time at Hibs, he knew what to expect in European competition abroad and he used his experience to help the others.

GEOFF ALLEN: Mind, if we hadn't had four goals and Ollie Burton and John McNamee at the back, we'd have been out. Feyenoord were that good. They were a tasty outfit with very good players. It was a bit of a difficult situation to be in, to go away and defend a four-goal lead. Do you defend? Do you try to go for a fifth?

You know they're going to say: 'Right, let's get an early goal and we've got a chance.' So they put all the pressure on us for the first 15 minutes, eventually got a goal and then they kept up the pressure and got a second. We didn't see much of it upfront because it was a backs-against-the-wall job with Ollie Burton and John McNamee heading that many balls away.
Willie in goal and David Craig, Ollie, John and Frank Clark at the back should have got medals for what they did that night... they did a fantastic job to get us through.

THE BRIDGE HOTEL, NEWCASTLE UPON TYNE, 15TH JULY 1969

Bill Gibbs and Tony Rodgers are at the bar

PAT (the pub's owner): What can I get you, gentlemen?
TONY RODGERS: Five beers please, Pat. **(glancing back at Bill)** I forget now, weren't you in Rotterdam too?
BILL GIBBS: Aye, that's right. Thirteen pounds it cost! Everyone found it hard, you know, unless you had money from your parents. It cost a lot to go to Feyenoord.
HARRY WATSON (as he passes the other two on the way to the toilet): You're not wrong. It was a week's wages, or more.
BILL GIBBS: We were in the upper tier called the Gallery of Sport – 1,500 of us – and there were another 1,000 of us on the other side. It was a great trip, mind. We flew over there with BKS Air Transport the same day, went by bus past all the windmills – we thought this was brilliant – and then they showed us the Feyenoord stadium. After that, we went on a ferry trip on the River Maas and got talking about England with a couple of Brazilian teenage girls. We even taught them to sing the Blaydon Races! They were fascinated by the Queen's head on our coins so we had a whipround and gave them a

handful worth about a shilling, I think. They thought this was great; they thought they were rich. We asked: '*Where are you from*?' They said: '*Brazil*', so my mate says: '*I can speak Brazilian - Garrincha, Vava, Didi!*' We quickly told him to shut up.

I was with a lad called Bobby Stowells, who was a bit pissed off that his mam wasn't happy with him. You see, everyone was wearing a collar and tie except Bobby, who had an old combat jacket on – but as you know, everyone normally goes away dressed in a collar and tie.

Anyway, we came away from the river and went to the city centre for a drink where they had these bands on and saxophones. Dinner was in a big café there and that was all paid for. In the nighttime, away we went to the bar in the stadium where we were all drinking schnapps. Nee one was bothering with beer; it was all schnapps and that was when it kicked off, because everyone had had a few. These coppers there were dressed like the RAF coppers, in like a light-grey uniform, and you could just see they didn't like us.

Then one copper suddenly went his ends. He was all flustered and he clipped one of our lads around the head for no reason and then dragged him away downstairs – I don't know what he did but it couldn't have been bad enough to warrant that.

This old man then turned around – who I later found out was Sammy Flynn, 77 years old. He shouted to the copper:

'*You! You b*st*rd!*'

It all went quiet.

'*We fought the war for b*st*rds like you and there was no need for that!*'

He and the rest of the crowd started to barrack this copper who came over all demoralised and then disappeared. The next minute, our lad came back up. They'd let him go. I think they were sensing there might be a barney. Everyone was really upset about that.

Mind, there were a few naughty things that Newcastle fans were up to... they were buying meatballs for sixpence and throwing them down onto these Feyenoord fans, who were under umbrellas because

of the rain, but somehow the coppers never saw it. That was crazy; I wasn't going to throw away meatballs I'd just bought. What a waste.
HARRY WATSON (on his way back to the table): They'd have been coming from a canny height, mind – with some force.
BILL GIBBS: I remember the match – we got absolutely plastered from pillar to post by Feyenoord. How we only lost 2-0, I'll never know. Honestly, I thought they could have possibly stuck 4, 5 or 6 past us 'cos they were really good, a strong side. They were just muscling in on everything, not giving you time on the ball and Newcastle seemed to be lightweight compared to them – they all looked big. I actually spoke to Big John McNamee some time afterwards and he told me that Tommy Gibb had come up to him saying their centre-back Israel had punched him. *'Punch him back then!'* retorted Big Mac, who then said he'd got a few in after that to make up for Tommy.

Pat returns with the beers and takes payment.

BILL GIBBS: Thanks, Pat.

He and Tony Rodgers return to the table and hand out the pints.

So, when we came out of the match at the end I was happy we were through, but I just wanted to get home really. We were on the bus when who should leap on but Spow, shouting:
'Come quick! We need help – the Feyenoord fans are causing mayhem!'
Luckily, the police had sorted it out by the time people had got off.
SPOW: Aye, we'd come out after the match and walked towards where the buses had been but someone told us they'd moved, so we had to walk across the car park. On the way though, we came across all these big dockers from Rotterdam who were just looking for you. They'd walk past and give you a couple of big whacks. I was only 20 then and there was no chance of hitting these guys back. They

were all six foot tall, probably weighing about 20 stone and I thought: 'If I hit one of them, they'll take my head off.' So there was a bit of hassle but the coppers eventually got us safely back on the buses.

When it came to going to Feyenoord, obviously at work you were entitled to two weeks' holiday so I thought: 'Right, I'm taking two days' holiday for the game and I'll cash in three days so I've got a little bit of pocket money.' There were about 3,000 Newcastle United fans over there and I remember a canny few brought back big rounds of Edam cheese on the plane home!

MICHAEL'S CLUB, NEWCASTLE UPON TYNE

The bar manager is interested to know if any of the competition's big guns fell at the first hurdle. His eager barmen are only too happy to oblige.

BARMAN 1: Now then, if we look at the right scrapbook **(flicks through a few hefty volumes)**... we can see. Yes, here it is. A few of the big guns did go out. Marseille went out on a coin toss after drawing 2-2 on aggregate with Turkey's Göztepe.
BARMAN 2: Bill Shankly's Liverpool suffered the same fate – death by metal – after trading 2-1 home wins with Athletic Bilbao.
BARMAN 1: The hopes of Dinamo Zagreb, the 1967 winners, were dashed by Fiorentina. Perhaps not such a shock since they were the best team in Italy this season.
BARMAN 2: Valencia won the Fairs Cup twice in 1962 and 1963 but their challenge ended straightaway at the hands of Newcastle United's 2nd-round opponents, Sporting Lisbon, while other big names to fall by the wayside included Athletico Madrid, Panathinaikos and Munich 1860.

BARMAN 1: Plenty of top teams did sail safely through though: Juventus, Lyon, Rangers, Leeds United, Bologna, Hamburg, Napoli and Eintracht Frankfurt were amongst those names in the last 32 of the competition, not to mention Újpest Dózsa, who benefited from minnows Spora Luxembourg withdrawing in protest at the recent invasion of Czechoslovakia by several Warsaw Pact countries, led by the Soviet Union.
BAR MANAGER: Right, well… thanks for the comprehensive news report, lads **(smiling)**. I'll look forward to the next instalment soon.

Turns away to serve a customer.

Yes, Sir, what can I get you?

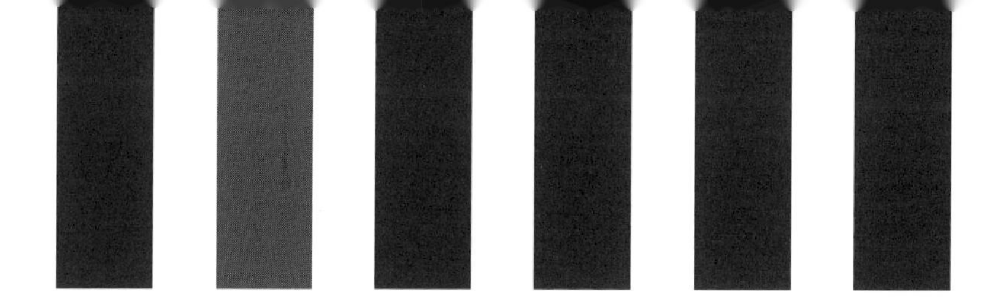

FAIRS CUP 2ND ROUND

NEWCASTLE UNITED
v
— SPORTING LISBON —

ÚJPESTI DÓZSA
v
ARIS SALONIKA

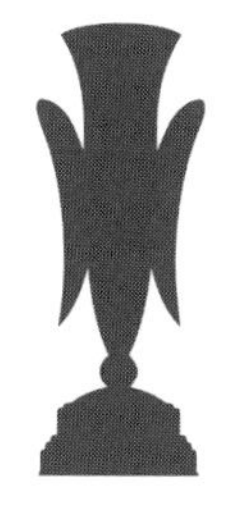

SPORTING LISBON AWAY...

INTER-CITIES FAIRS CUP 2ND ROUND 1ST LEG

SPORTING CLUBE DE PORTUGAL 1
NEWCASTLE UNITED 1

Kick-off: 21:45 CET, Wednesday 30th October 1968
Venue: Estádio José Alvalade, Lisbon, Portugal
Referee: Ervin Vetter (East Germany)
Attendance: 9,000

Sporting Clube de Portugal: Vítor Damas, José Carlos (c), Hilário da Conceição, Celestino, Armando Manhiça, João Morais, Vítor Gonçalves (Marinho, 46), Pedras, Lourenço, Chico Faria, Ernesto
Substitutes not used: Carvalho (GK) (others not known)

Newcastle United: Willie McFaul; David Craig, Bob Moncur (c), Graham Winstanley, Frank Clark; Tommy Gibb, Ollie Burton; Jim Scott, Wyn Davies, Bryan Robson, Alan Foggon (Keith Dyson, 73)
Substitutes not used: Dave Clarke (GK), Dave Elliott

Goalscorers:
0-1 Jim Scott (32)
1-1 João Morais (89)

MICHAEL'S CLUB, NEWCASTLE UPON TYNE

ANNOUNCEMENT: Ladies and Gentlemen, next to be served is the soup course, Minestrone a la Sporting Lisbon!

At the journalists' table

GIBBO: So it was a Tuesday morning in London airport, one of the busiest terminals in the world and Newcastle United were waiting to fly out to Estoril, the millionaires' playground on the west coast of Portugal.

Joe Harvey, outwardly calm and friendly, was worried about what lay ahead. So was coach Dave Smith. United were going blind into a foreign country to play some of the Continent's best ball players but they hardly knew a thing about the Portuguese; the chance to see them in had action slipped away when the match they'd planned to watch was postponed.

As we waited, a few of us drifted over to the book stall. Smith begin glancing casually through a number of football magazines. He was paying little attention as everyone chatted away until his eyes caught the words: 'An analysis of Sporting', on the front of an international soccer magazine.

Could it be the same Sporting? A quick look inside and there it was – a special two-page technical breakdown on United's opponents, perfect in every detail. Smith immediately bought it, showed it to Harvey and spent the two-hour flight studying the report. It was to form the basis of United's tactical fight the next night, a fight which was hailed in both the Portuguese and British Press as thoroughly professional.

The odds against United's coach accidentally finding the answer to his problems at a London Airport bookstall must be about a million-to-one, but that's exactly what happened. Here's Dave now actually – Dave, what about that book on Sporting Lisbon you found at the airport, eh?

▌2ND ROUND 1ST LEG▐

DAVE SMITH (passing the group on his way to order a drink): Well, that was a tremendous help to me, that was. At least we knew something about each player before we got on the field. No one can underestimate the importance of that, psychologically as much as anything else… it's the best shilling I've ever spent!

GIBBO: That must have been a big boost, given the injuries that had hit the squad since the Feyenoord tie, especially the hero of the first leg, winger Geoff Allen. His career's in danger now after a serious knee injury picked up at Nottingham Forest. John McNamee was also ruled out with a knee injury.

Then, 48 hours before flying out to Portugal, captain Bob Moncur had his nose broken in a league match at Liverpool and had to have it reset in the dressing room by club director Fenton Braithwaite, a respected surgeon.

This lengthening injury list contributed to the youthful look of the delegation which checked into the Hotel Palácio in Estoril on the shores of the Atlantic, the same plush accommodation in which Celtic had stayed when they won the European Cup two years ago.

There were four lads aged 20 or under: reserve keeper Dave Clarke, central defender Tot Winstanley, flying winger Alan Foggon and forward Keith Dyson and the squad of 14 featured no less than seven North-Easterners.

They trained at 21:45 in the José Alvalade stadium on Tuesday evening, to try to replicate the match conditions the following evening. Meanwhile, 11 club officials and the same number of Pressmen were entertained at a reception with a seven-course meal which can only be described as magnificent.

The next day, I had some spare time so after a crazy – and I mean crazy – ride in a green cab, I found myself at Benfica's stadium in search of Portuguese footballing superstar Eusébio and remarkably, I found him. He would be attending that evening's match because of his great friend Hilário, who is Sporting's left-back, so we agreed to meet after the match to see how the dice had fallen. He told me United's typically hard, professional English style would trouble Sporting and he was going with his Benfica teammates, Coluna and Torres, to see if he was right.

BRYAN POP ROBSON: Once we arrived, we stayed in a place called Estoril where there wasn't a lot to do – we just hung around, trained and ate. I don't know how many Coca Colas we must have drunk to pass the time, but it was just something we got used to. Some of the training areas weren't great but we just did a bit and stayed aware. Eating together, living together... it just helped build the team spirit even more, you know.

FRANK CLARK: I can't remember whether it was this time or the next time we visited Estoril for the quarter-finals, but one day, four of us were walking along the promenade when a bloke offered to sketch us for about half a crown each. He was a diabolical drawer and got worse with every one he did. I was last and I turned out looking like a vicious caricature of actor Jon Pertwee. It was worth twice as much for the laugh.

BOB MONCUR: Well, obviously I'd missed the Feyenoord games because of my cartilage trouble so this was my first match in Europe. Joe came up to me on the afternoon of the match and said to me:

'*I'm going to leave Ollie Burton out and put Dave Elliott in.*'

And I went: '*Whoa, I'm not sure that's a good idea, boss.*' Because Joe sometimes talks to me about team selection, you know.

'*Well, I've done it. I've told the press; I've done it.*'

'*Well, from where I'm standing, that ain't gonna go down very well with the lads. We like Ollie in the team because he's a worker, a grafter.*'

But typical Joe, he just said: '*He's in.*'

So, fair enough – there was nothing more I could do about it. A bit later, we have the team meeting and Joe goes: '*Right lads, here's the team*' and I'm ready to wince, thinking: 'Ooofff, boys, you're not going to like this.' But Ollie was still in the lineup! The Press boys though, they've already written their pieces before their afternoon deadlines and they've published the team that Joe had told them would start.
We get to the stadium and of course the Press boys are like: '*What's happened here?*' After the game, they quizzed Joe on what had happened, to which he explained:
'*Ah, when I got to the stadium and I saw it was raining quite hard, I thought it would suit Ollie Burton better...*'
Well, it was nowt to do with that; it was 'cos I'd said it wouldn't be popular, so that was typical Joe but he did it, he got away with it and the Press boys over there **(nodding towards the journalists' table)** fell about laughing when I told them later.
Now we know Joe's a great man-manager and obviously all the lads have great respect for him, but he's never a tactician. Later on in that meeting, when I thought he was going to announce that Dave Elliott was in the team, we asked him:
'*Boss, you've been away on these scouting trips – can you tell us a bit more about their team?*'
'*Don't you worry about them,*' he says. '*You just worry about yourselves. You get out there and do what you're good at and get stuck in.*'
'*But*', I protested. '*You must tell us something, Boss – perhaps about their centre-forward?*' And a couple of other guys ask the same question: '*Aye, what about the guy I'm playing against, Boss?*' '*Aye, me too, gaffer.*'
We keep pushing him to the point where he eventually gives in and admits: '*Well... the waitress in the hotel reckons the centre-forward's very sharp and my taxi driver thinks the goalkeeper's dodgy on crosses.*'
So that was his team talk and we just burst out laughing. But that was Joe. The Press boys over on the other table can confirm he would usually be sat on those foreign trips smoking instead of taking notes on the match.

It wasn't a problem though; Joe had Frank and me in this Fairs Cup team so Dave Smith would handle any tactical stuff before the game. Then, on the pitch, on the day, on the night, Clarky and I would sort it, more or less, because he and I were quite astute on the tactical side.

Joe would always say: *'Right, you're the skipper so you're the manager on the pitch'* and I then used to make the decisions. He's a great manager and he knows what the fans want – to watch entertainers – so that's why he's very popular.

KEITH DYSON: It was like a fairytale to be selected to go away to Sporting Lisbon. It was the chance of a lifetime. I was doing well – I was top scorer in the juniors and the reserves and then one Wednesday night, Joe came down to Huddersfield to watch the reserves. David Young was playing and I got this ball from him and flicked it on. I just ran on to it and hit it first-time on the half-volley from about 30 yards and it went flying into the top corner of the net.

Joe was watching and the next Saturday I was in the first team. I just bloomed after that. I think young players tend to run out of steam a bit after, say, 15 games, so Joe tries to use you well and not tire you out.

ALAN FOGGON: What do you reckon you're best at, Dyker?

KEITH DYSON: Well, I suppose I'm strong, particularly in my thighs, and I can shield the ball well. Joe has said I'm a bit slow off the mark but I think that's just mental in terms of seeing what's available at the time and going for it. Maybe I'm not quite good enough yet mentally to do it. I'm not the fastest, although I've played on the wing for a while, but I'm definitely strong and I can hit a ball really, really hard. Some of the goals I've scored – like that one in the reserves – have been, well, sensational. Not just tap-ins.

ALAN FOGGON: I can't disagree with you there and you're right about it being the chance of a lifetime too – all of it was just a big adventure. The hotels we stayed in were lovely, weren't they, and a bit better than we had here, so it was excellent. Do you remember, Dyker, there was that big casino in Estoril and we were rooming together. We could see the casino from our hotel balcony and I said to you: '*Eeeh, this is good, isn't it*?' We didn't get to go to the casino, mind, obviously.

RAY ELLISON (reserve-team player, sitting within earshot): Were you there long then? Didn't it get on top of you a bit?

ALAN FOGGON: Nah, it didn't intimidate us at all – maybe that's just because we're young and nothing bothers us at this age, eh? As for how long we'd be there, we'd usually travel on the Monday, train, then train again on the Tuesday, play the game on the Wednesday, have a night out and then come home on the Thursday morning.

KEITH DYSON: Tot **(nodding at Graham 'Tot' Winstanley on the same table)** was on that trip too so there were a few of us younger guys involved. Joe had blooded Geoff Allen against Feyenoord and we'd won 4-0 so he must have thought : 'Oh, well, I'll try somebody else in this time then.' So as well as me being in the right place at the right time, I think he just took a chance on us young kids, rode his luck and we all came good for him. The gaffer can spot a player, definitely, and as we know, he can rely on Benny Craig, the youth-team coach, to tell him who's ready.

And yeah, I do remember that hotel in Estoril – that area was the plush part of any holiday in Lisbon, and the Hotel Palácio was just like a fairytale – it was just so plush, looking down on the pool.

BOB MONCUR (overhearing as he passes in his way to the bar): So much so, actually, that it's been used in the James Bond film coming out later this year, 'On Her Majesty's Secret Service'.

GRAHAM 'TOT' WINSTANLEY: Aye, I heard something about that too. Overall, it was just the unknown, wasn't it? Dip your finger in, see what happens and the team did exceptionally well. We didn't have thoughts of winning it and, during the season, each step was one more step beyond our expectations, really. Newcastle were an unknown to others too. Whether that worked in our favour, I don't know but it probably didn't do us any harm.

Conditions were really quite atrocious in Lisbon, where we had a lot of rain and it was a bit of a monsoon really. Water was lying on the pitch so it was kind of a 'flick it up in the air and knock it the way you were facing' sort of thing, which was hopefully towards the other goal.

DAVE CLARKE: The one time I thought I was going to get on the pitch during the five matches for which I was sub keeper was when Willie got clattered in this game and I thought: 'Oh, I'm in here; this is my big chance.' He managed to get up and get on with the game though, luckily really, because I was just a young lad. I'd have backed myself and there was no fear but you want your first-choice keeper in these situations. He got a hell of a whack, mind, when a guy slid into him in those treacherous conditions.

DAVE ELLIOTT (passing by this table when he chips in): I won't forget the rain in Lisbon in a hurry either. Joe had told Keith to go on in the second half. We were the two outfield substitutes and I was wearing No 12 on my jersey but Keith had no number on his. After he went on, the referee insisted that the number 12 and 13 had to be shown, so you can imagine to us, it felt like hours for me to pull off a soaking wet jersey and for Keith to put it on.

GRAHAM 'TOT' WINSTANLEY: Things were really quite bad and it wasn't what you'd expect, but having said that, the only thing they could have done was abandon the game and that was probably never going to be on the cards.

There wasn't a massive crowd there and if you've just played at Liverpool with 40-50,000 fans there like I had, it was just another game really. While it was a new experience for us youngsters, all the team knew each other because midweek, we often play 1st team against reserves, so we'd played with and against everyone. And in all fairness, there are no egos – they're a good set of lads.

BRYAN POP ROBSON: That time in Lisbon it was absolutely bouncing down, thunder and lightning and it was in doubt whether the game was going to go ahead. On the way to the game on the coach, we were thinking: 'They'll do well to go ahead'. They put us under tremendous pressure from the start because they had to, they had to get on top of us.

Maybe they'd done a little bit of homework on what had happened at home to Feyenoord because obviously once you've beaten a team like that, you gain a little bit of a reputation. They started fast and we didn't get much joy upfront; all I was doing was chasing and trying to stop balls being played forward and we didn't get much to Wyn, so we were always under pressure. It wasn't anything like we'd experienced at home against Feyenoord.

LISBON, PORTUGAL, 15TH JULY 1969

Every summer, in a tradition going back well into the 20th century, Lisbon's professional footballers travel to the seaside town of Setúbal 40 minutes away to spend a day together in a seafront restaurant eating seafood, drinking red wine and talking about 'O Jogo Bonito', 'the Beautiful Game'.

1969 is no different. Several cars gather outside the Estádio José Alvalade ready to take the various members of the Sporting Club de Portugal team from Portugal's capital city to the idyllic town of 60,000 inhabitants on the shores of the Atlantic.

Young club official Henrique 'H' Roque is driving one of these vehicles with three of the players as his passengers: team captain and owner of the car, José Carlos, a rock-solid central defender and a 1966 World Cup bronze-medallist with Portugal; José's national-team colleague Hilário, a left-sided defender born in Mozambique who would eventually make over 600 appearances for the 'Verde e Brancos', and one of the team's rising stars, 25-year-old forward Marinho, who would also later play for Portugal.

José Carlos readjusts the windscreen wipers and removes a speck of dirt from the otherwise gleaming bonnet of his Opel Rekord.

JOSÉ CARLOS: Be gentle with this beauty, H. I bought it with my bonus money after we thrashed Manchester United in the European Cup Winners' Cup a few years ago – we were handed 25,000 Escudos – half our salary – for knocking George Best and Bobby Charlton out of that competition.
H: 1964! Already five years but it feels like yesterday. We beat a Hungarian team in the final, I remember.
JOSÉ CARLOS: That's right, MTK Budapest after a replay. João Morais hit the winner direct from a corner. Great days.
H: They'll be back soon enough.
JOSÉ CARLOS: Well, let's hope so. We didn't quite see them this year, did we?
H: Well, you knocked out Valencia in the first round of the Fairs Cup, at least…
MARINHO: True, that wasn't easy in the end either – we beat them 4-0 at home in the first leg and then they did the same to us in their stadium. We scored in extra-time to sneak through though and that gave us some extra confidence when we were drawn to face this English team… Now, of course, everyone will only ask us about this defeat.

H: Well, I'd barely heard of them, but then they went all the way and won it.
JOSÉ CARLOS: That didn't surprise me, you know. Newcastle is in a period when people are beginning to recognise them as a good team again. They've gone from being nondescript to becoming a very good team and it's always been a very well-known club.
MARINHO: Yeah, when you are knocked out by a team that goes on to win the competition, I suppose you have a feeling of pride. And to me it wasn't a surprise. We feared English teams; we wanted anyone but the English. It's difficult to play against them.
HILÁRIO (glumly): These games against the best English or German teams though, they're just losses for Portuguese teams. English football is a lot more advanced than Portuguese football. There isn't any comparison so we have to try to catch up.
The English have a different physical condition. As an example, I've never entered a gym. I've played more than a decade for Sporting and never set foot in a gym. No one expects us to win these games. Sporting thrashing Manchester United was unusual... no one expected it.
JOSÉ CARLOS: What we said immediately was: '*What we did to Manchester United is what these guys will do. They knocked us out and now they'll be champions*.' They had a good team and a very good defence. Their game in the air was impressive, both in terms of defending and attacking. You can't win these competitions by chance; you must be good.
H: Sorry for asking so many questions, but I'm really interested – I've always been fascinated by English football. In the home game – when it rained like hell – did you guys feel the lack of support from the fans because there were only 9,000 there in the 42,000-capacity Alvalade?
JOSÉ CARLOS: The weather didn't help. The European games always attract a lot of people but it wasn't the case this time. There were very few people. The fans who support us most go to the cheaper stands but there was no cover there.
MARINHO: It's true, there were very few people in the stadium. It was a terrible day – a lot of rain and wind. it reminded me of

the tragedy a couple of winters ago when hundreds of people died in floods here. We were supposed to play against Fiorentina that Wednesday but the match was postponed. That was terrible.

H: With all that rain, do you think the English players were lucky to have that weather in Lisbon?

JOSÉ CARLOS: In a way, yes. English teams were a lot more used to that kind of weather. They only didn't play if the pitch was a pool. They were a lot more prepared for the pitch we had that day.

MARINHO: Yes, you could say that. It played a part. Newcastle adapted better to the bad weather and the pitch. Although, the English players didn't need any of that. In England, they didn't play with any tricks or excuses. Even without the bad weather, they would have come here and had an attitude like: '*We are English, we're here to play football. We came here to win, not to draw*.'

H: Did it change anything in Sporting's plan?

JOSÉ CARLOS: No. It affected both teams. The pitch was flooded and in certain areas it didn't drain. Our training isn't scientific at all but one thing we do well is to read the opponent. Sporting was the first team in Portugal to watch recordings of opponents. Anselmo Fernandez was the first to do it. He was our coach when we won the Cup Winners' Cup in '64 and it was around then that we started doing it.

H: So the coach used it when you played against Newcastle?

JOSÉ CARLOS: We've done it ever since the first time and now other teams have started to do the same.

H: Ah, OK, so do you remember specifically watching recordings of Newcastle matches?

JOSÉ CARLOS: Yes, we watched some footage of a Newcastle game. Our old coach Anselmo Fernandez managed to get a hold of it. He had a friend in England who I think worked in the embassy.

H: I see. How did preparations for the game go – just as normal?

JOSÉ CARLOS: Pretty much, yeah. During the week, before the training sessions, we talked about the opponent. We were told who

were the stronger players, how they worked, their movements. Then we were told who were the weaker players, those we should press more. Anselmo Fernandez was a very smart guy when it came to analysing our opponents and we carried this on after he left.
Here in Lisbon, they played from the back and closed up in defence. The ball wouldn't roll on the flooded ground and they were good in the air so they cleared everything. Sporting's playing style was about having the ball on the feet, passing it a lot, using the roll of the ball on the ground. However, it was impossible on that pitch, so we had to change it and play high balls. They had the advantage there though, and Newcastle's defence was very good.

MICHAEL'S CLUB, NEWCASTLE UPON TYNE

The journalists' table

GIBBO: With McNamee, injured, 20-year-old Tot Winstanley came in for his European debut. And Alan Foggon lined up on the left wing for his first Fairs Cup appearance too. His evening was punctured somewhat by a heavy early clash with the Sporting goalkeeper. He needed treatment to his ankle and was later replaced by another young gun Keith Dyson.
Both teams had early sights of goal. Pop had a shot on the turn from Wyn's pass palmed around the post by Vítor Damas. Then Lourenço and Ernesto combined in the 17th minute to make Willie McFaul dive full length and tip the ball away for a corner.
IVOR BROADIS of The Journal: Then the skies wept gallons midway through the half and how United welcomed it. Their defence pinched the Portuguese for room and when they were trying to make the final telling pass, it was like trying to thread a needle with darning wool!

The Fairs Cup scrapbooks owned by the young barmen in Michael's Club

Bryan Pop Robson with his fiancé, champion table tennis player Maureen Heppell (Gordon Amory-Daily Express-Express Syndication)

Frank Clark, so often Newcastle United's entertainer off the pitch, was team captain against Feyenoord in Bob Moncur's absence (Gordon Amory-Daily Express-Express Syndication)

Jim Scott scores Newcastle's first-ever European goal at home versus Feyenoord (Mirrorpix)

Bryan Pop Robson on the attack against Feyenoord in the first leg (photo courtesy of Newcastle United FC)

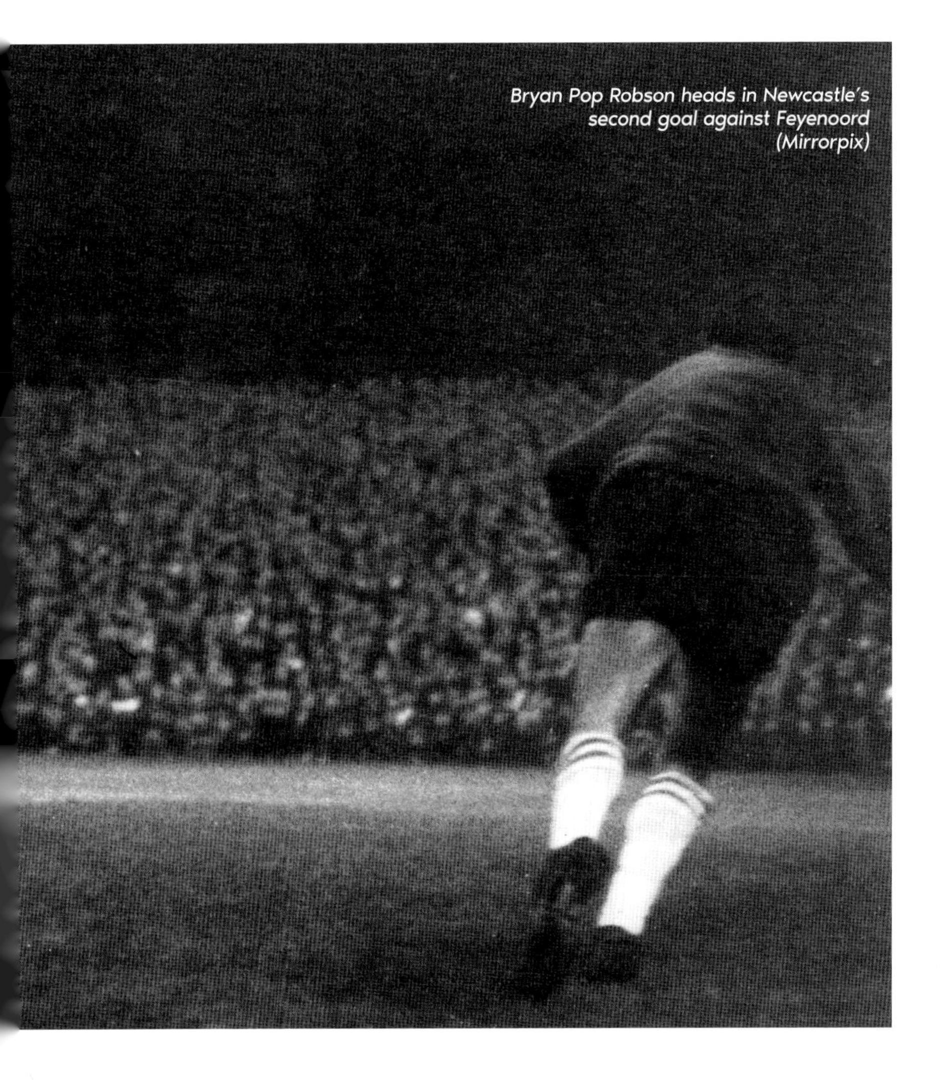

Bryan Pop Robson heads in Newcastle's second goal against Feyenoord (Mirrorpix)

Visiting goalkeeper Eddy Pieters Graafland stood no chance of saving Pop's diving header (Mirrorpix)

Intrepid Newcastle United fan Arthur 'Spow' Spowart

Newcastle United fan Spow was one of several thousand English fans who made the journey to Rotterdam for the second leg

Frans van der Heide bursts into the Newcastle penalty area and rifles in Feyenoord's second goal in Rotterdam (photo from the Frans van der Heide collection)

Willie McFaul punches clear under pressure from Feyenoord substitute Frans van der Heide in the second leg (photo from the Frans van der Heide collection)

Some of the Newcastle United players relax by the pool before the first leg versus Sporting in Lisbon (private photo by Gordon Amory, from the Dave Clarke collection)

Ollie Burton (left), Dave Smith and Dave Elliott brush up on their skills before the Sporting match in Portugal (photo from the Ollie Burton collection)

Sporting goalscorer João Morais advances with the ball towards goal as Newcastle United substitute Keith Dyson (left) looks on (photo from the Sporting club magazine, 1 November 1968)

United captain Bob Moncur exchanges pennants with his Sporting counterpart José Carlos (photo courtesy of Newcastle United FC)

Wyn Davies heads
the ball across the box
for Bryan Pop Robson
to spectacularly volley
an early winner
(Mirrorpix)

Bryan Pop Robson in the act of scoring his wonderful volley against Sporting at St James' Park (photo courtesy of Newcastle United FC)

Bryan Pop Robson scoring his rocket volley against Sporting from another angle (photo from the Bryan Pop Robson collection)

Central midfielder Tommy Gibb slides in to thwart a Portuguese attack in the second leg (photo courtesy of Newcastle United FC)

Wyn the Leap crashes home another header but this time the goal is ruled out for a foul on Sporting goalkeeper Damas (photo courtesy of Newcastle United FC)

An exhausted but jubilant Pop Robson toasts the home win over Sporting (photo courtesy of Newcastle United FC)

Lourenço did force McFaul into a great double save – firstly parrying a 16-yard shot and then smothering the rebound. But then, switching quickly from defence to attack, United incredibly went ahead on 32 minutes and it was Robson's courage that made it.
Earlier he'd been impressive in bringing the ball away on the break and he made something out of nothing when Davies failed to reach a long Clark free-kick, awarded for a foul on Foggon.
Robson saved the ball near the byline and, sending up the spray with a crisp square pass, he served Jim Scott, who celebrated his return after a three-week absence with the mere formality of a gentle side-foot home from almost under the bar.

JIM SCOTT: So now I was United's first home goalscorer in Europe and the first away goalscorer too! However, the two shots combined must have been from around eight yards – one from about six yards and the other from right close in.
FRANK CLARK: Doesn't matter, Jim – they all count.
JIM SCOTT: That's what I mean though. There've been some terrific goals scored by Newcastle over the years and I'm remembered for a goal from six yards and another from two.
BRYAN POP ROBSON: Your away goal was crucial, though – I mean we didn't realise at the time how crucial they were. You were adding up in your head and asking: '*How is this going to pan out?*' Then, in the home leg, you knew you'd likely have to score.

IVOR BROADIS: For the rest of the half, United contained the Portuguese in midfield and upfront, Scott, Robson and Davies stopped the home side staking everything on all-out attack.

Sporting actually came out for the second half having replaced their green hooped shirts with green and white halves. The need to pull back this United lead began to open up gaps in the Portuguese rear and on their breaks Newcastle looked just as dangerous, despite seeing far less of the ball.

The heavier the rain, the greater the Magpies grew in stature, while the Portuguese fans' ironic whistling showed what they thought of their team's disappointing performance.

GIBBO: The freak storm threatened to abandon the game at any time. The jagged streaks of lightning which flashed across the black, brooding sky were actually a sight to behold as thunder rumbled around us and the rain just lashed down on a flooded pitch.

I can still see Dave Smith sitting on a bench on the athletics track with a large, white towel over his head and the water creeping up the bench until his legs were nearly submerged.

IVOR BROADIS: But in the dying seconds, with the hosts launching desperate final attacks, a looping 25–yard drive from Morais beat McFaul off the underside of the crossbar. There was hardly enough time to restart the match.

GIBBO: Willie actually told me: *'I touched the goalscoring shot up onto the crossbar and as it came down it brushed my arm and went in behind me.'*

Nevertheless, it had been a wonderful all-round performance which saw United's name blazing defiantly across Europe. Joe Harvey summed it up by saying: *'The boys were magnificent. I don't think they deserved to lose that late goal and I think even the Portuguese would agree with me.'*

And of course I managed to catch a word afterwards with Eusébio, the 1966 World Cup's top goalscorer. He told me: *'Newcastle are a fine team – strong, courageous and skilful. I knew they would give Sporting a hard time.'*

Praise indeed from the best in the world.

WYN DAVIES: The thunderstorm actually came when we were completely on top and ready to grind Sporting into the ground. The result was that we were bogged down by the lush green turf and Sporting, completely out of the game, managed to force their way back in the closing minutes to grab an equaliser.

KEITH DYSON: When you're playing against continental teams like that, they like passing the ball around – you can't get the ball off them. They're a bit ahead of the English game and they pass a lot so you don't get a lot of chances. When we played Sporting, what we were trying to do was get a draw, so coming away with a 1-1 result was great.

After the game, we just decided to go out and have a good time – I think we just met up in a bar. It was all new to me as I didn't really drink. In fact, I might just have started drinking at that stage. Everybody got a bottle of Mateus Rosé – that was the drink we were all clued into that night - it had to be two or three o' clock by the time we got to bed.

GRAHAM 'TOT' WINSTANLEY: It was the early days of wine being introduced to the team in new places and of course it was pretty tame, but that Mateus Rosé we were drinking was in a dome-shaped bottle and it went down well. I think Willie McFaul decided to sample some on the night and then Pop had one and Bob and the rest, but really we just had a quiet night in and around Estoril. Willie was on good form and Estoril was a nice place. The hotel was lovely but it was just somewhere to sleep really before and after we played the game.

Then, on the way back, I remember this man **(Tot taps the arm of Jim Scott as he passes their table on his way to the**

gentlemen's room) dropping a bottle of brandy in Lisbon airport – it wasn't a pretty sight and he was most upset. There was a roar of approval. Unlucky, Jim. A bottle of brandy then would have been quite expensive but it was a gift from Sporting Lisbon, I think.
JIM SCOTT: Aye, and quick as a flash Moncs had everyone chortling with: '*What a Scot. Can't even hold his liquor!*'

THE BRIDGE HOTEL, NEWCASTLE UPON TYNE

SPOW: When it came to the Sporting away game I thought: 'Am I gonna go away again?' I did, and I got a bit of pocket money from me Ma as well. There were only just over a hundred on the Sporting trip. It was lashing down just before the match but earlier it hadn't been raining. We were going on the bus to the ground when one lad looked out the window and exclaimed:
'Hey, Spow, have you seen these lads? They've all got umbrellas. Maybe it's an offensive weapon that they use on the away fans...'
I replied: '*Well, I've got me Doc Martens so I'll be alreet.*' It got us thinking though and then of course the heavens opened and Jesus Christ, it literally lashed down for two hours at least. I thought the game would have been cancelled. We stopped in the hotel afterwards and just had a few beers until two or three in the morning.
Just like in Rotterdam, there was a sightseeing trip organised for the day after the match but one of the lads advised: '*Divn't gan on that, Spow. Best thing ta dee is jump in a taxi to Benfica's ground, have a look there and then cross the dual carriageway to see Sporting's ground.*'
So we did, and we walked into reception and starting talking to a guy there, who gave me a Sporting Lisbon badge, a pen, a photograph, a little pennant and offered to take us around.
He took us down into what looked like a dungeon, at which point we were thinking: '*What the hell's this we've got here*?' But what

was there was a brick wall in the middle with all these holes in it and a load of kids aged around nine or ten years old. They were just constantly kicking footballs through these holes in the wall and then running around and kicking them back through. It was a little training room but it was just unbelievable.

BOB MONCUR: After the game, we went to a little bar called the Galita bar down in the middle of this fishing village there – with the Press boys there as well. So we were all there having a sing-song because Clarky used to sing songs – he was the entertainer. We were all quite happy because we'd had a good result so we said: *'Right, let's have some 'Mateus Rosé, because that's what the Portuguese drink.'* Most of us had this wine and it cost peanuts.

However, unfortunately the lads were drinking them like pints – bottles of them – *'Oh, that's nice, isn't it?'* – 'cos it's easy to drink. And of course people... no incidents, mind, no problems...

Next thing I know, everyone's left and I'm left there to pay the bill. I thought: 'Oh, thanks, lads,' so I had to pay that, which wasn't a fortune and... oh, by the way, on that night... I'll come back to the story about the bill, but the next morning I'm lying on my bed, and remember I'd had a few drinks as well, when I get a phone call from reception which began:

'Hello Mr Moncur, The Evening Chronicle is looking for Mr Gibson.'

So I replied: *'Well, you've got the wrong room – this isn't his room.'*

'Yes, Sir, we know but we can't reach him – he's not answering the phone. Could you help us find him please?'

So back I came with a reluctant *'Urghh, OK'* and went across the corridor to bang on his door.

Now, the night before, when the game had finished, Gibbo had needed to write his match report to submit the next day to the

Chronicle by phone, but for some reason he hadn't done it at the stadium. So he's in the pub with us drinking and writing – I always notice he's left-handed – and he had this cheap, brown paper which he was writing away on.

Of course Gibbo, when he's had a drink, is a bit full of himself, so he's having a good drink and writing his report but we're chipping in all the time, saying things like: *'Another fine tackle by Moncur'* and *'a great save by McFaul'*, to which he'd exclaim: *'Oh yes, that's good, lads – we'll put that in!'* and he's writing all this stuff down.

Anyway, next morning and I go and find him:

'Gibbo, Gibbo! Get up! The Chronicle's on the phone!'

He's zonked out and cursing to himself as he gets up, barely knowing where he is. So he picks up his notes and reads out word for word over the phone what we'd told him the night before... what a report that was!

And the bill, so I'd been left to pay it, so on the bus to the airport the next morning I stood up and said: *'Everyone have a good night then?'*

'Aye Bob, good stuff, great...'

'Well, that's the good news,' I said. *'The bad news is the bill.'* The lads visibly slump back and sigh. *'Absolute fortunes. Does anyone want to have a guess? 'Cos you all left me on my own.'*

So they all have these guesses which are way over the top and I give them some high figure and say:

'Divide that by 35 and that's what I want off each of you.'

'Ah, Bob, we haven't got that kind of money on us now...'

'Well, the good news is, it was nothing like that – it was peanuts because Mateus Rosé only cost about 10 bob a bottle, so it wasn't silly money, but that'll teach youse to leave me on my own – I could've got a fortune from you!'

UNITED THE MASTERS IN LISBON DELUGE

Sporting Lisbon . . 1
Newcastle Utd. . . 1

THE Lisbon Lion was caged last night. As the golden sun of Portugal turned into a torrent of rain which threatened to abandon this amazing Fairs Cup match, Newcastle United swept contemptuously to the brink of resounding success, writes **JOHN GIBSON.**

A 1-1 draw, snatched in the dying seconds by Sporting Lisbon, leaves the Gallowgate victory parade an exciting near-certainty.

Some people may say the Lion, Sporting's proud emblem, was drowned by a freak storm in the city which, earlier this year, went four months without a drop of rain.

But, in my opinion, Sporting were washed out not by the weather, but by a much more aggressive, better-equipped and alert United side in full bloom.

Conditions were certainly amazing, especially in the second half.

Jagged streaks of lightning flashed across the black brooding sky as the thunder rumbled ominously for Sporting and the rain lashed down cruelly on a ground which quickly became like a flood area.

GREAT DEFENCE

I can still see coach Dave Smith sitting on a bench on the athletics track with a large white towel over his head and the water creeping up the bench until the legs were nearly submerged.

My one worry was that the referee would abandon a game in which United had Sporting by the scruff of the neck.

Bob Moncur, a skipper who typified United's spirit, threw off the effects of a broken nose to produce a display of defensive strength and skill that Sporting could never match.

He was ably backed up by a defence so magnificent that United were never in any danger of falling behind.

David Craig, a class full-back, found no problem in bottling up Morais, a man who kicked Pele out of the World Cup. It was not Craig's fault that Morais got a last-minute goal from 30 yards.

LOW CROSS

Tommy Gibb, Ollie Burton, Graham Winstanley . . . the list of credits goes on.

In attack the graft was distributed pretty well evenly, with Jim Scott more than justifying his return.

His goal in 31 minutes was the clincher. It came when Alan Foggon was grounded on the left as he tried to go through.

Clark pumped the free-kick over to Davies, standing on the edge of the penalty area, but the centre-forward failed to collect at the last moment.

Robson latched on to the ball like a flash to shove a low cross into the goalmouth, where Scott side-footed the ball home.

Manager Joe Harvey had earlier reversed his decision to axe Ollie Burton when the rain suddenly hit the city one-and-a-half hours before the kick-off.

Dave Elliott was left out, after all, and there was no doubt that, in the circumstances, the final decision was right.

United were completely in charge throughout, though 18-year-old Foggon was injured after quarter of an hour and another 18-year-old, Keith Dyson, substituted in 73 minutes.

Morais equalised seconds from time when his hopeful shot was pushed on to the bar by McFaul, but the rebound struck his arm and the ball flashed into the net.

John Gibson's report of the match against Sporting in Lisbon (credit: Chronicle Live)

SPORTING LISBON AT HOME...

INTER-CITIES FAIRS CUP 2ND ROUND 2ND LEG

NEWCASTLE UNITED 1
SPORTING CLUBE DE PORTUGAL 0

Kick-off: 19:30, Wednesday 20th November 1968
Venue: St James' Park, Newcastle upon Tyne, England
Referee: Gerhard Schulenburg (West Germany)
Attendance: 53,747

Newcastle United: Willie McFaul, David Craig, Ollie Burton, Bob Moncur (c), Frank Clark; Dave Elliott, Tommy Gibb; Jim Scott, Keith Dyson (Albert Bennett 78), Wyn Davies, Bryan Robson
Substitutes not used: Dave Clarke, Graham Winstanley

Sporting Lisbon: Vítor Damas, Celestino, Armando Manhiça, José Carlos (c), José Morais, Hilário da Conceição, Pedras, João Carlos, Chico Faria, Marinho, Lourenço (Sitoe 60)
Substitutes not used: Carvalho (GK), João Morais, Alexandre Baptiste

Goalscorer:
1-0 Bryan Robson (10)

Newcastle United win 2-1 on aggregate.

MICHAEL'S CLUB, NEWCASTLE UPON TYNE

The journalists' table

GIBBO: Young Alan Foggon still hadn't recovered from the ankle injury sustained in Lisbon three weeks earlier so Dyson again deputised. The only other changes to the lineup was Ollie Burton replacing young Tot Winstanley at the heart of defence and Dave Elliott taking the number 10 shirt in midfield.
Meanwhile, Sporting were rocked on the eve of their departure to England by the resignation of their coach Fernando Caiado. I remember he was an intense, handsome little man who had won his playing honours with Sporting's bitter city rivals Benfica. He also once had the job of – unsuccessfully, I may add – helping to stop Jackie Milburn in an England vs Portugal match in 1951.

KEN McKENZIE of The Journal: Newcastle actually turned out in an all-white strip with the Portuguese retaining their Celtic-style green and white hoops and black shorts. Joe Harvey said Sporting were entitled to keep their own strip and that it was our turn to change this time.

LISBON, PORTUGAL, 15TH JULY 1969

Three Sporting Clube de Portugal players are being driven by young club official Henrique 'H' Roque to an annual players' gathering in a seaside restaurant in nearby Setúbal. They are crossing the huge bridge over the River Tagus, which flows between the metropolitan area of Lisbon and the Setúbal peninsula. 'H' is keen to hear more about Sporting's Fairs Cup campaign that season, so attention switches to the team's visit to Newcastle for that crucial second round second leg.

▌2ND ROUND 2ND LEG ▌

MARINHO: We thought we could knock out Newcastle. Despite playing away, in that atmosphere, which we knew would be very difficult against an English team, we thought we could do it. In England, the atmosphere was terrifying – the fans were so close. Here in Portugal, they all have athletics tracks and obviously we, at Sporting, even have a cycling track, so the fans are very far from the pitch.
H: The boss Caiado left three days before the game in Newcastle. How did that affect the team?
MARINHO: Well, it didn't affect us negatively. It may even have been good for the Sporting players. At the time, we didn't like the coach Caiado. It's not that he wasn't a good coach – it's that he'd been at Benfica. He'd been European champion there as Béla Guttmann's assistant coach. He was a good coach and a good man but he was a bit old and he'd come from Benfica to Sporting; no one who does that is ever accepted in the same way as someone without that history; not by the players, the fans, anyone. When he left, it was probably a good change to make to try and beat Newcastle.
JOSÉ CARLOS: I agree with that – Caiado was never a coach who was universally popular at Sporting, simply because he'd come from Benfica. The fans were always reluctant to support him. What's more, and it's difficult for me to even say it, he was probably the worst coach I've had.
He'd talk to us in a strange way. He used to say to the defenders: '*This space is your little garden; no one can get in here.*' I've already studied a bit to be a coach and when I heard that I thought to myself: '*How is this possible?*'
H: Do you have any other examples of his weaknesses?
JOSÉ CARLOS: He couldn't read the game. It was horrible. Our system was very poor. He didn't say much to us other than: '*Go in there and take care of your little gardens.*'
H: I see. By the way, was it intimidating to play in Newcastle?
JOSÉ CARLOS: For some players, yes. Certain crowds affected some of the players. Not me. I even liked it.

HILÁRIO: Well, I remember we weren't used to the fans in English stadia. The English people live football. Here, there's only Benfica and Sporting. Not there. There, they really live football from the first minute until the last.
H: I guess the stadium was full?
HILÁRIO: Full, with everyone supporting their team. It was unusual for us.
H: Unusual, but was it intimidating for the Sporting players?
HILÁRIO: Of course it was. We're not used to that.
JOSÉ CARLOS: I remember they pressed us a lot during the game. We had a very good defence and we didn't concede easily, but they were very difficult to contain. I'm not very tall but I have a very good jump and I can leap very high, so being good in the air meant it would be most likely me marking their main striker.
MARINHO: In Newcastle, we had many chances to equalise. We'd have taken it to extra-time if we had, so it was all very even. In fact, both these two matches between Sporting and Newcastle were very, very even. Newcastle did better and knocked us out but I'm convinced that if we'd played the first leg in Newcastle and then in Lisbon, we'd have knocked them out in such an even tie as this. We thought that in a knockout format, playing the second leg at home was an advantage. The atmosphere in Newcastle was terrifying for the opponent. It scared the players.

THE BRIDGE HOTEL, NEWCASTLE UPON TYNE

BILL GIBBS: Our crowd made the difference. There were two things that beat the foreigners here – the crowd and Wyn Davies.
HARRY WATSON: Because of the layout of the ground, I think the very fact that the crowd practically sits on top of the players makes an impact; the fans are so close to the players and they can feel that – the crowd can almost reach out and touch the players and I don't think that's the same abroad.

For the fans, it is a case of you support them 100 per cent and you assume we'll win. On that basis, you're vocal from the start and you never stop. Coming away, the next day you're bloody hoarse. You can hardly talk because you've given everything as well, so your vocal chords are shot.
BILL GIBBS: Aye, if you've heard the Leazes End in full throat... I mean, if you'd heard them at top volume that night singing this:
'Aye, aye, ya-yaye...
McFaul is better than Yashin...
Wyn Davies is better than Eusébio...
And Sporting are in for a thrashing!'
HARRY WATSON: The thing is, it was so powerful and so loud coming from the Leazes End that if you were like me and my father in the corner-paddock, or even as far along the side as the centre-paddock, you could hear it loud and clear, so you just joined in. You sang along with the Leazes End even though you weren't in it, just because it was infectious. So it wasn't just that part of the ground, but more like three-quarters of the ground singing it in unison.

MICHAEL'S CLUB, NEWCASTLE UPON TYNE

DAVID CRAIG: Pop scored a fantastic goal early on; it just set the crowd alight. Do you remember, it was a volley quite high up off the ground and he absolutely rifled it in the back of the net, probably from a cross that Wyn had nodded down. They were a good side though, so it was a tight game after that.
BRYAN POP ROBSON: In fact, it came following Wyn's header from a Tommy Gibb free-kick… a training-ground routine. I always run over the ball and run behind their wall while the ball is being chipped to Wyn for him to head down into the middle. It worked beautifully and when I saw the ball coming to my foot I just hit it. I always anticipate that happening because I'm good at volleying.

DAVE SMITH: This was the first time this move came off for us and it couldn't have come at a better time. Week after week I'd been getting the boys to work this in practice to get it deep into their systems. A big disappointment in this game came after the first 20 minutes when we reverted to this bad habit of the big boot after showing so much controlled play. Nevertheless, the lads deserved every credit for making the game memorable.

KEITH DYSON: I wouldn't say Pop came out of his shell exactly, but he suddenly became the man of the tournament, if you like, because he hit some screamers and the volley versus Lisbon at home was an absolute bullet.

OLLIE BURTON: I went over on my ankle before the game had even started but I decided to carry on. It troubled me through the game but our opponents didn't pile on sufficient pressure to worry me. In fact, do you know what? I never even broke sweat. There was hardly anything coming through the middle so they had no penetration and I found it easy.

WILLIE McFAUL: It was actually one of the easiest games I've had. It seemed as if they didn't want to shoot. In Lisbon, they were going one-two and then having a crack at goal but at St James' Park I was expecting things which never came. I only had one real shot to deal with near the end.

▌2ND ROUND 2ND LEG ▌

FRANK CLARK: I didn't think we played that well, mind. For a time we were back to our old failing of last season of sticking too many long, hopeful balls up into the middle. It caused us to lose a lot of possession.
BOB MONCUR: Anyway, we were in the hat for the next round and that was the main thing. I suppose if we'd played really well and lost, there'd have been hell on.

AT THE JOURNALISTS' TABLE FOR THEIR MATCH MEMORIES

DOUG WEATHERALL: It was one of the greatest volleyed goals I've ever seen. It was fabulous – very, very high off the ground. Pop was in the air and he controlled the strike brilliantly – it was a wonderful volley. He timed it beautifully from around the edge of the penalty area.
IVOR BROADIS: I remember writing that he looked like a top-class hurdler as he smashed his volley high into the roof of the net. Earlier, the Lisbon players had immediately endeared themselves to the terraces by scattering club pennants among home fans and by way of a 'thank-you', Newcastle stormed immediately into the attack.
It was a characteristic start by a side obviously intent on an early goal – and they nearly grabbed one from the kick-off. A Moncur long ball was helped on into the box for Scott to set it up for Davies, but his shot from 14 yards had nothing like enough power to bypass Damas – he was down like a cat to his right.
There was no relaxation of United's early pressure though and on 10 minutes, Dyson, cutting into the middle, was tossed like a cork between left winger João Carlos and left-back Hilário before Gibb's free-kick led to the goal.
Lisbon, as I'd expected, proved themselves to be extraordinary ball players, but they sought their breathing space in zonal short passing – the sort of exhibition stuff that the Continentals turn on when they're in front. Even when Morais sent a searing 40-yarder from midway in his own half,

centre-forward Lourenço elected to check back instead of taking it on. He met the fate that Bobby Moncur reserves for most men who dally.

BOB CASS of The Sunday Sun: Then came a spell of attacking that promised more goals and had it not been for Sporting's keeper Damas, undoubtedly there'd have been more.

IVOR BROADIS: Yes, Jim Scott, coming in like an express train onto one Davies header, forced him into a great turn around the post and he and David Craig both went close. Inevitably, following 45 minutes of solid graft, United lost some of their rhythm and method after the break but Davies, dangerous as ever up aloft, did stir the pulses on the hour, nodding home a left-wing cross which was unfortunately chalked off for an infringement. There was the odd penalty box scare thereafter but they had done enough in that magnificent first half to take the next step. Out of the ball-playing Lisbon side, many an English manager would take the international José Carlos and the English-style Marinho upfront.

KEN McKENZIE: Three-time FA Cup winner Bobby Cowell was at Gallowgate that night too – but he never saw a ball kicked. *'I'd seen them play five times so far that season; two losses and three draws,'* the former Newcastle full-back told me. *'I didn't dare go up to the stand, so I just hung about the inside of the entrance.'*

BOB CASS: The rest of the game was a disappointment but the fact that Newcastle, so often called the backdoor entrants into Europe, had justified their Fairs Cup place by reaching the last 16, should have sent everyone home happy.

A few yards away at the bar in Michael's Club, our two young barmen can't believe their good luck at being able to serve their heroes and work at such an enjoyable event, but even this is superceded by their deeply-embedded enthusiasm for Fairs Cup nostalgia. We're about to discover just how far their reminiscences extend.

BARMAN 1: OK, so you've got your Fairs Cup scrapbooks and I've got mine, but what are all these bundles of letters and paper cuttings you've brought here?

BARMAN 2: Ahhh, yes, you'll like this. These are the letters I've received from my penpal.

BARMAN 1: (nonplussed) What penpal?

BARMAN 2: Haha, well, he's from Hungary – his name is Gyuri Lelkes – George to you and me. He's a big football fan like we are, but get this, he was actually at the 2nd leg of the final in Budapest.

BARMAN 1: (exhaling) The lucky son... of... a... gun!

BARMAN 2: Yeah, he likes all football really but he collected some of the stuff that came out over there on European football for me. It's mainly Újpest Dózsa-based because they were the only Hungarian club in Europe last season after the others were forced to pull out for political reasons. It's all explained in here **(points at the letters)** but there's a load of info on the final too. He's really good at English so he's translated some of it for me, so, you know, that's why I brought the stuff in…

BARMAN 1: OK, well, let's try and take a look if we can when everyone's getting stuck into the main course. What do we need to know first?

BARMAN 2: Well, look, I'll keep it short, but one thing that is interesting is that while England had seven clubs in Europe last season, Hungary only had one.

BARMAN 1: One?

BARMAN 2: Yeah, because of politics. Basically, Czechoslovakia was invaded by their Communist overlords, the Soviet Union, and other Warsaw Pact countries in August 1968, to crush a Czech move towards democracy. In the wake of this, possibly for political or security reasons, UEFA decided, to pair all Eastern European clubs with each other in the first rounds of the European and Cup Winners' Cups. The Communist-led football governing bodies in the likes of Hungary didn't like this one bit – perhaps because they felt disrespected or because it reduced the chances of overall success by a team from a Communist country – so they pulled out en masse. However, the Fairs Cup isn't run by UEFA – its head, Stanley Rous, is the FIFA president – so Újpest Dózsa stayed in it. Mind, their projected first round opponents, Spora Luxembourg, took the opportunity to avoid a thrashing by withdrawing too, in protest at actually having to play a team from the Eastern Bloc.

BARMAN 1: OK, so who did Újpest get in the 2nd round while we were taking care of Sporting?

BARMAN 2: Umm... OK, give me a second. From memory, they played a Greek team... yes, Aris Salonika... there's a bit here. They turned on the style at home, mind, and beat the Greeks 9-1. Here are George's match reports from the two legs, plus a couple of player interviews. Best to know now that the two Újpest players called Dunai aren't related – Antal, the striker, is known as Dunai II and Ede, the young, all-action midfielder, is Dunai III.

NOVEMBER 6TH 1968: IN-FORM ÚJPEST EDGE PAST ARIS

Goals from striking predators Ferenc Bene and Antal Dunai helped Újpest Dózsa battle to a hard-earned 2-1 away win against Aris Salonika in the first leg of their Fairs Cup 2nd round tie on Wednesday, despite a number of challenging obstacles.

Firstly, Lajos Baróti's team had only played one league match after a six-week hiatus, albeit they stuck five past Pécsi Dózsa last Saturday with no reply, and then they had to fly to Greece just yesterday morning for a match on a difficult sand-topped pitch this afternoon. Nevertheless, Hungary's title challengers exploded into life early on and took a seventh-minute lead when Bene exchanged passes with János Göröcs and thrashed the ball through the legs of Nikos Christidis, a Greek international goalkeeper, from fully 14 metres.

Christidis saved further efforts from Fazekas and Bene as the match reached half-time with no further score, but that was to change in the 57th minute when Gunaris outran the visiting defence and crossed for Konstantinidis to head into the net barely a metre from the goal line. An equaliser was no more than the Greeks deserved but Újpest overcame the awkward bounce of the ball on this uneven playing surface and scored the winner as the game entered its final ten minutes. Dunai II cut in from the right, beat two defenders and played a one-two with Fazekas before burying the ball past a hapless keeper from ten metres out.

NOVEMBER 20TH 1968: DOMINANT DÓZSA DESTROY DESPAIRING GREEKS

A 2-1 first-leg advantage was a notable if not decisive lead to take into this second match two weeks later in Budapest, but any doubts as to Újpest Dózsa's progress to the last 16 of the

Fairs Cup were dispelled within minutes of the kick-off against Aris Salonika at the Megyeri út stadium.

Midfield maestro Göröcs fed Antal Dunai for the first goal inside two minutes and his 19-year-old namesake Ede Dunai doubled the lead from just outside the box five minutes later. Antal then made it three on 16 minutes and Bene put the game and the tie beyond any doubt before the half-hour mark.

Siripoulos gave Aris a consolation goal on 40 minutes but that was merely a momentary trip in Újpest Dózsa's early-evening stroll, Antal Dunai grabbing his hat-trick and substitute Béla Kuharszki heading into the net within three minutes of the restart.

Centre-back Ernő Solymosi dispatched a clinical penalty for Dózsa's seventh on 55 minutes before a fourth goal for Dunai and a smart ten-metre finish into the right corner by another replacement, László Nagy, confirmed the home side's overwhelming superiority. The 9-1 result sees Baróti's charges sail into the third round 11-2 on aggregate.

• •

ANTAL DUNAI: I remember the Aris club president told someone to approach Lajos Baróti and ask for us not to score any more goals because they wouldn't be able to go home afterwards. It was very bad for them and the scoreline was already enough, given that we'd overwhelmed them in all areas, but we weren't the sort of side to stop. Our crowd was everything to us – how could we stand down? We didn't, but still, the president had asked us to ease off as much as possible.

PÉTER JUHÁSZ (Újpest squad member): Here in Budapest, Aris were an easy opponent for us. Their coach said on the touchline: *'OK, it's enough, Mr Baróti. You don't need to score any more.'*

Mr Baróti finished his cigarette and told us: *'Score more goals if you want.'* We scored more, they lost heavily and because of this, they didn't attend the official post-match banquet.

▌2ND ROUND▐

AGGELOS SPIRIDON (Aris Thessaloniki defender and prospective Greece international): Of course we already knew Újpest when we were drawn to play them. They were one of the best teams in it with a lot of players – six or seven – in their national team at a time when Hungary are one of the world's best.
In Thessaloniki, we played a good game but we weren't prepared for the second leg in Budapest. We'd travelled a long, long way by bus from Thessaloniki and had lots of problems in reaching the stadium, so we almost missed our pre-match training session the previous evening.
There'd also been a mechanical problem with the vehicle, which had meant we'd had to walk for some time. In the match, I think we were 4-0 down after the first 25 minutes. It was a really bad day for our team because actually, we're a really good side.
We didn't attend the post-match banquet in Budapest because of all these problems – the delay in reaching the stadium and because of the nine goals – the huge loss. Our president made a protest and insisted that nobody would attend the post-match banquet.
Playing against Újpest was like playing against Barcelona or Real Madrid, who are full of top internationals. Don't forget, we're amateur footballers and we don't get paid, so we have to go to work in the morning and only afterwards do we hold our games and training sessions.

SEVERIANO CORREIRA (Aris head coach): Újpest Dózsa are one of the world's most prolific teams. It was almost unbelievable how happy they were to score as many goals as possible. A scoreline of 3-0 or 4-0 wasn't enough – they wanted ten!

BARMAN 1: Blimey. Explosive stuff there then. And the Hungarians had served an early warning of intent.

BAR MANAGER: Are you two men of letters still chattering? How about some glass collection to break up your evening of leisure?
BARMAN 2: Yes Sir. Sorry Sir. We were just getting acquainted with Újpest Dózsa.
BAR MANAGER: There's plenty of time for that later when our waitresses are delivering the mains. All I want to know is what happened to the teams I've heard of? Go on, quickly.
BARMAN 1: Errr… quickly then… Chelsea – out. On a coin toss after two goalless draws with DWS Amsterdam. Olympique Lyon – out. Thumped 7-1 on aggregate by unknown Portuguese outfit called Vitória Setúbal. Bologna, semi-finalists last year – dumped out 2-1 by OFK Belgrade. Panathinaikos – out. Napoli – out.
And… Juventus – out! The battle of two 1966 World Cup finalists saw West German Helmut Haller and his famous Italian club concede a winner in the very last minute of extra time, that after more than 200 minutes of goalless football against Eintracht Frankfurt, for whom his international teammate, Hans Tilkowski, was in goal.
BAR MANAGER: That'll do. Who's up next for our lads then?
BARMAN 2: Los Magnificos!
BAR MANAGER: Que?
BARMAN 1: Real Zaragoza of Spain. Previous winners and they'd just knocked out Aberdeen.
BAR MANAGER: Great. Now – glasses, *please*!

FAIRS CUP 3RD ROUND

NEWCASTLE UNITED
v
— REAL ZARAGOZA —

ÚJPESTI DÓZSA
v
LEGIA WARSAW

REAL ZARAGOZA AWAY...

INTER-CITIES FAIRS CUP 3RD ROUND 1ST LEG

REAL ZARAGOZA 3
NEWCASTLE UNITED 2

Kick-off: 17:00, Wednesday 1st January 1969
Referee: Alfred Ott (West Germany)
Venue: Estadio La Romareda, Zaragoza, Spain
Attendance: 22,000

Real Zaragoza: Nieves; Irusquieta, Borrás, Santamaria, Manuel González, Santos (c) (Luis Violeta 51), Javier Planas (II), Bustillo, Moya (Miguel Planas (I) 77), Armando Martín, Marcelino
Substitutes not used: Alarcia (GK)

Newcastle United: Willie McFaul; David Craig, Ollie Burton, Bob Moncur (c), Frank Clark; Tommy Gibb, Jim Scott; Keith Dyson, Bryan Robson, Wyn Davies, Alan Foggon
Substitutes not used: Dave Clarke (GK), John McNamee, Jackie Sinclair

Goalscorers:
1-0 Santos (5)
1-1 Bryan Robson (7)
2-1 Bustillo (17)
2-2 Wyn Davies (32)
3-2 Planas (II) (57)

MICHAEL'S CLUB ON NORTHUMBERLAND STREET, NEWCASTLE UNITED'S FAIRS CUP VICTORY CELEBRATORY DINNER AND DANCE

ANNOUNCEMENT: Ladies and Gentlemen, please be seated for the Fish course, Sole avec sauce Real Zaragoza!

The guests are ready to continue their continental culinary adventure. Gibbo, Doug and the other journalists kick off their conversation with a look at why Real Zaragoza had been such a big deal during the Swinging Sixties.

GIBBO: Well, given who was left in the competition, it could scarcely have come any tougher than Real Zaragoza, could it? I mean, they'd knocked out Juventus on the way to winning the Fairs Cup in 1964 and their world-class forward line had earned the nickname of Los Magnificos, known to us here as the Famous Five.

There was Brazil international Canário, who'd won the 1960 European Cup for Real Madrid at Hampden Park with Puskás and Di Stéfano; left winger Carlos Lapetra, who'd lifted the 1964 European Championship with Spain; Marcelino, who sealed that win with an extra-time headed winner against Lev Yashin's Soviet Union; plus Eleuterio Santos and Juan Manuel Villa.

The problem was that the Famous Five, which had carried the club to eight successive top-five finishes in La Liga, two Spanish Cups and the 1964 Fairs Cup, had had its day. Canário had already departed for RCD Mallorca and Lapetra and Villa were both recovering from operations after serious injuries. This left Santos and an increasingly injury-prone Marcelino.

To compound the problem long-term, they'd sold striker Miguel Ángel Bustillo to Barcelona in exchange for £50,000 and two players, although he'd be available for this Fairs Cup tie because he wouldn't be moving until the summer. The next generation was slowly replacing these stars but Zaragoza didn't have time to wait –

it was already January and they were second-bottom of La Liga, so new coach César Rodríguez had some tricky decisions to make in terms of which competition to prioritise.

Interestingly, United's chairman Lord Westwood had sounded words of caution on this score too. He said in the build-up to this tie: *'The Fairs Cup is one of the luxuries of football and not our bread and butter. Our immediate aim is to improve our league position.'*

NICK SCURR of The Northern Echo: Nevertheless, Joe Harvey actually left Dave Smith in charge of United in their league match at Stoke in early December to spy on Real Zaragoza in their 1-1 home draw with Real Madrid. I know he was pleased about this because it meant they wouldn't go into this one as blindly as they had in the last round against Sporting Lisbon.

And that was just as well, because Zaragoza have a high-powered record against British teams. They beat Hearts, Dunfermline and Leeds on the way to losing the 1966 Fairs Cup final, then Everton the following year in the Cup Winners' Cup and now Aberdeen in this season.

GIBBO: Mind you, Rodríguez wasn't as lucky in his efforts to find out about us. His spy was thwarted when bad weather postponed United's match with Liverpool in late December.

NICK SCURR: That same weather meant Newcastle's delegation had to take a coach down the A19 because Newcastle Airport was snowbound. The plane left Teesside Airport around an hour later than scheduled and the pilot was Captain John Rush, nephew of Squadron Leader Jimmy Rush, a Newcastle United director.

GIBBO: Once everyone was safely ensconced in Zaragoza's smart Hotel Goya, it should have been plain sailing until the game but there was a scare early on the day before the match when all 14 players had to be treated for sore throats. Wyn Davies found it particularly troublesome. The central heating made the bedrooms like Turkish baths. Willie McFaul over there groaned to me: *'I never slept a wink. I'm not looking forward to another night like that.'*

THE BRIDGE HOTEL

At the Newcastle United Supporters' Club's first meeting of the new season, fans are reminiscing about the glorious Fairs Cup campaign. Arthur 'Spow' Spowart was the most well-travelled of the group, but even he couldn't go to Zaragoza after the costly festive period contributed to the cancellation of the fans' official trip due to lack of numbers.

SPOW: When it came to Zaragoza, I thought: 'Ah, damn, I've got nee bloody money.' But me mam and dad said: *'It's coming up to Christmas so we'll pay for your trip with the supporters' club – as your Christmas present.'* I said: *'Oh, great, thanks.'* But then the trip got cancelled on Christmas Eve.

There were 36 of us still wanting to go and there was this old lady at Boroughbridge, Miss Nelson, who knew Joe Harvey, so she asked him: *'Is there any chance of getting 36 of the fans on the plane, just so we can see the match?'* But he said: *'I'm sorry, we can't do it.'* So I thought 'Ah naa, what'll a dee now?' I was trying to get there somehow but I was working, yer naa, and I had to work on New Year's Eve.

I thought: 'Right, I'll finish work at 5pm. I wonder how much a flight is from Newcastle to Paris, from Paris to Zaragoza and all that.' By the time I'd worked it all out, I could see I'd get to Zaragoza by half-time on New Year's Day. Then I'd have to have got to the ground, so it wouldn't have been worth it and I'd have got back a day later. So I decided there was nee way a could dee it. It really pissed me off, yer naa.

Of course I got ma money back but I was still really frustrated. Me and ma pals went out for New Year's Eve and by 11 o'clock I was ratted – I'd just knocked them back all evening. We were at my mate John's girlfriend's house in Hebburn and one of my mates said: *'Howay, Spow, we'll get you home.'* But I said: *'No, I'm stopping here.'* I was just still so annoyed.

I said 'I'm gonna put me heed doon' so I went in a side part of the hoose and I must have just drifted off when one of the lads said: *'Howay, Spow, it's nearly midnight!'* so I said: *'Right'* and that was it – I was back up and supping until about 7 o'clock in the morning. They said: *'Spow, I divn't naa where the hell you're putting it,'* and I replied: *'I divn't naa either but it's gannin' doon like wildfire.'*

Just at that moment, two of Bill and Harry's other pals enter the bar. Their names are Peter Donaghy and Peter Ratcliffe.

BILL GIBBS: How, Spow, obviously we're all sad for you that you lost your 100 per cent attendance record there, but would you mind if we talked with one lad who *did* get to Zaragoza?
SPOW: Aye, gaan on then, I'll not spoil the party. How did he get there though?
BILL GIBBS: Hello, lads, take a seat here – a couple of guys have just left after signing up for the Hibs trip. We're just reliving the good old days of last season. Peter D, meet Spow, he went to 11 out of the 12 Fairs Cup matches but he missed Zaragoza.
SPOW: Hiya Peter, nice to meet you. So how did you get there then? I couldn't manage it after the Supporters' Club trip went down the swannie.
PETER DONAGHY: Well, as Bill might have told you, I'm a teacher at St Cuthberts and obviously a Newcastle fan but I lived in Spain for a year-and-a-half while studying for my degree, so when the draw was made, I immediately offered my services to the club and they took me to Zaragoza as their interpreter.
TONY RODGERS: Wow, that must have been exciting – what an opportunity.
PETER DONAGHY: It was. I was delighted to be helping the club. When we checked into the hotel I was given three tasks. I was to help Joe Harvey go shopping for a pair of shoes because he always liked to buy a pair abroad. Then, Alderman William McKeag, an ageing

club director, needed a new battery for his hearing aid. Finally Bob Moncur – who, like all the other players, was fantastic with me – wanted to make sure the kitchen staff wouldn't be cooking their meat and steaks in any cooking oils or garlic.
I had various other little jobs and on New Year's Eve a sing-song started in the hotel bar and all the players were singing 'Lily the Pink' before midnight. You know, the song by The Scaffold?
HARRY WATSON: Oh aye? With Paul McCartney's brother Mike in it?
BILL GIBBS (smiling): Don't get Harry started on music – he's an expert so we might never hear the end of it.
PETER DONAGHY (laughing): OK, I won't. Anyway, there was also a Spanish team staying there, Granada, on their way home after a friendly match in Barcelona. There was talk of us playing a friendly with them later in the season, but of course United were too bound up with the Fairs Cup. I went to bed shortly after midnight to be ready for a busy time at the match the next day.

MICHAEL'S CLUB, NEWCASTLE UPON TYNE

JIM SCOTT: Don't forget, everyone, I'd played for Hibs against the likes of Barcelona and Valencia. I rated the Spaniards as being just as skilful ball players as the Portuguese, but far stronger and more progressive.
FRANK CLARK: Aye, the games were getting harder all the time but Europe didn't frighten us.

On the journalists' table, the reporters are animated in recalling their memories of matchday.

GIBBO: Thankfully, all the players had recovered from their cold symptoms in time to take advantage of Joe Harvey's permission to have one drink to see in the New Year and to join in with the Spanish tradition of eating 12 grapes at midnight – one for good luck in each of the next 12 months.

I know some of you will remember this as well. The Granada team was staying in the same hotel. They were given ample freedom after midnight and proceeded to entertain the non-playing members of our party with an impromptu cabaret performance.

Two of their stars actually produced Beatles wigs and long flowing beards to sing Spanish pop songs accompanied by two guitars. They finished off by chanting *'New-cass-ell'* in true Leazes End style and when we responded with a version of *'Gra-na-da'* it brought the house down!

Joe Harvey's players would've have been fast asleep by then. They'd already trained at Zaragoza's stadium earlier that day and they were due to hold another session at 10am on New Year's morning, ahead of the match a few hours later.

Let's face it though – by that time there wasn't much to fine-tune. The squad selected had been virtually the same for weeks and there were no surprises in the team Joe picked. Ollie Burton got the nod over John McNamee as Bob Moncur's central defensive partner and youngsters Keith Dyson and Alan Foggon were providing teenage zest either side of Wyn Davies and Pop Robson in attack.

For the first time, there was no Supporters' Club trip abroad but the team still had some support. Two Spanish brothers, Julio and Luis Montero, travelled 250 miles by car from Madrid to support United against their fellow countrymen. Why? Because both of them had worked on Tyneside and become fervent Magpies fans during their stay.

Phone calls also arrived from Bilbao, Alicante, Barcelona and Madrid all wishing United well, all from Spaniards who had at one time visited Newcastle. Not that their good wishes had much effect initially. Rather the opposite, in fact.

IVOR BROADIS: United were shocked straightaway when Craig conceded a corner in the first minute and the team shipped an opening goal moments later. Left winger Armando Martín sent a corner sailing over the bunched mass in front of McFaul. And Marcelino – along with Santos, one of the two Famous Five fit enough for this match – nodded the ball back to Bustillo.

He first-timed a shot from close in that McFaul saved on the line but Santos, lurking on the edge of the box, collected the hurried clearance and fired a tremendous left-foot shot into the roof of the net.

NICK SCURR: Geordie hearts were lifted two minutes later though, when Tommy Gibb – he had a wonderful game – took the ball out to the left and put over a low centre.

The ball appeared to be going too far across goal. Their keeper Nieves came out but he was always failing to catch up with it and he was left hopelessly stranded when Pop Robson appeared from nowhere and hooked the ball, almost from the byline, into the net.

IVOR BROADIS: But Newcastle were looking shaky in the air in front of their own goal – they were too vulnerable to the long, flighted cross and they were behind again on the quarter-hour mark. Foggon's youthful exuberance led to a brush with Moya down the right. Full-back Borras stepped up to take the free-kick and Bustillo left McFaul groping when he powered a downward header past him from fully ten yards.

GIBBO: You know, Bob Moncur admitted to me later that the defenders were beaten in both cases because they didn't expect the light ball to carry so far in the air, but once they got the measure of it the iron curtain clanged down firmly. Then, enter Wyn the Leap.

IVOR BROADIS: You know, you could just tell from the confident strut of the long, lean Welshman that this was going to be his day. The Spaniards just hadn't a clue how to prevent him winning the ball in the air and United wisely looked for him with the bulk of the passes they played forward.

JOE CUMMINGS of The Sun: It was certainly a fascinating duel between Davies and their centre-half Santamaria. He was a big, muscular Spaniard, very much a local hero and he'd pranced and

preened at the start with cocky self-assurance. But after 90 minutes trying to mark Wyn, he looked sick and bedraggled.
It was the best and most exciting exhibition I've seen from him and he crowned it with a goal that was not only spectacular but also went a long way to putting United into the quarter-finals.
IVOR BROADIS: Yet again, it was Robson's courage which opened the door. His tremendous run took him almost the length of the field before he was unceremoniously halted on the edge of the box by their left-back Irusquieta. As Robson counted the bruises, Gibb stepped up and almost nonchalantly curled a short free-kick just over the defensive wall for Davies, moving quicker than his marker, to head in a splendid goal.
JOE CUMMINGS: Yes, it really was – it screamed into the net. Meanwhile, Santamaria dropped to his knees and tore his hair in anguish.

ZARAGOZA, SPAIN, 15TH JULY 1969

Next to the Estadio de la Romareda there's a small precinct full of quite smart cafés, bars and restaurants. It's where players often go for smaller functions or parties, especially on non-matchdays when it's much quieter.
This time, the squad has come together for two reasons – firstly, to toast their successful battle against relegation from La Liga; and secondly, to bid farewell to Miguel Ángel Bustillo, their explosive centre-forward who has finally moved to Barcelona in a deal agreed last winter.
After a while, the subject of the Fairs Cup and the Newcastle tie arises, not least because the genial owner of the bar they're in, Juanjo Laporta, has visited England in the past and is keen to know what his guests experienced. He was also at the home game and could scarcely believe his eyes when he saw how high the opposing centre-forward could leap.

MANUEL GONZÁLEZ (Santamaria's central-defensive partner for Real Zaragoza): Basically, Davies was tall and difficult to defend against. One example stands out. There was a free-kick just before half-time. I was stood next to him in the box when Santamaria came marching over: '*Stop! I'll mark him! You go over there.*'
So I did. The ball came in, Davies rose highest and headed the ball inside the far post for the equalising goal. Then he did something even more amazing.
He came over to Santamaria, who is a Zaragoza legend and a Spanish international, smiled at him and then lightly ruffled his hair as he knelt on the ground. Santamaria nearly exploded in anger and humiliation.

MICHAEL'S CLUB, NEWCASTLE UPON TYNE

As his plus-one, Wyn Davies invited to the celebratory banquet the young nurse, Angela, who looked after him so well in hospital while he was recovering from the broken cheekbone, which he suffered from throughout much of the final tie.

Naturally they're enjoying themselves and at this moment she playfully says with a smile: 'Now, Wyn, I didn't realise when you asked me here that everyone would be talking about how good you are!'

DAVE ELLIOTT: Ah, well, my good mate Wyn here was at the forefront of everything last season. I tell you, he's so good in the air, a player who gives his all – always 100 per cent. He makes a lot happen for our top goalscorer Pop Robson, who's over there on Bob's table, and we basically rely on him as our spearhead up front. One season, you know, Wyn played all 42 league games so if he wasn't in the team, he was a big miss.

DAVE CLARKE: Wyn Davies was fantastic... absolutely awesome. When we played away, they didn't know what to do with him. The continentals had never seen anybody like him, jumping as high as he could – six foot tall and he could jump another six foot. Unbelievable!

Against Zaragoza, we were taking a free-kick just before half-time and Wyn was standing at the back of the penalty area waiting to run in. I was sat on the bench next to Joe Harvey and I said to Joe: '*Look. Look what they're doing to Wyn!*'

Two players were stood right next to him – not even looking at the corner flag – but kicking his legs. Literally kicking his legs. Joe jumped up, grabbed the linesman and shouted: '*Eh! What's gannin' on here?*' But nothing happened.

Anyway, the corner comes in… bang, goal. Wyn's thumped in another header. He came off and honestly, his legs were black and blue. They were just hacking him because they couldn't jump with him.

GEOFF ALLEN: He's just a phenomenal player; he plays his heart out for you. Once he'd put that shirt on and was upfront, he gives everything for you. Phenomenal in the air – it doesn't matter how or which way the ball comes across – he has a go for you. It's priceless what he does for you if you could get a cross in. You can't get players like him every day and what he did in this campaign for Newcastle has made him a legend.

Hey, I'll tell you a story. I'll always remember when I'd just started – and it was the biggest wind-up ever – he said to me: '*When you cross that ball, just make sure the lace is away from my head.*' I was only 17 and I thought: 'How the hell am I going to do that?' He kept a straight face but this was worrying me sick. I thought: 'He plays for Wales. He's a Welsh international and I'm just starting.'

Anyway, a little later, he put his arm around me and said: *'It's a joke, you know...'*

IVOR BROADIS: Into that second half, the home side switched wingers and it worked after 57 minutes. Martín and Planas II moved like a couple of trains on parallel tracks. Martín raced down the right wing with Planas in the middle and the cross came in so accurately that the latter didn't need to check his stride before sending an unstoppable half-volley, high past McFaul and into the net from just inside the box. It was a fitting goal to win a match – any match – and so it proved. That was despite a great chance for young Dyson to level with five minutes to go when Robson left him with just the keeper to beat as he arrived in the box. An awkward bounce meant his first swing at the ball was missed and he was caught by a recovering defender. Then, his second effort lacked power as Nieves turned it round for a corner. This was an incredibly brave United performance against a team of high quality. Wyn did enough battling to underline his immense value and the men at the back took some hard knocks, but they did a great job after that nasty early shock.

WILLIE MCFAUL: To be honest, we weren't very happy after the game on New Year's Day. If one game went against us, that would be the one where we thought maybe we couldn't pull it back. To concede three goals wasn't us. We're tight-knit. We may argue with each other on the pitch – they might say: '*Are you gonna come for that ball or are we going to get it?*' There was always a lot of communication but that game put a question mark against us when we conceded those three goals. If there was one game in the whole run that worried me, it was this one.

BOB MONCUR: I still thought we could go on to beat them at home, but that it wouldn't be easy. I didn't enjoy seeing that third goal go in either, but I must admit it's the greatest I've seen in years.
FRANK CLARK: I didn't know whether to clap or cry when that went in. You almost wanted to stop and applaud because it was such a good goal, such a great passing movement from within their own half. It was one of those moves that we couldn't have done anything about really. Simply, Zaragoza were a very technical, short-passing team with a lot of pace. Some of the football they played in the game out there when they beat us 3-2 was really terrific; they were a really good side.

JOE HARVEY: Zaragoza were a most skilful team with plenty of power too. They were certainly the best side we'd faced in Europe by that stage. I was highly satisfied with that result, believe me – two goals away from home takes some getting. The team were marvellous. A lot of the lads took hard knocks but they kept fighting back when behind – they are a side who will never admit defeat. Zaragoza's third goal was one of the best I've ever seen. The build-up and finish was tremendous.
NEWCASTLE DIRECTOR STAN SEYMOUR: It was certainly a great result for us. We still had to remember they were a great side when they came over to Newcastle, but I thought we'd be too strong for them, especially if ground conditions would give a little and be more to our liking.

GIBBO: Then came the 15 minutes of fame for our much-valued translator on this trip, Peter Donaghy. He and schoolboy Stuart Rush, a relative of our director Jimmy, were perhaps the only United fans who'd travelled from England to Zaragoza for the match. It all started when we got back to the Hotel Goya after the game. Peter's a native of Newcastle and had helped tremendously with communications ever since the draw. But he'd never been so important to us as when we found two pistol-packing, plain-clothes policemen waiting in reception.

I remember when I wrote about it, Peter told me: *'A list of the members of our party staying at the hotel had been sent to police headquarters in Zaragoza. On checking the list, they discovered the initials and names of Jim Scott and coach Dave Smith coincided with those of two Englishmen wanted for failure to pay fines for offences committed months earlier in Spain.*

'Of course, Jim and Dave had both been to Spain before, so this increased the suspicion. These two tough-looking detectives insisted on seeing the pair and we had to check dates of birth, addresses and other personal details before they were satisfied they didn't need to make any arrests and it was just a case of mistaken identity. It was a bit frightening at the time though, I can tell you.'

THE BRIDGE HOTEL

SPOW: Eventually I got back home from the New Year's Eve party in Hebburn and went to bed. Later in the afternoon, I was lying on the settee when my dad came in and told me:

'Youse are gettin' beat.'

I replied: *'Ahh, no! What's the score?'*

'3-2', he says.

'Oh, great.'

'What do you mean? They're getting beat,' my Dad repeated.

'Yeah, I know', I said. *'But we've scored two away goals which can count double if it's level after the second leg, so now we only need to win 1-0 or 2-1 at St James' Park.'*

REAL ZARAGOZA AT HOME...

INTER-CITIES FAIRS CUP 3RD ROUND 2ND LEG

NEWCASTLE UNITED 2
REAL ZARAGOZA 1

Kick-off: 19:30, Wednesday 15th January 1969
Referee: Roger Barde (France)
Venue: St James' Park, Newcastle upon Tyne, England
Attendance: 56,055

Newcastle United: Willie McFaul; David Craig (Ron Guthrie 46), Ollie Burton, Bob Moncur (c), Frank Clark; Jim Scott, Tommy Gibb; Keith Dyson, Wyn Davies, Bryan Robson, Alan Foggon
Substitutes not used: Dave Clarke (GK), John McNamee

Real Zaragoza: Nieves (Alarcia 30); Santamaria, Rico, Manuel González, Luis Violeta, Irusquieta, Borrás, Santos (c), Fontenla (Tejedor 73), Armando Martín, Bustillo.
Substitutes not used: Moya, Diaz

Goalscorers:
1-0: Bryan Robson (2)
2-0: Tommy Gibb (29)
2-1: Armando Martín (43)

Newcastle United win on the away goals rule after drawing 4-4 on aggregate.

MICHAEL'S CLUB, NEWCASTLE UPON TYNE

AT THE JOURNALISTS' TABLE

TONY BOULLEMIER: In my short time at the Journal and in the company of you gentlemen, I've always had to defend my taste in ties. When Real Zaragoza arrived in Newcastle, their forward Moya – clearly a very discerning chap – made a beeline for me and asked where I'd bought my flower-power tie. My Spanish isn't as hot as my tie collection so I had to use sign language to tell him where the first stop on his shopping expedition should be.
GIBBO: Don't listen to the doubters, Tony. But please don't get me a tie for Chistmas – a card will do! **(chortles from the rest of the hacks as they tuck into their house wines).**

Some of the younger lads have been asked what it's like on a match evening as they wait to get out there onto the pitch in front of a capacity crowd. Keith Dyson takes the table through his routine on a Fairs Cup evening.

KEITH DYSON: You just see so many people outside as you're coming in and you can just feel it – the whole city's buzzing. People are just pouring in. With me getting into the team so quickly, having only signed as a professional weeks earlier, I didn't have a car so I got the bus in for league matches.
Actually, Foggon might have a car because he's a bit ahead of the game, you know **(smiling)**. For league matches, I get the bus in and have to listen to fans saying: *'Ah, you had a shocker there'* or *'Weren't you good?'* Or just trying to talk to me. In the end, I have to ignore them and not take what they say to heart too much.
For the Fairs Cup matches though, I've managed to get one of my dad's friends to give me a lift in. It's always around dusk so you're just getting that night-time feel with the floodlights coming on. You can

feel the anticipation of the fans milling around in Strawberry Lane and Barrack Road and this really helps everyone play out of their skins. There's definitely a bit of pressure – it makes you alert; you're just up for it; that's what it is. You see their smiles as you drive into the club car park with a barrage of people either side of you, who wave at you. Then you have a 50-yard walk to the players' entrance through the crowd, so you feel the crowd all the time and hear their good luck shouts.

We're told to be there an hour beforehand – half-six for a half-seven kick-off – and everyone's always on time. You go in through the entrance in the main stand, turn right and head into the dressing room – we don't usually carry much in. Then you try to pass the time getting a massage or saying there's something wrong with your boots or whatever.

Alec Mutch does all the massages – he's a hard nut in a good sense, in that he doesn't have any nonsense or timewasters. But once you're a bona fide person needing a massage, he does it properly and I think he's good, although I hardly ever need one. You can get stripped in five minutes so you have to draw out the time by going to the toilet, having a word with Alec... you're never drinking anything like tea or water.

Ah, I know what we do... we read the match programme. There are always 20 or so placed in the dressing room and you're dying to see who you're playing against and what's been said about them and you. Or to find out who you're playing in the next round or if the draw's been made, what the previous results were, did they get the stats right from the last league game, all that kind of stuff... the programme's a big thing actually.

Everyone tries to get a programme to slip away with for the evening, just for their personal collection and to prove they've played in that game. The other big thing is that after the matches, we're absolutely buzzing that we've won through to the next round.

There's little or no coaching or technical stuff on matchday, mind. Joe's like a gangster: '*Right, lads, you've got to do what I say, you do this, you do that...*' There's no actual substance in it. He relies on

Dave Smith to produce any technical advice. Joe comes out with a rallying cry, then he's away and it's Dave giving the instructions individually. Or it might be the other way around. Dave might start with the instructions then with about 20 minutes to go to kick-off, the boss would be in with a final *'Let's get stuck in.'*

There aren't any warm-ups and there's no kicking balls around – there are no balls or facilities – no gym or anything – so there's nothing to do like that. All you do is stretch or try to walk a few yards to see what Alec Mutch's doing or who he's treating. There's no going out onto the pitch and then coming back in.

And when we're out there, it's a ball between three, passing; a few sprints; stay in your own half; then off we go.

GIBBO: There were plenty of VIPs at Gallowgate this time, and not just from the world of football either. Tory party leader Edward Heath watched the game from the directors' box as the first stop on his tour of the North East last year, despite his plane only landing at 6:45pm. I had to laugh when I remembered United secretary Denis Barker saying before the match that:

'We are delighted to welcome him to the game. I understand that he could miss the first few minutes but that doesn't really matter.'

How wrong you were this time, Denis. How wrong you were!

THE BRIDGE HOTEL

PETER DONAGHY: This time, at home, my main role was to interpret for the dignitaries as they entertained their Spanish counterparts. Zaragoza had actually been staying at the Station Hotel in town but I remember the official pre-match dinner was at the Gosforth Park Hotel.

There, Lord Westwood seemed intent on telling as many jokes as he could to Real's president but, as any interpreter will tell you, translating jokes is the hardest task out there. Evidently, the Scottish sense of humour didn't marry with what the Spanish found funny, because eventually he gave up trying to make his guest laugh and told his jokes to me instead.

The most memorable part of my day came later though. One special guest was Edward Heath. He arrived from the airport just before kick-off and I had interpret for him as he circulated around the directors' box greeting other dignitaries.

On seeing the president of Real Zaragoza across the room, he asked me to deliver this message:

'I hope it's a good game, but that the forces of democracy triumph against the forces of totalitarianism.'

Well, I couldn't possible make a political statement like that, so I improvised: *'I hope it's a good game and that the best team wins.'*

TONY RODGERS: Brilliant. I love it!

PETER DONAGHY: The Right Honourable Gentleman's mischief didn't end there, mind. On the final whistle, he told me to relay a question:

'Should I send a telegram to my great friend General Franco, asking him to spare your lives on your return?'

I mean, how can you say that? It was bonkers. I translated it as:

'I hope you have a good flight and you get home safely.'

Heath clearly likes a good laugh and it must have been the first thing that came into his head. I think he thought he was being quite hilarious. The Spaniards though, would not have been amused at all.

BILL GIBBS: Crikey, that's a belting story, Peter. I was at the match too – as I guess we all were. I remember hearing about this away-goals rule and being a bit baffled by it all at first. We were in the Leazes End and the whole place was getting fed up with some of the Spaniards' antics, especially when they didn't come out straightaway for the second half. We were all singing: '*You can stuff your Spanish onions up your a***!*'

IN THE BAR NEXT TO ESTADIO DE LA ROMAREDA

JOSÉ RICO, REAL ZARAGOZA DEFENDER: Our centre-forward Marcelino was really a key player so his absence due to physical problems hit us. He was one of the best strikers in the world and had headed the winning goal for Spain against Lev Yashin in the 1964 European Championship final. Real Zaragoza always played with the aim of serving him and Los Magnificos, so without him we lost our focal point in attack.

Marcelino, Carlo Lapetra, Santos, Villa, Canario. When we had these five players in good condition, playing together, we were unbeatable and the thing is with Marcelino, you have a different tactic, you have a team playing for him and it changes everything. You have more confidence too.

Without him, we had to change the tactics, everything. We lost our reference point and with that we lost our goalscorer, our man who could jump two metres to head a ball and who was sharp in the penalty area too. Of the five Magnificos from the club's golden period in the 1960s, only Santos played in Newcastle.

MICHAEL'S CLUB, NEWCASTLE UPON TYNE

AT THE JOURNALISTS' TABLE

GIBBO: Real Zaragoza flew in without several key players – injury claimed Marcelino, Villa, Lapetra and both the Planas brothers. Furthermore, travelling Spanish journalists told me they expected Zaragoza to be eliminated because of their failure to hit any consistent form away from the Romareda stadium. Only one away win in La Liga – 1-0 against bottom club Cordoba – and losses in both Fairs Cup away legs bore that out.

TONY BOULLEMIER: Joe was having none of it though. He told me: *'They've got a first-team pool of 25 over there and they never seem to play the same team two games running. No. These so-called reserves will be just as good as the men we know about.'*

GIBBO: Joe showed true faith in the team that had fought so hard in Spain a fortnight earlier, selecting the same starting eleven with the only difference being Ron Guthrie on the bench in place of Jackie Sinclair, who was ill. And of course this time, it was United's turn to strike early.

IVOR BROADIS: That's right. There was no time for speculation about how long they'd need to chalk off that one-goal deficit from the first match. While small boys were eluding policemen to shin over the stadium wall and late-comers were still filing through the turnstiles, Bryan Robson was already pumping those sturdy legs in from the right wing in a quick zig-zag.

First to the right of one man, a quick feint, then left of another at breathtaking speed. Then, without breaking stride, a tremendous 30-yard left-footer, rising all the way. It hit the roof of the net and left goalkeeper Nieves flat-footed.

Truly something out of nothing – a goal that took us back more than a decade to Jackie Milburn here.

JACKIE MILBURN (legendary former Newcastle United centre-forward and now a journalist with the News of the World): That's very kind of you, Ivor. The thing is, Pop keeps it simple. He does what I used to do. He looks up briefly to note where the goal is and then looks down to concentrate on hitting that ball as hard as he possibly can. That brought me 200 goals for Newcastle.

DOUG WEATHERALL: I remember many of them well, Jackie. Yes, it was a stupendous goal. Astonishing. And after only two minutes. It was hard to tell who was the more overjoyed – the players or the crowd. Both went crazy and Robson was mobbed by his teammates. It was clearly going to be a night to remember.

CHARLIE SUMMERBELL of the Daily Mirror: Zaragoza were working the ball cleverly in midfield while Newcastle, remembering Wyn's success over in Spain, constantly lofted the ball to him. This time, he was given close attention by Borras. Santos was booked in the eighth minute for arguing with the referee while, at the other end, Newcastle wasted no time on finesse when danger threatened. One of Real's goalscorers in the first leg, Bustillo, showed his power for almost the first time in the 23rd minute when he out-jumped the home defence to a long free-kick from Rico, but the striker could only head over the bar.

ARNOLD HOWE of the Daily Express: After 29 minutes though, Newcastle were two up. And the second really was a gift. Robson took an inswinging corner kick from the left – earned by Clark – and Nieves, with no one near him, only had to grab the ball. Unaccountably, he punched it clear with two fists and Tommy Gibb raced in from the edge of the penalty area to head it straight back into the vacant goal.

CHARLIE SUMMERBELL: Quite right and it was a bullet-force header. Zaragoza were far from finished though.

IN THE BAR NEXT TO ESTADIO DE LA ROMAREDA

GONZÁLEZ: Shortly after their second goal, I saw Alan Foggon career at high speed into our goalkeeper Nieves. Our teammate went down injured after a knee landed in his chest and I could see the pain on his contorted face. It was all going wrong for us. We were heading out of the competition. We were struggling in the league and it seemed the end of a glorious era was nigh. And for Nieves, there was now nothing he could do about it.

'*Nieves*', I said. '*Where does it hurt? What's the matter?*'

All he said was: '*I think they've broken my heart.*'

He was stretchered off the pitch, not to be seen again.

On came his replacement, Alarcia. He wouldn't stand for any nonsense. At the first cross he faced, he jumped up and punched a Newcastle player full in the face. Two or three of them looked on, shocked. After that, they didn't touch our goalkeeper for the rest of the match and, in fact, he had a great game. He made some splendid saves. Then, shortly after Alarcia's entrance, came some hope.
ARMANDO MARTÍN (Zaragoza's 22-year-old winger from Argentina): A Newcastle defender who had been making a lot of tackles was marking me as a cross came in, just before half-time. But he wasn't quick enough to stop me stealing in and scoring. I remember him, because he played quite dirtily and I remember jumping for joy in celebration after I'd scored. I was up against someone bigger and more likely to win the ball that I was, but I managed it somehow. It was one of the best moments in my career to score a goal in Newcastle, especially as it was the club's 100th goal in European competition, in the 50th match. At half-time, our coach César Rodríguez was very calm – he never used many words or told us to do this, this and that. He wasn't motivational in the way that, say, Alfredo Di Stéfano was. And to this day I've no idea why we were delayed in emerging for the second-half.

MICHAEL'S CLUB, NEWCASTLE UPON TYNE

DOUG WEATHERALL: Martín had cut United's lead with a well-taken goal. Violeta's low through ball was deliberately left by Santos for the winger to control with his right foot and shoot in low with his left from ten yards.
CHARLIE SUMMERBELL: If we're honest, gentlemen, Newcastle were badly shaken at that point and were back-pedalling until half-time. Ron Guthrie, Joe's late choice as substitute, took over from hamstring injury victim David Craig for the second-half. The European debutant went to left-back and Frank Clark switched to the right.

DOUG WEATHERALL: Let's remember too, knowing that conceding another goal could end their European run could hardly have been comforting for United.
TONY BOULLEMIER: Especially given that the Newcastle players were left to contemplate this all alone on the pitch for fully five minutes before a linesmen went into the dressing room to call out Zaragoza. They still didn't come out and it needed the referee to go in and give them a roasting before they turned up.
IVOR BROADIS: But in that second half, Newcastle were like a pack of hounds at a wounded deer, don't you think? Worrying away for the kill and giving the Spaniards no time to settle.
ARNOLD HOWE: But these skilful Spaniards eventually started showing what they could do and the pressure was on the home side. This is when skipper Bob Moncur, Ollie Burton and the others battled magnificently to keep them out.
DENIS LOWE of the Daily Telegraph: In the last 20 minutes though, Newcastle again took over. Alarcia brought off four excellent saves from Gibb, Dyson, Robson and Davies and in the end, Joe Harvey's men were good value for their place in the quarter-final.

RON GUTHRIE: You could tell by their ball control they were really good – they had a lovely touch. You had to make sure you got there straight away so they couldn't turn you. It was a press – we got really tight to them so they didn't have time on the ball. We kept them at bay well and I can't remember them having a shot on target in the second half.
KEITH DYSON: Yes, Zaragoza were very good actually. They kept the ball more, so when you got it you had to keep it too. Dave Smith would shout to the others: *'Get the ball to Keith so he can shield it and take up a bit of time.'* It was more akin to the style of Don Revie's Leeds in winning a game rather than being expansive.

3RD ROUND 2ND LEG

These two games against Real Zaragoza were really hard-fought. The home game in particular wasn't open like it had been against Feyenoord when we won 4-0 and were cruising. This time, we really had to scrap. But we were through.

BACK IN THE BAR NEXT TO ESTADIO DE LA ROMAREDA

GONZÁLEZ: When Newcastle beat us, the dream came to an end.
MARTÍN: At the end of the match, lots of the Newcastle crowd came streaming onto the pitch. They came on once but it wasn't over – it was just a free-kick had been given. Then they came on again. We were all scared but actually they were friendly. They were celebrating but without touching the players – they were so respectful.
JOSÉ RICO: They defeated us on away goals but a year or two earlier, a replay would have decided the tie. We were very sad that a new rule meant we didn't have another chance.
NIEVES: It had been 50/50 which of these two teams would win – there was no favourite and in the end we weren't totally surprised that Newcastle beat us because they were good and we were struggling at that time.
Marcelino was our focal point. He was as important to us as Bobby Charlton is to Manchester United. And when he and other key players such as Lapetra were absent, there was no plan B. No plan B because there wasn't the same calibre of player in reserve. There was a huge difference in quality.
GONZÁLEZ: After the match, both teams were having a drink in the refreshments room and Davies beckoned to me to come over. I thought: 'Uh oh, are we going to continue hitting each other here?' but he just asked the barman for two beers – he just wanted us to drink together. He was a nice guy.

AT THE BAR IN MICHAEL'S CLUB

BRYAN POP ROBSON: When I got the ball for my goal, there was a gap. I moved between two defenders and I was surprised that no one came to meet me. I just cracked the ball without aiming for any particular spot and I was delighted when it flew in. I actually feel it was a better goal than the one I scored against Sporting Lisbon. It gave me greater satisfaction anyway.
TOMMY GIBB (who's popped over for a moment): It was great seeing both ours hit the net. For mine, I'd seen the cross come over just in front of their keeper. I thought he might be forced to punch it out so I ran in and kept hoping. It came to me at shoulder height so I bent and headed it as hard as I could.
DAVID CRAIG: Both of yours you've mentioned now, Pop, were both absolute crackers, so they were, and this was another tight game. I was really disappointed to have to come off but I'd pulled a muscle in the back of my leg about ten minutes before half-time – my usual injury hoodoo.
WYN DAVIES: After we'd played Real Zaragoza, I was told Ted Heath wanted to meet me. He said he'd had a good seat right in the middle of the stand, so I said: '*What about getting me one in the summer?*' Mr Heath looked puzzled, so I explained that he probably had more chance than me of getting seats for the investiture of Prince Charles in Caernavon, my home town.
FRANK CLARK: Overall, Újpest were the best team we played but Real Zaragoza would have run them close. We were a little bit lucky right through the campaign – we did get a lot of breaks – sometimes you get them, sometimes you don't. But Real Zaragoza had a really excellent team which had been doing really well in Europe. They were just on the cusp of fading away when we played them but they were still excellent.

▌3RD ROUND 2ND LEG▐

JOE HARVEY: Pop Robson's goal was the most important of the 20 he'd scored until that point of the season. I was a little bit worried just before half-time but the second half belonged to us. With any luck, we could have had five goals. I wasn't as worried as in some of the other Fairs Cup games; I only smoked nine cigarettes, which is good going for me. I knew for the next round we wanted to steer clear of Leeds and Rangers. These foreign trips are the ones which stir up interest for everyone so another continental team suited us fine.

While the guests are enjoying the fish course and the drink flows, the bar manager is tickled by how his young barmen keenly analyse each round of the Fairs Cup using their scrapbooks and memorabilia.

BAR MANAGER (while tidying up empty bottles and glasses): I guess you were there too, lads. It really sounds like that was an exciting night.

BARMAN 1: It was. Incredible. Tense too. One goal and we could have been out. My father was with me but my uncle couldn't watch – he was stood outside with Bobby Cowell, who wouldn't watch again as he still thought he was a jinx.

BARMAN 2: We were all nervous during that second half. Mind when I wrote about it to my penfriend Gyuri in Budapest, he wrote back saying it had been even worse watching Újpest Dózsa struggle against Legia Warsaw, who turned out to be a real class act.

BAR MANAGER: That's the team who won the Polish league this last season, right?

BARMAN 1: Yes, that's them. So what did Gyuri say about Újpest this time then?

BARMAN 2: Read for yourselves – here are his match reports:

POLE-AXED! LATE DRAMA AS DUNAI DOWNS LEGIA
23rd FEBRUARY 1969

Arctic temperatures and a frozen pitch couldn't stop Újpest Dózsa unexpectedly securing a narrow victory in their Fairs Cup third round, second-leg encounter away at Legia Warsaw on Sunday, Antal Dunai scoring the vital goal in the 85th minute of a contest which last season's Hungarian league runners-up could easily have lost.

Rustiness in their first competitive match of the new year was compounded by footwear which couldn't stop the players sliding around on an icy surface. The need to play this tie before next week's quarter-final dates meant that another postponement (the teams had already needed special dispensation from the Fairs Cup committee to play this tie later than planned) was out of the question.

A combination of poor Polish finishing and heroics from Újpest goalkeeper Antal Szentmihályi rendered the hosts' effective crossfield passes and long forward balls unrewarded and the game remained goalless at half-time. At this point, Lajos Baróti's men changed their boots and become much more adept in these conditions.

It was much more even after that and gradually the 10,000-strong crowd – of which approximately 100 were Hungarian supporters – started to see the real Dózsa. Five minutes from time, the unmarked Antal Dunai finished calmly from seven metres following László Fazekas' corner kick.

On the plane home, head coach **LAJOS BARÓTI** told how pleased he was with his team's defensive resolve:

'This was our first serious match of the year and our team showed how to battle it out. It surprised me a little, since this isn't generally a characteristic of Dozsa's game. We learnt from the footwear situation too. We could not stop ourselves in those plastic studded boots in the

first half so we gave up territory to Legia to counter the problem. After the break, with rubber-studded boots, we were a different proposition. In defence, Noskó did a great job neutralising Brychczy and this contributed to the win. Of course Legia could still have won, but if they'd have scored, we'd then have become more attacking. I'm delighted with the victory. It's a great advantage to have won away because Legia Warsaw are an exceptional team.'

ANTAL SZENTMIHÁLYI, the Dózsa goalkeeper who denied the Poles at least six or seven certain goals with fabulous saves, had this to say: '*To win on such an unrealistic surface for football is a huge achievement. It was a great surprise to see Dózsa play in a spirited way that I've never seen before. Legia were a much better team than we expected. We had some great luck.*'

Meanwhile **JÁNOS GÖRÖCS** hailed his goalkeeper before sounding caution ahead of the second leg in Budapest three days later: '*We certainly can't be sure of progression against Legia at Megyeri út. We really need to take care in the first half on Wednesday. However, if we score at least two goals, I don't think there can be a problem.*'

BACK FROM THE BRINK! DÓZSA RECOVER FROM TWO DOWN TO REACH FAIRS CUP LAST EIGHT, 26th FEBRUARY 1969

LEEDS UNITED SPIES LINDLEY AND OWEN WATCH ON AS DUNAI CONTINUES HOT SCORING STREAK

On another surface more like winter farmland, Újpest Dózsa overcame the inclement conditions and a two-goal half-time deficit against Legia Warsaw to take their hard-earned place in the Fairs Cup quarter-finals.

A single-goal advantage from the first leg in Poland three days earlier gave Lajos Baróti's men a little comfort going into this return match on Wednesday. But that positivity was replaced by rampant panic by half-time on a muddy Megyeri út pitch, as Legia's attacking prowess finally bore fruit.

Firstly, Władysław Stachurski's 28-metre howitzer of a free-kick crashed into the top left corner of the net via the crossbar in the 41st minute. Then, two minutes later, Poland international midfielder Janusz Żmijewski cut in from the right wing, by-passed several defenders and slid the ball past Szentmihályi to double Dózsa's trouble.

Legia were now 2-1 up and in sight of the competition's last eight, but Baróti's charges had other ideas. It helps when you have a goalscorer in red-hot form and last year's European Silver Boot holder Antal Dunai is certainly that. The Hungarian international forward reduced the arrears in the 67th minute, nodding in a flick from his namesake Ede Dunai, after a clever chip by Ferenc Bene.

Eight minutes later, László Fazekas was felled in the Warsaw penalty area and central defender Ernő Solymosi dispatched the spotkick with aplomb to hand his team a 3-2 aggregate victory.

LAJOS BARÓTI (Újpesti Dózsa head coach): *'I'm very happy that we fought through to qualify but I didn't like how we played. I'll admit it – we were lucky.'*

JAROSLAV VEJVODA (Legia head coach): *'The best team doesn't always win. We were on top in Warsaw and also in the first half here. Luck and to a certain extent the referee helped Újpest.'*

BAR MANAGER: It sounds like never-say-die spirit was in abundance at both ends of European football. Did this third round sort out the men from the boys?

BARMAN 1: I suppose so. Eintracht Frankfurt were again goal-shy and lost 2-1 on aggregate to Athletic Bilbao. Turkey's Göztepe edged past OFK Belgrade on away goals, as did Hamburg against Hibernian.
BARMAN 2: Scotland's last representative are Rangers – they cruised through 4-1 against DWS Amsterdam. Elsewhere, Leeds United sent out some real tremors with a 7-2 shellacking of Hannover 96. The biggest surprise of the round was Vitória Setúbal unceremoniously dumping out Italian supremos Fiorentina 4-2 over the two legs, despite being down to ten men for part of the second match when their captain Conceição was sent off.
BAR MANAGER: Yes, it definitely feels like we're starting to get to the business end now. What was the draw:
BARMAN 1: Újpest vs Leeds pretty much paired the two favourites together.
BARMAN 2: Bilbao-Rangers looked tasty too. Göztepe drew West Germany's Hamburg, European Cup Winners' Cup finalists the previous year.
BARMAN 1: So that left us and Vitória Setúbal. We'd be going back to Portugal, but not before some fun and games at St James' Park.

FAIRS CUP QUARTER-FINAL

NEWCASTLE UNITED
v
— VITÓRIA DE SETÚBAL —

ÚJPESTI DÓZSA
v
LEEDS UNITED

VITÓRIA DE SETÚBAL AT HOME...

INTER-CITIES FAIRS CUP QUARTER-FINAL 1ST LEG

NEWCASTLE UNITED 5
VITÓRIA DE SETÚBAL 1

Kick-off: 19:30, Wednesday 12th March 1969
Referee: Curt Liedberg (Sweden)
Venue: St James' Park, Newcastle upon Tyne, England
Attendance: 57,662

Newcastle United: Willie McFaul; John Craggs, Bob Moncur (c), Ollie Burton, Frank Clark; Tommy Gibb, Jim Scott; Bryan Robson, Wyn Davies, Arthur Horsfield (Jackie Sinclair 68), Alan Foggon
Substitutes not used: Dave Clarke (GK), John McNamee

Vitória de Setúbal: Vital, Herculano, Carriço, Carlos Cardoso (c), Alfredo Moreira, Vagner, José Maria, Jacinto João (Fernando Tomé 63), Figueiredo, Arcanjo (Petita 56), Vítor Baptista
Substitutes not used: Torres (GK)

Goalscorers:
1-0: Alan Foggon (23)
2-0: Bryan Robson (36)
3-0: Wyn Davies (60)
4-0: Bryan Robson (75)
4-1: José Maria (84)
5-1: Tommy Gibb (89)

MICHAEL'S CLUB, NEWCASTLE UPON TYNE

ANNOUNCEMENT: Ladies and Gentlemen, the main course – Roast Duckling a la Setúbal Portugaise with side dishes of Potato a la Harvey, Green Beans a la Smith and Brussel Sprouts Moncur – is about to be served.

The guests are back in their seats. At the journalists' table, Gibbo kicks off the discussion on their second experience of a Portuguese team on this amazing journey.

GIBBO: Setúbal's a little fishing port 25 miles south of Lisbon, sandwiched between the Arrabida mountain and the Atlantic Ocean, but there was nothing small-time about their European record at that point. Northern Ireland's Linfield, Olympique Lyon of France and Italian league leaders Fiorentina had all felt the lash of Setúbal's goal-hungry forwards, who'd rattled in 17 goals in three rounds.
Fernando Vaz, Setúbal's diminuitive, English-speaking boss used to be a Lisbon banker. He flew into Newcastle and charmed everyone with his courtesy and friendliness but in spite of being a strong-willed disciplinarian, he was about to encounter an unexpected problem that not even he could solve.
For a week before they arrived, the sun shone brilliantly but by the time they booked into the Five Bridges Hotel in Gateshead, threatening, grey clouds were creeping across the sky. The next morning – 24 hours before the game – it happened. Snow, tons of it, came cascading down to completely change everything.
Honestly, I'll never forget the scene when I took a photographer to see them. There were the players, clamouring by the door, obviously excited by the sight of snow actually falling out of the sky. When they spotted us, they rushed forward begging us to take their photographs. What souvenirs these would make back home in Setúbal, where snow hadn't fallen for 25 years!

But while the players pranced around like schoolboys on an outing, Vaz was standing in the foyer, ashen-faced. He alone knew what this meant for Vitória. He sent someone outside to record the temperature and loudly appealed for the match to be called off: '*We don't want snow. It is very bad for us. We want the match off until it is fine.*' But it was all to no avail.

TONY BOULLEMIER: Aside from the weather, Vaz told me his big fear was Wyn Davies: '*I saw your Geoff Hurst score three goals in the World Cup final. But for me, Davies is better – more dangerous in the air and more worrying for defences.*'

At the pre-match press conference he came out with a quaint expression: '*When I look out of my window this morning, I see the snow and think at once of your English pop singer Cliff Richard and his song 'Congratulations'. So I say 'Congratulations Newcastle – it snowed last time I was here when your recent match with Wolves was called off, and now it does it again.*'

ARNOLD HOWE: The Portuguese players regarded football in this weather as an entirely new form of purgatory. Some of us had been with Joe Harvey to watch Vitória draw 1-1 with lowly Leixões, prior to their visit to St James', and while I hadn't marked them down as anything special, I was well aware of the skill shown by some of them.

DOUG WEATHERALL: That was when the vice-chairman invited our group to his wonderful fish restaurant and everyone was given a hammer to break open the shellfish. '*By, that was lovely,*' I said afterwards, but then someone piped up: '*Doug, it's only just started!*' The feast must have lasted four or five hours with drinks after every course… it's easily the best meal I've ever had in my life… it was fabulous.

ARNOLD HOWE: Once a week that's where the Setúbal team is selected, between courses of peeled prawns, mussels and lobster. Anyway, over here, we hoped a liberal helping of English mud might slow down some of their ball players. It was beyond our wildest dreams when a blizzard started to rage, turning everything white. It turned red-blooded spectators into snowmen and that was the night I took my cap off to the Newcastle fans; they were as magnificent as their beloved Magpies.

15TH JULY 1969, 'O RAMILA' RESTAURANT ON RUA DE SAUDE, THE PICTURESQUE SEAFRONT STREET IN SETÚBAL, PORTUGAL.

Every summer, in a tradition going back well into the 20th century, Lisbon's professional footballers travel 40 miles to the seaside town to spend a day together in a seafront restaurant eating seafood, drinking red wine and talking about 'O Jogo Bonito', 'the Beautiful Game'.
1969 is no different. Players from capital-city clubs SL Benfica, Sporting and Belenenses amongst others, have joined footballers from the local Primeira Liga side Vitória de Setúbal to relax over a seafood banquet and a few glasses of the superb local wine. As ever, conversation quickly turns to how everyone had fared in Europe that season. Everyone is curious to know what it had been like for Vitória against the English after notable victories earlier in the competition.

JOSÉ CARLOS: Tomé! Hey, you guys didn't do badly at all this year! You beat Linfield and then thanks to your hat-trick, Lyon were taken care of. Then you bundled out Fiorentina, this season's Italian champions. So what happened after that?
FERNANDO TOMÉ (Vitória midfielder): Ah, Carlos, when we were drawn with Newcastle... well, we all know the English teams are always somehow superior; they have this style of play to which our Portuguese teams can't adapt. We were confident we could fight

against it, but we didn't reckon on encountering those conditions that day in England. In this aspect, they had a real advantage over us.

WAGNER (Vitória's Brazilian-born creative midfielder): It was really snowing a lot over there. For us to be able to see both goals, we had to be on the halfway line. If we were on the edge of one of the penalty boxes, for example, and looked towards the other goal, we couldn't see it.

We were going to train the day before to adapt to the pitch, but in the end we didn't; the pitch was just dirt, grass and snow... a lot of snow. It was the first time we'd been in such a situation. We were like sailors on their first trip, in these conditions.

TOMÉ: We're obviously not used to this. In Portugal, as you know, it only ever snows on the Serra da Estrela mountains in the north. I remember we went for a walk by the hotel and we were throwing snowballs at each other. One of the players, Alfredo, slipped and fell on his backside **(everyone chuckles)**. But then, in the game, it was really bad.

HENRIQUE 'H' ROQUE (the popular Sporting club official): So how did you guys react when you saw the pitch?

HERCULANO: Well, you know, the conditions of the pitch didn't necessarily mean that we were going to lose the match, but, for example, our boots were not suitable for that surface, even though we'd brought several pairs. When we tried to anticipate and get in front of an opponent, we'd slip and fall. And they're a lot more used to that situation than we are. The English play in rain, snow... anything. Here, we have a good climate and we're used to good grass.

TOMÉ: When we arrived at St James' Park, we checked the pitch conditions and the weather and became quite demoralised. We weren't ready for it. There were players who couldn't run; the cold didn't let us do it and we couldn't feel our feet. Jacinto João you know is a fabulous player. Arcanjo had circulation problems and even took some medicine to help with it. Eventually, they just had to be substituted.

CARDOSO (with a hint of frustration): Look, I was captain that day. They were stronger and we'd never played in such conditions in that kind of atmosphere.
WAGNER: 'Jota', Jacinto João, played around an hour. He couldn't move. There was a big pool full of hot water in the dressing room so they put him in it and ordered him: *'Stay there and defrost.'* **(laughter)**. It was frustrating because Jota's a fantastic winger with the ball at his feet.

AGAIN, WE'RE A FLY ON THE WALL IN MICHAEL'S CLUB, LISTENING TO CONVERSATIONS BETWEEN NEWCASTLE UNITED PLAYERS, OFFICIALS AND THEIR PARTNERS AT VARIOUS TABLES

BENNY ARENTOFT: I was still waiting for my transfer from Greenock Morton to be ratified by the FA because that's the case with all foreigners, but I saw both the Setúbal games, home and away.
In the winter, there's no grass in St James' Park. I remember I got cramp in one match because it was all mud. Your boots were disappearing in the mud and you couldn't play on the ground – you had to lift the ball with your foot because you couldn't run with it normally.
I said to myself: 'C'mon! You have to hide this; they can't see this on the bench,' because the competition for a place in the team is bloody hard. Even in training you have to do well, very well, because it isn't like everyone is friendly on the pitch. The reserve-teamers don't mind kicking you… hard tackling and the like.
ARTHUR HORSFIELD (a Scotswood-born centre-forward who signed for United earlier that winter from Middlesbrough and left for Swindon before the end of the same season): Ahh, but it was great to play in the Fairs Cup. While I'd been at Middlesbrough I'd actually gone to see some of the earlier games. There were two or

three of us who used to go, including Frank Spraggon who was a big Newcastle fan from Marley Hill in County Durham. The atmosphere at those matches was absolutely unbelievable. And to actually play in one... The weather the night we played Setúbal was dreadful. I've never been so cold on a pitch in all my life and some players came out wearing football socks all the way up their arms. They hadn't all brought gloves. We'd played in similar conditions before, of course, but they didn't look like they wanted to come out of the tunnel.

WILLIE McFAUL: Once we arrived at the ground and it became apparent the weather was probably on our side, we had a bit of a joke with Joe, by saying: '*We see you've had your prayer mat out again, Boss!*'

JOHN CRAGGS: I was only 19 years old and in and out of the team. The player ahead of me at right-back was David Craig, a Northern Irish international, so I generally only played when he was injured, like here against Setúbal. We saw the Vitória players standing shivering and Joe Harvey said to us before kick-off: '*If we have our heads screwed on today, we could score three or four past this lot.*' And that's what happened.

DAVE CLARKE: I went out for the warm-up in that blizzard – in front of the Leazes End – and I said to Willie: '*Corrr, you'll have to get your body behind the ball here*'. You know, to make a second barrier. Willie dabbed a bit of whisky on his wrists as he would do on a cold night and had a little swig in the dressing room. He's a smashing bloke. Anyway, it was absolutely perishing – and it was probably even worse sitting in the dugout.

They came out onto the pitch shivering, looking up at the sky... they must have been thinking: '*What the hell is going on here?*' They just didn't adapt, did they?

ARTHUR HORSFIELD: It was a good atmosphere as well, mind – it's always a good atmosphere at St James'. The crowd roars you on because they can see they're there for the taking. They certainly made a lot of noise and I'm not sure whether the Portuguese were used to anything like that.

BRYAN POP ROBSON: The lines had to be cleared and there was snow on the pitch but it was slushy and it generally mixed into mud, but it was freezing and they had socks on, gloves on, anything they could get. We just steamrollered them and they didn't want to know. There wasn't much physical contact and we battered them really.

ARTHUR HORSFIELD: And yet, in the first half, they played OK, even though they looked absolutely frozen and petrified.

BRYAN POP ROBSON: Everything fell into place with the team spirit and the energy that we had. Europe was new to us and I don't think the away teams came with any trepidation – they must have thought it was just another cup-tie that wouldn't be too difficult for them. They didn't realise until they got here what we were capable of.

Mind, we started to get some really good results in the league as well, especially at home. Willie McFaul was really starting to perform well, becoming more confident and the back four was settled, certainly with David Craig, Ollie Burton, Bob and Frank. And there weren't ever many changes or different patterns of play. It was all very simple and basic for us, but it was really dynamic.

ARNOLD HOWE: The art of possession play was evident early on though. The Portuguese monopolised the ball but they couldn't get in with a telling blow and gradually the Newcastle defence began to settle.

IVOR BROADIS: That's right. While the ground kept its 'iced-cake' look and their blood was still running warm, they stroked it around accurately. However, once it churned up into a slide, they must have wished they were back among their orange groves.

ARNOLD HOWE: And when the blizzard started, the tide turned.

GIBBO: The visitors were missing their captain, right-back Conceição. He'd been sent off against Fiorentina in the last round and they must surely have missed his leadership skills.

IVOR BROADIS: Alan Foggon gave a taste of what was to come with a ninth-minute shot that sent up spray and snow before it was gathered by their keeper Vital. And while the Setúbal defence were still arranging their forces for an indirect free-kick, given against the keeper for carrying, Gibb slipped it quickly to his right and Robson's point-blank shot was turned round the post by Vital – the only man to react quickly.

In quick succession, the Vitória number one had to scoop a long ball from Clark from under the bar; an offside decision saved Horsfield's blushes when he fired Robson's low cross against the keeper; and a Davies headed chance skipped narrowly wide. Then, a huge roar greeted a picture goal.

JEFF HODGSON of the Sunderland Echo: Wasn't it just? A brilliantly-worked move put United in front halfway through the first half when a Davies-Horsfield-Craggs combination set Craggs free on the right wing. He crossed perfectly and Foggon timed his header beautifully. Eleven minutes later, a long-range shot from Cardoso almost caught McFaul unawares, but he recovered to palm the ball over the top.

NICK SCURR: Then, in the 36th minute, United went two up. Craggs was pushed in the back almost on the right touchline and took the free-kick himself from 40 yards. He lifted the ball into the penalty area but just as Vital was about to catch it, Carrico went up to head it clear. He only succeeded in putting it at Robson's feet and our top

The Newcastle United squad with interpreter Peter Donaghy outside the Hotel Goya in Zaragoza (private photo by Gordon Amory for Peter Donaghy)

NEWCASTLE UNITED FOOTBALL CO. LIMITED.,

HOTEL GOYA - ROOMING LIST

30th DECEMBER - 3 nights

12 Singles with private bath - 7 twin bedded rooms with private bath

Full Pension Terms

Name	Room type	Room
Mr.S.Seymour	(Single)	507
Mr.W.McKeag	do	512
Mr.R.R.McKenzie	do	517
Mr.F.Braithwaite	do	518
Mr.J.Rush	do	519
Mr.J.Harvey	do	520
Mr.D.Smith	do	521
Mr.J.D.Barker	do	522
Dr. [illegible] J.K. STRAUGHAN	do	523
~~Mr.P.Donaghy~~	~~do~~	
MR P DONAGHY	do	524
MR A. MUTCH	do	525
W.S.McFaul / D.J.Craig	Twin bedded room	502
F.A.Clark / ~~T.Gibb~~ Robson	do	503
A.D.Burton / ~~R.Moncur~~ Clarke D.	do	504
A.Foggon / ~~J.Scott~~ Dyson	do	506
~~R.Robson~~ GIBB / W.Davies	do	508
~~[illegible]~~ SCOTT / J. ~~[illegible]~~ SINCLAIR	do	511 604
~~D.Clarke~~ MONCUR / J.McNamee	do	604
Mr.H.Sedman	(Single)	610 ~~609~~

Invoice to Viajes Melia - Zaragoza

The Newcastle United room allocation list in Zaragoza (courtesy of Peter Donaghy)

Newcastle United's squad on the pitch before the third round first leg in Zaragoza (photo courtesy of Luis Fando)

Real Zaragoza on the attack at home as Newcastle United defend in numbers (photo courtesy of Luis Fando)

Bryan Pop Robson after sliding home United's first equaliser in Zaragoza (Gordon Amory-Daily Express-Express Syndication)

Wyn Davies beats Santamaria to the ball and scores United's second equaliser in Zaragoza (Gordon Amory-Daily Express-Express Syndication)

Santamaria kneels in frustration after Wyn Davies scores United's second equaliser, then stands upright in anger after Davies ruffles his hair (Gordon Amory-Daily Express-Express Syndication)

Bryan Pop Robson on the attack in Zaragoza (Gordon Amory-Daily Express-Express Syndication)

The Newcastle United and Real Zaragoza teams greet the crowd at St James' Park (photo with kind permission of Newcastle United FC)

Bob Moncur exchanges match pennants with Real Zaragoza captain Santos (photo with kind permission of Newcastle United FC)

Real Zaragoza goalkeeper Nieves desperately tries to save Bryan Pop Robson's early thunderbolt in the second leg at St James' Park (Mirrorpix)

Frank Clark sends over a cross against Real Zaragoza at St James' Park (Mirrorpix)

Alan Foggon contests the ball with goalkeeper Nieves, who sustained a match-ending injury in the collision (Mirrorpix)

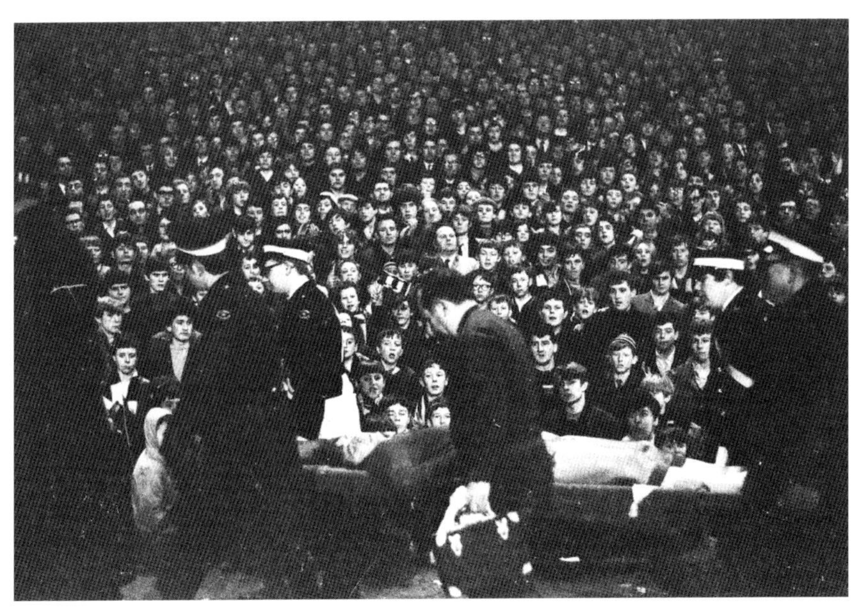

Real Zaragoza goalkeeper Nieves is stretchered from the pitch after being injured in a collision with Alan Foggon (photo with kind permission of Newcastle United FC)

Real Zaragoza winger Armando Martin gives his team hope with a goal just before half-time at St James' Park (Mirrorpix)

Tommy Gibb unleashes an effort on the Real Zaragoza goal in the second leg in Newcastle (photo with kind permission of Newcastle United FC)

Newcastle's captain Bob Moncur exchanges pennants with his Vitória counterpart Carlos Cardoso at St James' Park (photo courtesy of Newcastle United FC)

The Newcastle United v Vitória Setúbal clash took place in arctic conditions despite it being mid-March (photo courtesy of Newcastle United FC)

Alan Foggon heads Newcastle United into a first-half lead at home against Vitoria Setubal (photo courtesy of Newcastle United FC)

Bryan Pop Robson doubles Newcastle United's lead at home against Vitoria Setubal (photo courtesy of Newcastle United FC)

Bryan Pop Robson aims to score
for Newcastle United in the quarter-final first leg
(photo courtesy of Newcastle United FC)

Wyn Davies controversially nets Newcastle United's third goal against Vitória in the snow (photo courtesy of Newcastle United FC)

Vitória Setúbal players surround the referee to claim that Wyn Davies' first-leg goal should be ruled offside (photo courtesy of Newcastle United FC)

Bryan Pop Robson scores his team's fourth goal against Vitória Setúbal at St James' Park (photo courtesy of Newcastle United FC)

United players Alan Foggon (left), Wyn Davies and Bryan Pop Robson pictured after the 5-1 quarter-final 1st-leg win over Vitória Setúbal at St James' Park (Mirrorpix)

Joe Harvey and physio Alec Mutch survey the festivities before the away match against Vitória Setúbal in Lisbon (Gordon Amory, Daily Express, Expresss Syndication)

It was a carnival atmosphere before and during the quarter-final away leg against Vitória Setúbal (Gordon Amory, Daily Express, Expresss Syndication)

scorer added one more to his tally by slamming it into the net off a defender's leg.

ALAN FOGGON: They just couldn't cope. We knew we had an advantage and we had to make it count. I scored early on with a header – I rarely ever headed goals. But that started it off and it just got progressively worse for them. They weren't up for it.

ARTHUR HORSFIELD: I came off in the second half and to be honest I felt I'd hardly had a kick. It was just one of those things where I felt that wherever I went, the ball didn't come. You have times like that and I wasn't surprised to come off. I thought Joe had to make the change even though we were winning at the time. I think we gradually got on top of them and hammered them into the ground in the second half.

There wasn't much to say at half-time either. Joe never used to say a lot. He isn't the sort of bloke to have a chalk board. You were prepared and went out and played and you gave everything you had and that was it. He isn't a massive tactician. I think his attitude is *'Get it up the other end of the park, stick it in the box and put it in the net.'*

ARNOLD HOWE: This was a lead that Newcastle certainly deserved but when they got a third on the hour, there was a mass attack on Swedish referee Curt Liedberg. Frank Clark put the ball over, it was touched on by Robson and turned into the net by Davies. The Portuguese players protested that Wyn was offside and I thought they had a case, but there was no need to tear the referee's jacket halfway off his back.

GIBBO: Absolutely no need! Their manhandling of Liedberg left me astonished. He was set upon by Setúbal defenders and carried bodily to the touchline for a consultation with linesman Ewart Färgh that he didn't want. When he tried to object, his collar was torn and his neck badly scratched. I remember Joe saying: *'He was a brave man to stick with his decision. I was amazed at the Setúbal players.'*

Before that third goal, Vaz had brought on Petita for Arcanjo in midfield and soon Setúbal's coach was ringing the changes again, Fernando Tomé coming on for the ailing Jacinto. Joe also shuffled his pack, bringing on Jackie Sinclair for European debutant Horsfield.

IVOR BROADIS: The Setúbal switch certainly produced a little more direct running but their newly-found drive left them vulnerable to sweeping diagonal balls picked up on either flank. It was no surprise when the fourth goal came on 75 minutes and it was Robson's courage that earned it.

Vital came out of goal quickly for a low Clark free-kick but failed to gather it cleanly and from under his nose, Robson belted the ball home from the left of the penalty box.

JEFF HODGSON: Setúbal did pull one back though, in the 84th minute through José Maria. Striker Figueiredo had worked the ball past Clark on the right and when he neatly cut it back into the middle, McFaul stood no chance with the winger's shot. Tommy Gibb then made it 5-1 for United with the best goal of the game, thrashing home a 25-yarder.

NICK SCURR: Yes, that was a fine left-foot shot but only after great work by substitute Jackie Sinclair.

TONY BOULLEMIER: Understandably, Vaz looked glum as the happy crowd streamed away from St James' Park. He said: *'God saved Newcastle by supplying the weather. And the linesman helped. As soon as I saw the pitch I knew we had no chance. I thought Newcastle played brilliantly under the conditions and their four-goal lead looks too much for us to pull back. For my men though, it was like playing three hours of football out there.'*

O RAMILA RESTAURANT IN SETÚBAL

Stars of Setúbal are telling their group of mainly fellow top-flight footballers from Lisbon clubs about their extraordinary experience in the Newcastle snow a few months earlier.

HERCULANO: It was actually snowing a lot during the game too. One of the linesmen seemed like he was missing a hand! When he was running the line level with our defence, there were three or four goals we thought were offside but which he didn't call. We were playing well but every time they sent a pass behind our defence we would concede a goal.
TOMÉ: Herculano says three goals were offside and I'd have to say at least two were. They were long balls sent forward and their players were already there, in behind us.
HERCULANO: All our players encircled the referee and kicked him so much.
TOMÉ: That happened just after the third goal. That was a defining moment. At 2-0, it was still just about OK, but at 3-0 our task was really starting to get difficult.
JOSÉ CARLOS: Were you already on the pitch as a substitute?
TOMÉ: Not yet. When Fernando Vaz told me and Petita to go and warm up, we went into the dressing room and opened the doctor's medical bag. Petita pulled out the bottle of medical-strength alcohol. '*What are you doing?*' I asked.
So he showed me. He used the alcohol and a match to set alight all the cotton wool that was in the bag, so that we could start a fire and warm our hands and feet. Only after that, did we go back pitchside. When we got back in the dressing room after the game, the doctor wanted the alcohol to help treat some wounds, but there wasn't any left...
MARINHO: Wow, Tomé, that's incredible. So then you came back out to the pitch. What did you see of the protest?

TOMÉ: We were by the bench on the other side of the pitch so I couldn't see much. I just saw our players complaining. The television didn't show much of it later either.
H: But everyone encircled the referee, right?
HERCULANO: Everyone, from the goalkeeper to the left winger.
TOMÉ: Yes, and some of them kicked him. José Maria grabbed him by the neck but still the referee didn't send anyone off.
HERCULANO: The ref was right in the middle and he didn't know exactly where the kicks were coming from.
TOMÉ: Our lads lost their minds a bit because it really felt like a decisive goal. And it was. It was the third. Then, because the team was affected, the fourth and the fifth came.
H: After the game, were the players in the mood to create a scene?
TOMÉ: Oh yes. The one who calmed things down, because he was a gentleman, was our coach Fernando Vaz.
MARINHO: That doesn't surprise me – he's a good man. What did he say?
TOMÉ: He said he'd warned us many times that we shouldn't complain about the referee's decisions. The referee is sovereign and if they, the referees and linesmen, make a certain decision, it's because it's the right one. He never likes to use the referee as an excuse and he told us it's just not worth complaining.
TOMÉ: Petita was warming up with me. Then, when he went on, he took a free kick – he had a really powerful shot – and the ball thudded at tremendous speed into a Newcastle player's face. He fell and there was a lot of blood. Petita ran over to the bench and piped up: *'Mr Fernando, I've killed one already.'*
'I wanted you to score, not kill the opponent,' came the reply.
H: Ha, well, a fair point, I suppose. Do you remember much about Newcastle's goals?
TOMÉ: The first goal was a header. They played a lot of direct balls up front. Fernando Vaz told us English football is played

a lot on the wings followed by very good crosses into the box. Because they played 4-4-2, we played a 4-3-3 formation with the priority being to stop them playing from the wings, so there wouldn't be any crosses to their strikers. The first one was like that – a ball played out to the wing – and the rest were long balls up front.

HERCULANO: In the second half, we were defending in the half where there was that linesman who only had one hand and it was then that those offside goals happened. They played just as we expected them to, really.

TOMÉ: Yes, Vaz had known in advance about Newcastle's team. He told us Davies was physically very strong and played very well with his head, so he warned us to be careful with him.

JOSÉ CARLOS: Yes, we remember him too, of course.

H: I suppose Davies met your expectations then, based on what Mr Vaz had said?

TOMÉ: He was a great player. A proper striker. A typical British or German centre-forward, who was very strong and had an important presence in the box. In Portugal, we only have one player like that, José Torres over there, at Benfica **(nods to Torres eating with some others on the other side of the room)**.

He makes the difference. Eusébio benefits a lot from him and Davies had the same characteristics as Torres.

H: Fernando Vaz didn't come to talk to us at Sporting to get information about Newcastle, did he?

TOMÉ: No, he didn't do that. The knowledge he had was from reading. He reads a lot, often buying foreign newspapers. They'd arrive with a few days' delay but he would study them intently. He also used to tell the goalkeepers that if there was a penalty, a certain player would take it.

JOSÉ CARLOS: That late away goal must have at least given you guys some hope for the second leg, didn't it?

TOMÉ: Yes, it did, because we all know away goals are important. We thought if we could play brilliantly and win 4-0 at home, we'd go through. It's always good in knockout competitions to score an away goal but 5-1 was a very uneven result. It was never going to be easy to come back from that.
And then also what Herculano said about the unfortunate refereeing. We felt it was something which contributed to the scoreline.
HERCULANO: Yes. But we knew how good we were; we'd knocked out other strong teams before so there was still hope.

THE BRIDGE HOTEL, NEWCASTLE UPON TYNE

BILL GIBBS: There are three things I remember about the Setúbal game here: One is us demoralising them with that thrashing, the second is the snow and the third is the smell of the old brewery mash as it came over from the brewery near St James' Park.
HARRY WATSON: Aye, you can smell the hops brewing and stuff like that...
BILL GIBBS: It's funny, for a while I didn't know what that was... what a smell!
HARRY WATSON: Oh, it's lovely.
BILL GIBBS: If the brewery's working at full pelt, it drifts ower St James'.
HARRY WATSON: Well, yes, 'cos it's right next door.
BILL GIBBS: That's part of Wednesday nights, that is. The weird smell.
TONY RODGERS: What's it close to, do you think?
HARRY WATSON: If you know anyone who's done any home brewing, ask them. It's the mash, the smell of hops.
BILL GIBBS: And it's not there so much on a Saturday but much more in midweek for some reason. Now, you expect it to drift ower, 'cos you're only, what, 100 yards from the brewery.

HARRY WATSON: Aye, just across Barrack Road. And you know they've a social club in the grounds of the brewery too, don't you? There's an underground pipeline which goes straight from the brewing centre to the club, so that the Brown Ale for the men and Amber Ale for the women is piped straight through. There's still that smell though.
BILL GIBBS: Magic. Fairs Cup Mash!

MICHAEL'S CLUB, NEWCASTLE UPON TYNE

ALAN FOGGON: Things had gone for us throughout – firstly against Feyenoord when Geoff played so well and then the snow coming against Setúbal so you're thinking: *'Ooh, we've got a chance here.'* But the return leg was a completely different kettle of fish, because they were a very good side.

VITÓRIA DE SETÚBAL AWAY...

INTER-CITIES FAIRS CUP QUARTER-FINAL 2ND LEG

VITÓRIA DE SETÚBAL 3
NEWCASTLE UNITED 1

Kick-off: 21:45, Wednesday 26th March 1969
Referee: Othmar (AKA Dittmar) Huber (Switzerland)
Venue: José Alvalade Stadion, Lisbon, Portugal
Attendance: 35,000

Vitória: Vital, Joaquim Conceição (c), Carriço, Carlos Cardoso (Petita 47), Alfredo Moreira, Vagner (Tomé 46), José Maria, Jacinto João, Figueiredo, Arcanjo, Vítor Baptista.
Substitutes not used: Torres (GK)

Newcastle United: Willie McFaul; John Craggs, Bob Moncur (c), Ollie Burton (John McNamee 66), Frank Clark; Jim Scott, Tommy Gibb; Jackie Sinclair, Bryan Robson, Wyn Davies, Alan Foggon
Substitutes not used: John Hope (GK), Dave Elliott

Goalscorers:
1-0: Arcanjo (27)
1-1: Wyn Davies (40)
2-1: Petita (60)
3-1: Figueiredo (66)

Newcastle United win 6-4 on aggregate.

O RAMILA RESTAURANT IN SETÚBAL

Tomé, Herculano and others from Vitória Setúbal are recounting to a few Sporting Lisbon players and their friend, club official Henrique 'H' Roque, how they tried to stay in the Fairs Cup by overturning Newcastle's shock 5-1 win in the snowbound North-East of England.

TOMÉ: We hosted them in a borrowed stadium – at Sporting's in Lisbon – because we didn't have floodlights in Setúbal. So winning 3-1 must give us some credit.

CARDOSO: And we could have scored more goals.

TOMÉ: Do you remember, our club president held a press conference before the match asking people to support us because we believed we could turn the result around? He used the example of Sporting a few years earlier, when José Carlos and Hilário here helped overturn a deficit against Manchester United. They lost 4-1 in England but won 5-0 here. That game was used to try and motivate us. He asked everyone here to support us.

H: And they did. Are you guys used to having so many people watching the European games?

TOMÉ: Yes, we're used to having a lot of fans. When our stadium's full, they say it holds 32,000 but in the Alvalade there may have been more – they told us around 35,000 were there.

H: I saw the pictures of the big parade around the pitch and people on motorbikes with flags. That looked fun…

TOMÉ: Yes, there was a party there before the game with cheerleaders – a group of girls from local schools. It took place on the running track around the pitch before the game.

H: So was all that staged because of the game?

TOMÉ: Yes, to raise people's spirits in the stadium. By the way, they didn't let us play in our home kit of green and white stripes because it looked too similar to Newcastle's black and white. As our kit man

hadn't brought our second kit and there wasn't enough time to go back to Setúbal and bring it over in time for the start of the game, we had to play the first half in Sporting's shirts.
Here, it was a little different psychologically to being in Newcastle. Despite conceding just before half-time, we were confident. When we scored the third goal, I remember I went to get the ball from inside the net and ran quickly back to the halfway line, telling my teammates to do the same because we could do it.
CARDOSO: Wyn Davies, he opened up my eyebrow with an elbow early in the second half and I had to go off. I believe if we'd only lost 2-0 or 2-1 in Newcastle we'd have had a much better chance of knocking them out here.
HERCULANO: And we could have scored more than three.
TOMÉ: We scored first – a far-post header by Arcanjo from Figueiredo's right-wing cross. Then they equalised before half-time. We grabbed the second after an hour – a typical free-kick from our specialist Petita just outside the box – and then a third five minutes later through Figueiredo. He nodded in a cross from Jota, but we couldn't snatch a fourth or fifth despite our best efforts.
MARINHO: OK, but after losing 5-1 there, what could you really expect from the game over here?
TOMÉ: Well, the coach told us that nothing had been lost yet. We had to play our football and try to score early. We started well and we did score first but then Davies equalised and we broke down a bit. When we scored the third goal, my team mates were all hugging. Suddenly, we only needed two more to take it to extra-time.
H: About Davies' goal, do you remember anything?
TOMÉ: It was from a corner. The one who usually marked the taller opponents was Alfredo because he was taller than Herculano.
JOSÉ CARLOS: Davies was a real test. Were you given any instructions to mark him in a specific way?

TOMÉ: Man-marking at free kicks and corners. There were certain players in Portugal whom Fernando Vaz wanted to be marked with two players. One in front and one behind. Like a sandwich. The one in front would jump to disturb his action and the one behind would give him a slight touch to stop him reaching the ball freely. Davies was a focal point for Newcastle up front. He screwed us **(laughs)**, but we were warned that he was a good player.
H: When he scored the equaliser…
TOMÉ: Then our spirits were dampened a bit. If we could've made it 2-0, maybe it would have been Newcastle who would have disintegrated but it wasn't the case. They equalised and that wasn't good for us. In the second half we found a second wind but we were already halfway through the second half when the third goal came. That's why I was running back to the centre-circle with the ball. There wasn't time to celebrate.
H: We read reports in the newspapers that the second leg became a bit aggressive from both sides and they specifically mentioned Conceição, who was back in the team after suspension.
TOMÉ: Conceição has his style of play. It's tough but it isn't meant to motivate his colleagues to be aggressive. It's just he's our captain and he sets an example by playing his own way. It's normal. There were tackles during the game but the British are also known for being tough in such situations.
MARINHO: What did Vaz say at half-time?
TOMÉ: I only heard a part of it because he'd told me to go and warm up, but he did say if we were going to be knocked out, we still had to be standing by the end of it; we had to justify how far we'd gone already in the competition. We couldn't finish the first half in front but we needed to play our football in the second half to make it as close as we could.
H: And I suppose you guys were still confident you could turn it around?

HERCULANO: Yeah, we were actually. We had a lot of chances to score and at least go to extra time. They totally closed up at the back. I think we're known as one of the best football-playing teams here, along with Académica and you guys at Sporting and Benfica. I'm not saying Porto because currently Porto aren't even close to us in this respect. So this made our fans believe we could turn around the bad result and for that reason, a lot of people travelled to Lisbon. We began the game trying really hard to score early on.

JOSÉ CARLOS: Newcastle's goal came at just the wrong time then?

HERCULANO: Yeah. I don't remember it exactly but it was against the flow of the game. We were always attacking and they scored on one of the very few occasions they made it into our box.

H: And Newcastle then just played more defensively in the second period and tried to block you out?

HERCULANO: Of course. The result at half-time was fine for them so they tried to keep it.

H: How was the atmosphere after the game?

HERCULANO: The fans applauded us. They were happy with our performance.

H: That's good – at least they'd seen you win and restore some pride. How do you feel about Fernando Vaz moving to us at Sporting this summer?

TOMÉ: In my opinion, he's the coach that has left the biggest mark on this club in terms of technique, tactics and physical preparation. During his five years here, he's made the team play in a way that people really talk about. We play lots of short passes but we're always moving forward. We don't pass it to the sides and back.

And we whistle to one another. If I have to ask Herculano for the ball, I don't have to say anything, I simply whistle and he knows it's me. Three new players came to our team recently and we asked if they could whistle. One said he couldn't, so we've told him to clap his hands.

H: Haha, OK, we'll look forward to that. And yes, it's true you guys are always tough to play. We lost our coach Caiado between the two games against Newcastle and just fell short. What did you think about Newcastle's team?

TOMÉ: You know, we respect every team, but English football is always feared. When a Portuguese team is drawn against an English team we say: 'We're gone.' In this match at home, we just tried to show it wasn't necessarily like that. For us, it's an honour to see that Newcastle have won the Cup. Just like you, we know we've been knocked out by the winners.

MICHAEL'S CLUB, NEWCASTLE UPON TYNE

ARTHUR HORSFIELD: Yet when we played them away, they looked totally, totally different; they looked a good side. Obviously they had their own support too.

BRYAN POP ROBSON: Yeah, the second leg was totally different; they battered us back in Lisbon and we had to be so resilient. They seemed like different animals – they were so much more aggressive. I was totally surprised by it. We didn't do any real attacking as such; it was all backs-to-the-wall defending. It was like chasing shadows, trying to stop them playing forward balls.

They hadn't wanted to be at St James' in the snow and obviously it was an embarrassing result for them, so they had to do something and they certainly made it difficult for us.

ALAN FOGGON: You'd have to play really badly to lose the tie after the first leg, but they started off like a house on fire and played really, really well, so we thought: 'Aye, aye... it's not going to be as easy as we thought.'

We were a team that played for each other and got stuck in and that's how we managed to get through. And we had big Wyn so if we were struggling, we could always just bang it up to him. European sides weren't used to that because they were a bit more subtle and play it on the ground.

That combination of British lion-hearted spirit and direct, effective football was almost unbeatable against the continentals. This stood us in good stead all the way through. We played for each other, you know, and in the latter stages of the tournament it was the same 11 or 12 players so we were all used to it.

BOB MONCUR: We were back in Lisbon's Alvalade stadium and before the game, there were these bloody motorbikes going round the pitch with clowns standing up on the back of them trying to intimidate us. It was Europe, our first time in it and it was easy to get distracted.

One thing we knew about them was that they were deadly from free-kicks. During the game in Lisbon, Ollie Burton got injured and things were getting a bit nasty, a bit naughty. The crowd was right on their backs and getting them going, so it was very intimidating.

Anyway, Willie had been saying to us all: *'Don't give free-kicks away. Don't give free-kicks away.'*

Then Ollie has to go off and who should I see warming up but John McNamee... and I'm thinking: 'Oh... free-kicks!' because John wasn't the most gentle, so he comes running on, the big man from Glasgow, and the first thing I said to him was: *'John, whatever you do, do not give any free-kicks away!'*

So he says: *'Aye, alright, Bob.'*

First tackle... Whoosh. The player goes up in the air – free-kick! We battled on through though.

Then there was that famous incident with their well-known right-back Conceição, who was playing against Alan Foggon and Alan was giving him a hard time on the wing. At one stage, Alan fell down and this guy stamped on him. No doubt, he stamped on him.

Everyone was really annoyed, to say the least, and Ollie Burton, who was now off the pitch injured, was limping up the touchline to have a go at him! Ollie's short-tempered too – it's like a red rag to a bull with him at times – and Big Mac was there as well. They were infuriated and it became a bit nasty, the whole game, especially after that incident.

Anyway, after the match, we had to go behind one of the goals to get to the dressing rooms and when we get there, I look around and say: *'Where's Foggon?'*

Someone says: *'He's still out there.'*

*'Oh, f****** hell!'*

So I run back out up the tunnel – there'd been people on the pitch when we'd left – and there's Foggon, still out there, arguing with people.

So I get a hold of him and tell him: *'Come here!'* And I remember us backing off and backing off, keeping an eye on the crowd right in front of us when... crash! We finish up in the back of the net.

So I just shout: *'Run!!!'*

We charge back down the tunnel and there are all sorts coming after us. But we got back to safety.

A couple of yards away, Alan Foggon is listening from the adjoining table with a cheeky grin on his face.

BOB MONCUR (smiling): Honestly, Foggon, what were you doing?

ALAN FOGGON (laughing): I don't know... talking to somebody. I can't really remember much about it, to be honest. But if you say it's true, Moncs, it's true.

BOB MONCUR: Aye, well, I got a fright out there – the police weren't helping at all and with people gathering around the edge, it had been a nasty experience.

BRYAN POP ROBSON: It hadn't been a great evening so everybody was just relieved… and absolutely knackered.

BOB MONCUR: Then, the following day – Foggon's only 19, remember – we get on the plane to go back to Newcastle and all of a sudden there's a bit of a kerfuffle and the plane's been delayed. The gaffer comes up and I say: *'Howay, let's b*gger off'*, to which he says: *'Ah no. Can't. Something's going on.'*

Well, it turns out that this right-back Conceição wants to apologise to Alan Foggon. So this message comes through and we say: *'Tell him to f*** off! Tell the pilot, let's go. Stuff him – he did what he did and that's it.'* But eventually the directors and Joe get involved and he's on the plane. So we say *'Aye… OK then.'*

So this right-back holds out his hand and in his best English, says: *'I'm very sorry.'* However, he doesn't really understand our language so Alan shakes his hand, smiles and calmly replies:

*'That's OK, you dirty, cheating b*****d'* and starts to laugh as, all innocently, the Portuguese player politely goes along with it: *'Oh, yeah, yeah, yeah.'*

The plane was in uproar and I was like: *'Oi, you!'* But it was very funny from him with the guy not knowing and the Press on board taking photographs... I'll never forget that.'

THE BRIDGE HOTEL, NEWCASTLE UPON TYNE

Just as with the away game against Sporting, Spow is the only supporter in the Bridge that evening who actually travelled abroad for the quarter-final 2nd leg against Vitória Setúbal. Unsurprisingly, he has a few stories to tell.

SPOW: So we got back on the bus after the match and went back to the hotel where probably at least one of the two busloads went to bed, but the rest of us, about a dozen of us, asked the porter if there was any chance of a beer.

He said the bar's shut now but we persuaded him to sell us some and we sat doon at a big roond table and were just chatting and ordering more rounds. So he'd go downstairs and come back with more and more beers until it got to about five in the morning when the last of us decided to go to bed. I had all this loose change in Escudos left on the table so I asked: *'What'll a dee with this?'* Someone said: *'Ahh just give it to the man'*, because he had a young'un with him too. So that's what I did.

The next morning at breakfast, the guy was still working and he came straight up to me and shook my hand. I didn't know what was up but one of the other lads asked: *'Spow, did you give any money to that waiter last neet?' 'Aye,'* I said. *'A load of left-over coppers on the table.'*

'Spow, you've just given him about two weeks' pay!'

HARRY WATSON: Crikey, Spow, he must have thought it was Christmas again.

SPOW: Then, on the plane on the way back from Setúbal, Bobby Cowell, who won the FA Cup three times in the '50s with Newcastle, is sitting next to me and on the other side is the reporter Tony Boullemier from The Journal. Tony asks me: *'So, who makes up all the terrace songs?'*

'Anybody,' I replied. *'You've just got to have a catchy tune.'*

He says: *'So could you make one now?'*

I ask: *'What, right now?'*

'Yes.'

'Ummm, well, I'll think aboot it.'

Well, the flight was aboot four hours long, so half an hour later, I said: *'I've got one!'*

He says: *'Great, let's hear it then.'*

'It's to the tune of the Twelve Days of Christmas':
On the twelfth day of Christmas Joe Harvey gave to me:
Twelve Alan Foggon
Eleven Jackie Sinclair
Ten Ben Arentoft
Nine Wyn Davies
Eight Pop Robson
Seven Jim Scott
Six Bob Moncur
Five McNameeeeee
Four Tommy Gibb
Three Frank Clark
Two Davie Craig and
McFaul is our go-o-oa-leeee!

And can you guess what Tony said to me afterwards?

EVERYONE IN UNISON: Absolutely superb, Spow!
SPOW (beaming): Eee, thanks, you lot. Oh, Bill, by the way, I've still got the programme from the Setúbal match you asked me to get for you.
BILL GIBBS: Champion! I'll give you the money now. How many did you bring back?
SPOW: I got loads, Bill, 150. I'd that many requests for them. And when I got back to Newcastle at half past ten on the Thursday night, do you know what happened? The bloody security guy at the airport wanted to go through my whole bag.

I said: *'Howay man, me last bus from Worswick Street's at 11:20pm...'*

But he insisted on looking through every bloody programme. Time was passing and I was raging. I asked him what he was looking for...

He says: *'Oh, we're looking for porn.'*

'PORN? PISS OFF!!'

MICHAEL'S CLUB, NEWCASTLE UPON TYNE

BAR MANAGER: So then there were four. Who was left by now, lads? Leeds and who else?

BARMAN 1: No, not Leeds! They may be champions of England now but they met their match against the unknowns of Újpest Dózsa. Honestly, most people don't know too much about Eastern European football because their teams only ever come over for the occasional European tie. Those players on the other side of the Iron Curtain are forced to live under Communism so they aren't allowed to move to Western teams, nor can their clubs welcome Western touring sides. They only ever go on tours of their own to South America or maybe to four-team tournaments in Spain during the summer or winter breaks.

BARMAN 2: But Újpest Dózsa are a team for the ages. They beat Leeds home *and* away. Thanks to George, we've got his match reports here again:

LEEDS SLIP TO SHOCK DÓZSA DEFEAT
5TH MARCH 1969

Failure to convert a barrage of presentable chances and a powerful strike from the prolific Antal Dunai propelled Újpest Dózsa to a shock one-nil triumph over Leeds United at Elland Road last night and left the English club with a mountain to climb in Budapest to stay in this year's Fairs Cup.

An unfamiliar sight greeted Yorkshire supporters when their favourites turned out in all-blue and the Hungarians wore Leeds' all-white home kit, the French referee having decided that there would otherwise have been a colour clash.

This quarter-final first leg proved to be an open affair from the start, the visitors forcing three corners in the first five minutes and keeper Gary Sprake pulling off a fine save from midfielder Ede Dunai.

Don Revie's team soon settled though, looking for the three goals their manager said they would need to see the tie through in Budapest. Rod Belfitt and Jack Charlton (twice) both struck the woodwork when well-placed, while Eddie Gray and Paul Madeley also missed good opportunities.

These pale into the background though, when compared to the penalty awarded for Ernő Noskó's debatable handball in the 58th minute. Noskó himself commented: *'The ball struck my side, not my arm. I even showed the mud print of the ball on the left side of my all-white jersey, but he was having none of it.'* Johnny Giles struck the ball well to the keeper's left but Antal Szentmihályi displayed outstanding athleticism to hurl himself to his right and turn the ball around the post.

Then, 19 minutes from the end, came the sucker-punch. Stylish forward László Fazekas surged down the right and crossed for his Hungarian international colleague Antal Dunai to turn and fire the ball venomously into Sprake's net.

There were to be no more goals before the final whistle, Újpest happy to milk the applause of a gracious home crowd at the end while Revie was left to wonder how his team could possibly still engineer a fourth Fairs Cup semi-final in a row.

ÚJPEST USURP FLU-STRUCK LEEDS 19TH MARCH 1969

A second-half penalty from Újpest Dózsa spotkick specialist Ernő Solymosi and a fine strike from quicksilver forward Ferenc Bene deservedly sent Leeds United tumbling out the Inter-Cities Fairs Cup last night, but the English side were not disgraced.

Not least because a flu epidemic had deprived Don Revie of three England internationals in Paul Reaney, Jack Charlton and Mick O' Grady, while five others played on, despite displaying clear symptoms. One-nil down after the first leg, this was a night when chances needed to be taken, but unfortunately Leeds couldn't make their marginal first-half superiority count, shots from Giles, Jones and Gray all flying narrowly wide.

The first goal was always going to be crucial and it fell to the hosts in the 63rd minute when Göröcs sent the ball forward, Paul Madeley illegally halted Ferenc Bene's breakaway in the box and central defender Solymosi planted the spotkick firmly in the bottom right-hand corner of the net.

This was also the ball's destination for the killer second goal 12 minutes later, after Bene cleverly exchanged passes with Antal Dunai in a tight space and buried the ball past a despairing Sprake.

DON REVIE: *The best team won but I was proud of my men. We held them well in the first-half and then Újpest became a bit panicky. It might have been a different story if we'd been at full strength. Their attack was very good in the second half and individually, I liked midfielder Ede Dunai the best.*

ERNŐ SOLYMOSI: *Everyone is nervous before a penalty kick. I'd decided to aim right, even though Szentmihályi saved Giles's penalty in that same direction in Leeds. Luckily, Sprake moved left.*
FERENC BENE: *I got the ball from their defender, exchanged passes with Antal in a tight space and then I just needed to kick the ball. I hit it well and this goal ensured we'd go through.*

LEEDS, ENGLAND, 15TH JULY 1969

Leeds United's Glaswegian winger Eddie Gray is taking his younger brother, budding footballer Frank, home after the 15-year-old had visited him for a couple of weeks. As a favour, he also agrees to take his two Geordie teammates, Norman Hunter and Jackie Charlton, north to see family for a few days, before pre-season training starts. The plan is to drop Norman and Jack in Newcastle town centre, take the A69 towards Carlisle and then head north to Scotland.

EDDIE GRAY: Now then, Frank, how long until these two start to pine for their pease pudding? Northallerton? Darlington?
NORMAN HUNTER: Ah, you can't beat being back home, Eddie. You know that.
JACKIE CHARLTON (smiling): Pity Wor Kid wasn't driving home from Manchester – I could have hopped across there and avoided your jokes, Eddie!
EDDIE GRAY: Well, I know you can take it, Jack. Anyway, while you two are up there, you can see if they're looking after that trophy they took away from us.
JACKIE CHARLTON: Aye, the Fairs Cup? I still can't believe they won that – I'd been backing the other team in my Evening Post column

before the game. Beat those Hungarians in the final – the ones who beat us, didn't they?

NORMAN HUNTER: They did. Remember what we called them because we couldn't say their name properly? Ups-a-daisy.

JACKIE CHARLTON: I do.

FRANK GRAY: Haha, someone told me it's You-pesht – they knocked out Dunfermline a few years ago when Jock Stein was manager there. Top team, so Eddie says.

EDDIE GRAY: Oh, aye, they were magic against us. Both here and over there. Bene was some player. Especially the second time we played them. He was brilliant.

NORMAN HUNTER: Was he the older-looking one? Bit thin on top?

EDDIE GRAY: Aye. Quick.

NORMAN HUNTER: That's right.

FRANK GRAY: How quick was he, really?

EDDIE GRAY: Like lightning. You know, I never thought I'd see anyone outrun Paul Madeley, but Bene did. What I thought they were so good at was keeping the ball moving so quickly, one-touch, bang, bang, and then Bene would be off. I always remember him running down the side of defenders, his teammates playing balls in to him, and his pace taking him away from people and bringing others into the game.

They just played great football that night. We were just about to be league champions *and* we'd beaten Napoli earlier in the Fairs Cup, so it wasn't as if we weren't battle-hardened. They're a hard team to beat physically too. Solymosi can take players out, mind – he's a hard boy.

JACKIE CHARLTON: You call *that* hard?

EDDIE GRAY: Alright, Jack, by my standards, eh? And I don't think it was complacency, do you? I just think they played well.

JACKIE CHARLTON (looking out of the car window): Well as you know, I wasn't in Budapest this time 'cos I had the flu, so I don't know. But I do know that we'd learned to respect Hungarian football when we first met Újpest Dózsa three years ago, hadn't we?

He looks back into the car.

Frank, we beat them by three goals on aggregate at the same stage of the Fairs Cup in 1966, but if that sounds easy – well, it wasn't. Things went well at home but we were lucky to get even a draw out there. We could have been four goals down in the first ten minutes.
EDDIE GRAY: Ah, you know, I think the first time we played Újpest we beat them quite comfortably, but this time round it was completely different. They'd grown up as a team; they're a top team now. We expected to win, but we expect to beat everyone we play. Over the two legs though, I don't think there was any doubt that the Hungarians deserved to go through.

MICHAEL'S CLUB, NEWCASTLE UPON TYNE

BARMAN 1: When they staged the semi-final draw in Zurich the day after United returned from the Setúbal match, a new Battle of Britain was announced: Glasgow Rangers versus Newcastle United. This meant Újpest Dózsa would meet Göztepe in the other semi-final – the Turkish team who'd knocked out Marseille earlier and got lucky when Hamburg had to withdraw because of a fixture pileup.

Gibbo has come over to order some more wine for his table. He sees the two barmen poring over some papers while the bar manager tries to pay attention to both them and the guests.

GIBBO: What's happening, gentlemen? **(sees all the match reports, cuttings and memorabilia spread out over the end of the bar)** Blimey! What's all this then?

BARMAN 1: Ah, Sir, well, we're just reading our scrapbooks and things as we go through each round. Reminiscing, like, you know.

GIBBO (looking at the bar manager): Crikey! They're keen, aren't they? **(looks back at the barmen)**. What's your name, son?

BARMAN 1: It's Bolam, Sir.

GIBBO: Oh aye. As in *The Likely Lads*. And that's what you two are, eh? Making these scrapbooks must have taken up plenty of your weekends. What do you do with your time apart from reading football memorabilia?

Just at this second they see his attention is drawn to a corner of green baize hanging out of one of the barmen's bags. On it, a Subbuteo logo is clearly visible…

GIBBO (shaking his head and feigning disbelief as he walks back to his table with a new bottle of house white): Do NOT answer that question!

BARMAN 2 (as everyone still chuckles): Well, anyway, now there were just six matches left of a thrilling competition. Little did our players and supporters know, the most dramatic moments still lay ahead of us.

FAIRS CUP SEMI-FINALS

NEWCASTLE UNITED

v

— GLASGOW RANGERS —

ÚJPESTI DÓZSA

v

GÖZTEPE

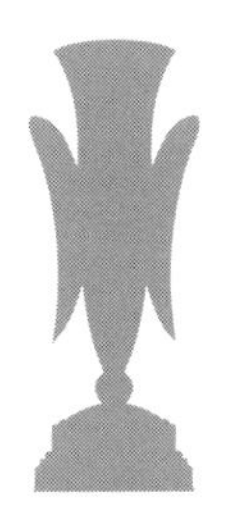

GLASGOW RANGERS AWAY...

INTER-CITIES FAIRS CUP SEMI-FINAL 1ST LEG

GLASGOW RANGERS 0

NEWCASTLE UNITED 0

Kick-off: 19:30, Wednesday 14th May 1969
Venue: Ibrox, Glasgow, Scotland
Attendance: 75,580
Referee: John (AKA Jack) Adair (Northern Ireland)

Glasgow Rangers: Gerhardt Neef, David Provan, Kai Johansen, Sandy Jardine, Colin Jackson, John Greig (c), Dave Smith, Örjan Persson, Andy Penman, Willie Henderson, Colin Stein.
Substitutes not used: Norrie Martin (GK), Alex MacDonald, Alec Miller

Newcastle United: Willie McFaul; John Craggs, John McNamee, Bob Moncur (c), Frank Clark; Tommy Gibb, Preben Arentoft; Jim Scott (Jackie Sinclair, 75), Bryan Robson, Wyn Davies, Alan Foggon.
Substitutes not used: John Hope (GK), Ollie Burton

(Newcastle's **Willie McFaul** saved a 35th-minute penalty from Rangers' Andy Penman)

MICHAEL'S CLUB ON NORTHUMBERLAND STREET, NEWCASTLE UNITED'S FAIRS CUP VICTORY CELEBRATORY DINNER AND DANCE

ANNOUNCEMENT: Ladies and Gentlemen, please retake your seats; dessert – the Glacé Glasgow Rangers Flambe – is served.

The guests start making their way back to their seats after a short interval. Gibbo, Tony Boullemier and several of the players open up the conversation with their first thoughts on the Rangers tie.

GIBBO: Well, United were in the semi-final and when the draw came through, it was a plum! Newcastle United v Glasgow Rangers, 34-times Scottish champions, renowned around the world and the only other British club left in the competition. This was a bestseller on both sides of the border.

BOB MONCUR: I think until that point none of us had got ahead of ourselves. We'd just thought: 'Right where are we off to now? Right, let's go.' A match, a night out in whichever country it was, and that's how we did it.

It was an experience, not just in terms of playing football but also in going abroad to different countries. So actually, in a way, we were a little bit disappointed with the draw: 'Hmmm, Rangers, Glasgow. Yeah.'

But of course it *was* a great thing because it was Scotland v England and fortunately I was on the English side this time.

BRYAN POP ROBSON: It certainly wasn't as exotic as flying away. It was very close to home and a bit more hostile. But I thought this would be a hard game. This game worried me. You'd just hear the name Glasgow Rangers and the crowd and the quality of the team…

FRANK CLARK: Well I'd have to deal with their right-winger Willie Henderson – that's what worried me! Mind, by this time, we thought we had a chance of winning. We'd beaten some good teams so we thought we had a chance. Newcastle supporters thought we had a

chance. The rest of the country still thought we had no chance. We knew it was going to be a difficult game up there though, and it was.
TONY BOULLEMIER: The watchword amongst the Press squad was stick together and don't wander off on your own. We found the hostility in Glasgow quite concerning. I'm the youngest member of our group at 23 and my older colleagues seemed quite keen to make sure nothing happened to me.
KEITH DYSON: Lucky you. I was on the reserve-team bus taking the reserves and juniors to Rangers to watch the game. We were going along this road to Ibrox which was packed either side with Scots people, when some idiots sailed some big bricks through the windows and smashed a whole set of them!
Everybody ducked down. We had to dive under the seats, get on the floor and cower, in case anything else came through. We could have been mauled. We didn't stop and just drove straight into the stadium.
BRYAN POP ROBSON: Blimey. Mind, with Glasgow being so close, at least it meant our families could go to the game and it was good for our Scottish lads too.
BENNY ARENTOFT: Jim, Jackie, Tommy, Bob… they all said the same about Rangers. A top, top team but big-headed. So it would be so nice to beat them, especially at home. I don't think we ever beat Rangers when I was at Morton and I'd never beaten Celtic. Against Rangers or Celtic it was only ever a question of how many you'd lose by.
DAVID CRAIG: It was certainly special for our Scots players but it was also special for me too against Rangers, a club I'd have loved to have played for. I was a Linfield fan from Northern Ireland and Rangers were the equivalent in Scotland of Linfield. Obviously our Scottish lads wanted to win – you Moncs, Scotty, Sinky, Tommy Gibb, Big Mac... especially Big Mac, having played for Hibs and being a Celtic fan.
BOB MONCUR: They were all under pressure, mind. I remember walking into Ibrox – and don't forget, I'd come down south as a

15-year-old from Scotland so I'd never had to play them. But they were all used to going there and getting hammered.

I could see Jimmy Scott, Jackie Sinclair, Big Mac and Tommy Gibb going: *'Ohhh...'* Even Big John. He wouldn't like to show it, but I just knew he was a bit worried about playing against Colin Stein.

So I kept saying to our Scots boys: *'Look, we're better than them. Scottish football is not as good as the stuff we play every week, so we can beat them.'* I was confident we'd beat Rangers.

OLLIE BURTON: I didn't play at Rangers, you know, after what happened to Dave Elliott in the lead-up to the game. I'd seen Dave have a fit in London before the West Ham game the previous season and I'd never seen anyone have a fit like that. When he had another fit before the Glasgow game, I knew I wasn't in the right frame of mind. So I think Joe Harvey made the right decision not playing me. Big John played instead.

GIBBO: That's all true, Ollie. You and Dave Elliott had decided to take a breath of fresh air when Dave collapsed on the pavement once more. You sprinted back to the hotel and David Salkeld, our club doctor, rushed out to look after Dave. He was put to bed in the same room as you.

Obviously when a top footballer dramatically collapses, not once but twice on the streets of great cities on the day of combat, it naturally causes a tidal wave of panic.

Joe decided he couldn't play Ollie in such a massive match, given his state of mind and how he'd reacted on the field the last time it happened in London. You didn't have your best game there, Ollie. So this meant a dramatic call-up for Big John, who'd been struggling for fitness and was actually visiting family down the road in Coatbridge.

Ollie, weren't you worried you'd lose your place for the return leg because of this?

OLLIE BURTON: Well, this is it, isn't it? But after the game Joe said: *'Don't worry, Ollie. I'll give you a bit of time and you'll be playing in the second leg.'* So he assured me I'd be playing.

GIBBO: It was all happening for you then, wasn't it? I reported at the time that a few hours before kick-off against Liverpool the following Saturday, your wife Sue presented you with your second child, a son! Craigy, you'd just come back from a hamstring injury so you weren't risked in the first leg at Ibrox, but you replaced your understudy John Craggs in the return match. What did you think of your chances?
DAVID CRAIG: Rangers were a good side, Gibbo, with some very good players but we fancied our chances against anybody, home and away. The aggregate system seemed to suit us because we knew we wouldn't give many goals away and we knew we could score goals.
BOB MONCUR: Big Mac had made a classic quote before the first game. He'd been struggling a bit with an injury but when a Glasgow reporter asked him how he felt about coming up against Stein, Big Mac growled: *'I'll play Colin Stein on one leg!'* And that was the headline in the paper on the night of the game. He's a character, but that's the spirit we play in.

They arrive at the journalists' table first:

GIBBO (taking his seat): You lads had slipped into a convincing groove too, losing only two First Division games out of 12 and shooting up the table. I remember the lads training at Barrowfield Park before the game, the Celtic training ground.
Aside from Ollie, Dave Elliott and Geoff Allen, United were almost at full strength with Craggs keeping his place ahead of Craig and Danish international Benny Arentoft, our new signing from Greenock Morton, operating in midfield.
GEOFF ALLEN: I remember Joe Harvey was talking to one of the Rangers staff before that semi-final when he pointed at me and said: *'We haven't got him, but I wish we had.'*
GIBBO: Rangers weren't in prime shape, mind. They'd lost the league to Celtic and the same team had just thumped them 4-0 in the Scottish Cup Final as well. What's more, they'd been forced to go into this match

without inside-left Willie Johnston, banned after a red card against Athletic Bilbao in the previous round, and two injured defenders, Ron McKinnon and Willie Mathieson. To cap it all, it wasn't clear which of their goalkeepers would get the nod to start.

BENNY ARENTOFT: It was such a big game. The feeling when you're going out onto the pitch is like you're buzzing.

GIBBO: Benny, was it excitement and motivation, or nerves and fear?

BENNY ARENTOFT: It was everything. Joe Harvey was always nervous during these big games – he'd smoke non-stop.

GIBBO: And his mood would only have worsened on the morning of the match when Wyn Davies sparked off a 4am scare. The 'One-man Welsh Air Force' needed sleeping tablets from the doctor because of the noise outside our hotel. He also complained of feeling unwell after all the travelling he'd done in the past week with the Welsh squad during the Home Nations tournament.

Wyn trained a few hours later in long trunks and trousers with a towel bound round his neck. Joe had admitted Wyn had him worried. He'd said: *'This sleeping business is vitally important before a match of this size. People underestimate a problem like this – we need Davies badly and I'm not happy with this sort of preparation.'*

THE BRIDGE HOTEL, NEWCASTLE UPON TYNE

The lads have finished their beers and signed up for the Supporters' Club trips to Hull and Hibs in early August. They get ready to leave and continue their Fairs Cup reminiscences on the way through town up to their bus stops.

SPOW: I'd decided early on that I'd go to whichever matches I could afford and obviously with Glasgow being so near, the Rangers game just cost me coppers really. We got the bus to Glasgow and parked down the street from Ibrox. There was a Rangers bus in front of us and one behind us too.

We got out and someone said: *'What now?'* *'Well,'* I said: *'There's nee bars aboot here,'* so we headed to the ground and went in. In came some Rangers boys with big carrier bags of alcohol, full of bottles of sherry and God knows bloody what and they were canny drunk already, singing their songs. Next thing you know, a bottle of sherry comes out and one says: *'Have a drink, Jimmy!'*

'No, no,' I said.

'HAVE A DRINK, JIMMY!'

'Alreet, mate...'

MICHAEL'S CLUB, NEWCASTLE UPON TYNE

At the journalists' table

TONY BOULLEMIER: Ibrox was like a bear pit. They treated John McNamee like a pantomime villain because he was ex-Celtic. There were more than 75,000 in the ground including 12,000 Newcastle fans and the tension was unbearable.

IVOR BROADIS: United's early plan had looked to be 'Get a quick goal, then sit on it' and it should have succeeded. Jardine let Davies get a shot away that he pulled wide and Robson failed with his first clear chance on nine minutes.

I suspect he might have felt a non-existent challenge at his back as a shrewd lob from Craggs left him perfectly set-up eight yards out. Their keeper, Neef, stayed put. But Robson leaned back in his attempt to lob into the far corner and the ball sailed over.

At this stage United were beating Rangers to the punch, going in to meet the ball while the home side stood off. United looked as immovable as

Grey's Monument until Andy Penman began to make his presence felt. A ball stroked immaculately inside Clark had Henderson coming in along the byline, but his final pass was cut back too far. Then the move was repeated for Persson on the opposite flank with Henderson firing his square pass against a defender.

TONY BOULLEMIER: Willie Henderson had started off for Rangers like a runaway train.

IVOR BROADIS: And Penman again found the a gap for the pitter-pattering Henderson to go through and hit a shot against McFaul, angling cleverly and diving right. It was all a bit untidy but there looked to be nothing between the teams until a decision by Northern Irish referee Jack Adair threatened to turn the game Rangers' way. Smith had aimed a great long ball over Craggs for Persson to chase.

GIBBO: What happened then depends on who you listen to – McFaul or referee Adair. Our keeper reckons he went to punch the bouncing ball, punched it against Persson's chest and his fist caught the flying winger as he went down. In other words, McFaul played the ball and not the man. Adair's story is straightforward. He says Willie, in his view, deliberately brought down the Rangers player. And as the man in the bright scarlet jersey was in charge, it was a penalty.

As Persson was being dowsed with water to bring him round, United's first-team coach Dave Smith leapt from the bench and frantically gestured to John Craggs.

Lord Westwood had shown Smith a picture of John Greig taking a penalty for Rangers with the ball going to the right of the keeper and Dave had forgotten to mention it to McFaul. Hurriedly the message was passed via Craggs to the keeper: *Greig will take it – dive right.*

Imagine the surprise when up stepped Penman to place the ball on the spot.

'I could have died,' Willie told me afterwards. *'But I'd made up my mind to dive right and it was too late to change it.'* Penman, reckoned to have the hardest shot in Scotland, lashed the ball low, just inside

the right-hand post… and there was McFaul at full stretch, pushing the ball around the post for a corner.

WILLIE McFAUL, passing at that moment on his way to order at the bar, throws in a thought as he goes: Well, sure, the penalty save at Ibrox was critical but Joe Harvey had said I had to save the kick because I'd given the penalty away. Joe's one-liners are always top-drawer!

TONY BOULLEMIER: Seriously, though, that save must have been a massive tonic for your teammates.

IVOR BROADIS: And let's not forget that right on half-time another fantastic McFaul save kept United alive. He couldn't have seen much of Penman's half-volley from 25 yards, hit with ferocious power as he met a headed clearance from a free-kick. But somehow he got to it to flash it round the post.

Rangers did the bulk of the attacking in the second half but there was a lack of imaginative craft about them. United refused to be drawn and instead erected a black and white shield in front of McFaul.

TONY BOULLEMIER: Yes, Frank Clark at left-back had weathered the initial onslaught from Henderson and by the end, he had the Scottish international well taped. Colin Stein is obviously a fine player and roamed far and wide, but when he came down the middle, McNamee shut him out as well.

GIBBO: It was a match of fierce tackling but the only player booked was home skipper John Greig when he fouled Arentoft on 73 minutes. Five minutes later, Jim Scott limped off to be replaced by Jackie Sinclair as they hung on, amazingly, magnificently, luckily, call it what you like. And Joe's men even nearly nicked it at the end.

IVOR BROADIS: Yes, the final thrill came in injury time when Robson cut inside from the left and Neef, surprised at the pace and swing of the 25-yarder, could only fling up an arm to divert the ball for a corner – and then it was over. No praise was too great for the iron-clad defence, marshalled by Moncur the Governor. Upfront, Davies was as brave as ever and he did a useful stint in defence for every corner kick.

TONY BOULLEMIER: Actually, both Davies and Moncur came off the field with bloodstained faces and shirts after heavy blows on the nose. Director Fenton Braithwaite, a surgeon, had to reset Wyn's broken nose in the dressing room but he told me he was sure he'd be back to face Liverpool in the last league match of the season three days later. It has to be said, the feeling amongst the Press corps was that we were going to go through.

BENNY ARENTOFT: We'd ended up on top but we were all bloody tired. We stayed in a hotel near the main station and went back the next day by bus. It was certainly a great journey back to Newcastle and training was great after that too, just great, because we knew we would beat them.

The coach and the manager had seen this game and had seen their players against our players, and they knew what we could do at home, at our home ground. The feeling was: '*This is us; we will beat you... just come to Newcastle and we will beat you.*'

THE ALBION TRAINING GROUND, GLASGOW, 15TH JULY 1969

It's the second day of pre-season training for the Rangers squad. Seven weeks of holiday couldn't have come soon enough after the disappointment of the previous season's trophyless exertions, culminating in a Fairs Cup exit in the North-East of England.

Now it's time to reset and start again. Several of the players are standing outside the shower building, waiting for the rest of their teammates to get ready before they take lunch, back at Ibrox. A young workman is up a ladder fixing the guttering, when a tool he's using falls harmlessly to the floor nearby.

YOUNG WORKMAN (in a softer accent than a typical Glaswegian one): Oh sorry, gentlemen.

Willie Henderson is nearest. He kindly picks up the screwdriver and hands it back up to the young man.

YOUNG WORKMAN: Thanks. I'd be struggling up here without that.

WILLIE HENDERSON: That's alright, laddie. What's your name? You're not from round here, are you?

YOUNG WORKMAN: Nice to meet you, Sir. My name's Monty. No Sir, I'm from the borders. Berwick.

WILLIE JOHNSTON: Oh, dear! **(glancing to the sky, clearly remembering an infamous Scottish Cup defeat there a couple of years earlier)**

MONTY: But I follow Newcastle United.

COLIN STEIN: Even worse! **(only half-joking)**

MONTY: My uncle's from Beith, Ayrshire, so I've come up for the summer to stay with family. I'm doing a few jobs for my uncle's pal who's a handyman around here. I was at those Fairs Cup matches last season. Hard luck – they were very, very tight.

WILLIE HENDERSON: Don't you worry, laddie. There are no superstars in that team of yours but they all played for each other, and it worked, it really worked.

MONTY: You must have fancied your chances though, no?

COLIN STEIN: We were a far, far better team than Newcastle at the time and it hadn't mattered who we'd drawn in the semi-final. The Hungarians have a great reputation, mind, and were probably the favourites to win the competition.

Newcastle though… it's always nice to have an England versus Scotland game which is always quite competitive, isn't it? And I used to play with Jim Scott at Hibs so I knew him quite well. He's been ribbing me ever since because they beat us.

I played with John McNamee at Hibs as well. He told me in the tunnel at Ibrox that it wasn't true about him saying he'd play me on one leg or have me in his pocket during the game; it was all just paper talk. It didn't bother me... but he *did* have me in his pocket! Mind, I didn't get any ammunition, especially in the game at Newcastle. We didn't do a lot there but we should have won at Ibrox. I'd been suspended in the lead-up to the game and if you're not playing every week, it does hold you back. I hadn't played club football for about four weeks.

MONTY: Did you feel an opportunity had been missed at Ibrox because of Andy Penman's missed penalty?

COLIN STEIN: Aye, but Pop Robson came close as well at Ibrox, didn't he? If we'd got a lead there though, it'd have made a big, big difference.

WILLIE JOHNSTON: On that night in Newcastle I didn't play well, nor did others play well... but the game at Ibrox was a turning point.

COLIN STEIN: I don't think it was a turning point. I think we should have done a lot better, especially in front of nearly 80,000.

MONTY: Just a shade over 75,000 fans. Incredible. That's a Fairs Cup record too. Why did Penman take the penalty instead of John Greig, the normal penalty-taker?

WILLIE JOHNSTON: Didn't Andy Penman also take penalties all this spring?

COLIN STEIN: I could'nae tell yer.

WILLIE JOHNSTON: Aye, Andy took them.

COLIN STEIN: I could'nae tell yer if there was a change or not.

MONTY: My family here kept a few of the newspapers for me to read. Apparently you'd been given the job, Mr Stein, if there'd been another penalty in the 2nd leg. How was Andy afterwards? Did he apologise in the dressing room or did people just say *'Don't worry, these things happen?'*

WILLIE JOHNSTON: Aye, that's it.

COLIN STEIN: And we had another 90 minutes to make things better...

GLASGOW RANGERS AT HOME...

INTER-CITIES FAIRS CUP SEMI-FINAL 2ND LEG

NEWCASTLE UNITED 2
GLASGOW RANGERS 0

Kick-off: 19:30, Wednesday 21st May 1969
Venue: St James' Park, Newcastle upon Tyne, England
Attendance: 59,303
Referee: John Gow (Wales)

Newcastle United: Willie McFaul, David Craig, Bob Moncur (c), Ollie Burton, Frank Clark; Preben Arentoft, Tommy Gibb; Jim Scott, Wyn Davies, Bryan Robson, Jackie Sinclair
Substitutes not used: John Hope (GK), John Craggs, Alan Foggon

Glasgow Rangers: Gerhardt Neef, Ronnie McKinnon (David Provan 65), Kai Johansen, Willie Mathieson, John Greig (c), Dave Smith, Örjan Persson, Andy Penman, Willie Henderson, Colin Stein, Willie Johnston
Substitutes not used: Norrie Martin (GK)
Other named substitutes not known, but the other squad members in the travelling party were: Alex MacDonald, Alec Miller, Sandy Jardine and Colin Jackson (note: Alex Ferguson also travelled with the squad but, in line with pre-match expectations, he played no part in the game)

Goals:
1-0: Jim Scott (52)
2-0: Jackie Sinclair (77)

Newcastle United win 2-0 on aggregate.

BENNY ARENTOFT: There was a big fear in advance that the Scottish fans would attack Newcastle. All the shops were told that they should barricade or close up. The players were told: '*Don't take your car into the stadium. Leave your car far away.*' I parked on the other side of the river and took a taxi.

GIBBO: There were plenty of nerves though, amongst that huge crowd of just under 60,000, mainly to do with whether the team could complete the job. There'd have been even more nerves if they'd known at the time that one of the linesmen, J.D. Williams of Wrexham, owned a house named 'Ibrox'!

There were plenty of football's top brass there to watch. Liverpool boss Bill Shankly, Everton manager Harry Catterick and intriguingly, the Újpest Dózsa head coach Lajos Baróti. He was given an interpreter by the club, Hungarian-born Veronika Griffiths, a Ponteland housewife, as he sought to complete his preparations for the first leg of the final eight days later.

Baróti would have seen that Sandy Jardine had made way for forward Willie Johnston – now free from suspension. Experienced centre-back Ron McKinnon had returned from a knee injury to replace Colin Jackson and left-back Willie Mathieson had come in for Davie Provan, who dropped to the bench.

Newcastle also made three changes. Fit-again David Craig took his normal right-back berth from John Craggs, for his first match since the home win over Real Zaragoza in January. Ollie Burton replaced thigh injury victim John McNamee and Jackie Sinclair slotted in on the left wing in place of Alan Foggon.

DOUG WEATHERALL: Rangers had nine skilful internationals in their side and the fanatical backing of 12,000 Scots.

GIBBO: And the rest! They seemed to be everywhere.

DOUG WEATHERALL: Added to that, Rangers are the most experienced European campaigners in Britain.

BACK AT THE ALBION TRAINING GROUND IN GLASGOW AS THE LAST OF THE RANGERS PLAYERS BEGIN TO EMERGE AFTER TRAINING

COLIN STEIN: The crowd that night at St James' Park was unbelievable, especially the Rangers following in the Gallowgate End. It was phenomenal for us but we didn't perform on the night. We went to Newcastle thinking we could still win the game – we didn't look upon ourselves as second favourites or anything like that. We thought we'd win the game.
MONTY: And it was the same type of hard, physical battle at St James'...
WILLIE JOHNSTON: Oh, aye...
COLIN STEIN (with a wry smile on his face): It was a Scotland v England game, wasn't it? For your information, Willie Henderson didn't turn up that night either!
WILLIE HENDERSON: Ah, Frank Clark played me really well.
MONTY: Did he?
WILLIE HENDERSON: Oh yes. Good player, Frank Clark.
MONTY: What did he do to stop you that others didn't?
WILLIE HENDERSON: Well, he had his machine gun, you know... **(everyone breaks out into laughter)**. Ah, honestly, he played me well – twice. A very good player; one of the best I've played against.

MICHAEL'S CLUB, NEWCASTLE UPON TYNE

At the journalists' table:

TONY BOULLEMIER: The day before the match, I'd gone up to meet the Rangers squad at the Gosforth Park Hotel. Alex Ferguson was in the squad but couldn't displace Colin Stein from the team. He didn't play and he wasn't on the bench but he thought he might have a chance, so he was pumping me for information to try to find who was likely to be playing at centre-back with Bob Moncur – whether it would be Ollie Burton or John McNamee. Even if I'd known, I wouldn't have told him. He was very pleasant though, the way he went about it.

NICK SCURR: It wasn't a great game and good football was at a premium. There was plenty of action, plenty of big boot and far too many niggling and nasty fouls, but the only name to go into the book was that of Jim Scott for what looked like an accidental trip.

Scott had the last laugh though, because it was he who put Newcastle on the victory trail in the 52nd minute. Tommy Gibb, who had looked good in flashes and not so good for long periods, slipped the ball neatly out to his right for Scott to sweep onto, cut inside and then, from just inside the box, hit a tremendous cross-shot which left Neef helpless. It was a great goal and it sent the Newcastle fans wild with delight.

In the 64th minute, Rangers suffered a severe blow when Ron McKinnon, who had just about shared the honours in his battle with Wyn Davies, had to come off when his knee broke down, Davie Provan coming on in his place.

The Scots were throwing everything at the iron-hard Newcastle defence but in the 77th minute, came the clincher. A free-kick against Stein midway in the Newcastle half was thumped upfield by Ollie Burton. Davies again got up to head it on and Jackie Sinclair was on to it in a flash.

GIBBO: It was perfect – he darted foward and blasted a close-range shot past Neef.

NICK SCURR: Yes, right into the roof of the net. It happened so fast there was simply nothing the Scots' defence could do about it.

BOB MONCUR: To be fair, the Rangers team were fine – Greigy, Willie Henderson, Steiny – I knew them from playing for Scotland so they were all great. There was nothing untoward on the pitch from the team and they had fantastic fans too, up to the point of them going *onto* the pitch, which was a bit out of order.

I still forgive them a little bit because they called it a riot, disgraceful and all the rest of it. But in fairness, what happened in the Gallowgate End, where they'd put all the Rangers fans, was that people at the back were throwing bottles but these weren't going on the pitch. They were hitting their own supporters on the back of their heads, so they were getting rained on.

Their team was 2-0 down at the time so the Rangers supporters spilt onto the back of the pitch. But it wasn't like a riot. There might have been a few who got on the pitch and then the police with the dogs came on, but the spectators at the front had nowhere else to go. You cannae keep taking bottles to the back of the head. So it was unfortunate and it was caused by the Rangers supporters, but only an idiotic minority.

Just by the table now is Barman 1, who's collecting a few empty glasses from the table.

BARMAN 1: Mr Scott, if I may ask, which is your favourite goal from the Fairs Cup?

JIM SCOTT (smiling): Actually, it has to be the one I scored up here in the semi-final against Rangers.

FRANK CLARK: Is that the one that caused the riot?

JIM SCOTT: It was about the only kick I got in the match. Wee Sinky doubled the riot when he scored the second!

WILLIE McFAUL: It was alright for you lot. You guys were at the other end of the pitch.

FRANK CLARK: I've told a story about you on that night, Willie. I think I've stretched the truth a little bit but it's a funny story. When we came off, we got to the tunnel, but you turned round. You were going to go back when I said to you: '*Where are you going?*' To which you said: '*I'm going back for my hat and gloves.*'

WILLIE McFAUL (laughing): That's true. That *is* true!

FRANK CLARK (laughing too): Well, I'm pleased about that... and I said: '*Don't be silly – I'll buy you a new pair!*'

As for how it started, we'd just gone 2-0 up with not long to go when play was temporarily held up down the other end. I was standing inside our 18-yard line when a couple of bottles whizzed past my ear. The atmosphere was electric. One hurried glance over my shoulder at the hordes beginning to clamber over the wall onto the pitch and I was off. I hared for the centre circle and then, as the referee also realised what was happening, I dived for the tunnel. I was first man off.

BENNY ARENTOFT, who's come over to chat: I was running too. I wasn't very far from the tunnel as I'd been playing on the left. It was terrible. I was just thinking about getting inside.

WILLIE McFAUL: Ollie was facing me and I was spending most of my time on the edge of the box anyway, because they (the Rangers fans amassed in the Gallowgate End) were throwing all sorts at me, and suddenly, all I could hear from Ollie was: '*RUN!*'

OLLIE BURTON overhears his name and leans over from his adjoining table to join the conversation: The referee was a Welshman, John Gow – I'd been introduced to him before, when I'd been playing for Wales – and he said to me: '*Ollie, I'm going to abandon the game.*'

I responded: '*You're bloody not!*' But he replied: '*Yes I am; they're throwing bottles.*' To which I pleaded: '*No! We're winning 2-0.*' I convinced him that we could go back out again after it had calmed down. But if you hadn't seen it, you wouldn't realise just how bad it was.

BARMAN 1: A lot of them had certainly had a lot to drink throughout the day. Had any of you ever experienced anything like that before?

WILLIE McFAUL: No, and I never want to again.

FRANK CLARK: It was the most frightened I've ever been on a football pitch. It was crazy, frightening, especially when we came back out. We had to play the last 15 minutes or so with police dogs ringing the track and if you look at pictures of the game, you'll notice the track around the pitch wasn't very wide, so the kids were sitting on the wall, the track was not very far away and the pitch was ringed by yapping police dogs. So nobody was volunteering to take throw-ins either.

WILLIE McFAUL: Before that though, the chairman of Rangers had come in to the dressing room and said to us all: '*As far as we're concerned, the game's over.*' But the referee wouldn't have it and said the game had to be finished.

FRANK CLARK: He did say though, that they'd withdraw from the competition if anything happened like a Rangers recovery, which was nice of him really.

BARMAN 1: Yes, I think that was John Lawrence and he was quoted in the papers as saying that: '*The exhibition by a small percentage of Rangers supporters had brought disgrace on our grand old club.*' Strong words.

WILLIE McFAUL: Yeah, but the biggest blunder was when we scored the second goal and that guy came on the tannoy...

JIM SCOTT: Aye.

WILLIE McFAUL: Because they'd already been on the pitch, so he said: '*If you come on again, the game could be abandoned.*' So of course, whoosh, they were on.

FRANK CLARK: So that's when they all came on? Ahh, right.

WILLIE McFAUL: Yes, that's what encouraged it. And the goalmouth was full of glass.

BARMAN 1: I read Nick Scurr's report that three previous 'minor' invasions – two by enthusiastic Newcastle supporters greeting the goals – had caused the referee to announce by loudspeaker that a repetition would stop the game. He said it was a well-meant warning, but probably ill-advised.

Did you ever get your hat or gloves back?

WILLIE McFAUL: Never! I'd had them for years, back to when I'd been playing in Ireland. I was superstitious about them. I probably never even wore the hat; it was just there.

OLLIE BURTON: Well, I've never seen anything like it, you know. You get crowds that boo you but not being dangerous – anyhow, we got through it.

TONY BOULLEMIER: We were told that they had 12,000 tickets allocated to them but it was estimated that 20,000 fans had come down. When the pubs closed at ten past three, they formed up into a marching band with bagpipes, flutes, drums and King Billy banners. We watched them come past the Journal offices in Groat Market and they just went round and round the city for the next three hours.

They then went up to the ground, smashed down a gate and got in. So although the official attendance was 60,000, I'd say there were nearer 70,000 that night. They were up the rafters in the stands, the floodlights and the trees behind the Popular Side. You've never seen such a packed ground.

GIBBO: It was heaving. They were even perching by the chimneys on the four-storey rooftops behind the Popular Side.

TONY BOULLEMIER: It just shows the lengths fans will go to. But it was Jackie Sinclair's goal that really provoked them to complete idiocy. They'd started throwing bottles earlier, in fact, they'd hit their own goalkeeper Gerhard Neef with a bottle in the first half. Once it became 2-0 and the writing was on the wall, they poured out of the Gallowgate End to attack our fans.

And of course, gentlemen, we all remember watching it from that old Press Box on top of the main stand – the biggest fire hazard in the whole Football League. Doesn't climbing that spiral iron staircase ever worry you chaps? We even have to push the older reporters up, to get them in!

ARNOLD HOWE: Tony, dear boy, rest assured all propulsions are gratefully received **(guffaws around the table)**.

TONY BOULLEMIER: Hmm, well, it really is an horrendous firetrap. Anyway, we were sitting on top of this scene, watching all these Glasgow fans pouring out of the Gallowgate End and heading toward the Newcastle die-hards at the Leazes End.

Luckily the cops had the whole situation under control. They sent in the dogs and they took down the Rangers' ringleaders and halted the charge in its tracks. This was a very good job because the Newcastle fans had started to come out of the Leazes End to meet them. Had it not been for the dogs and the mounted police who followed them, there would have been a pitched battle in the middle of the pitch. Of course, the players had been taken off by that time and were off for nearly 20 minutes. They came back to see out the last few minutes of the game and we were through.

GIBBO: You didn't hang around for long after that, did you?

TONY BOULLEMIER: No, I left sharply. I phoned my story over from the Press Box and set off for the office. But I was pretty soon ringing in another story from a phonebox at the bottom of Gallowgate. I was surrounded by Rangers fans who were running wild. It was like the sacking of a medieval city. They smashed in the windows of just about every pub in town and there was glass everywhere. It was a major riot. The police just didn't have a prayer. It was probably the worst outbreak of violence in Newcastle since the Scots captured it in the Civil War.

RAY ROBERTSON of The Northern Echo: Lord Westwood had actually been in the South of France on an important business appointment, so he was lucky not to witness the scenes of thuggery and violence.

DOUG WEATHERALL: And I never thought I'd see the day when genuine football-loving fans would give one of their biggest cheers to the police who eventually brought order at the Rangers end of the ground.

GEOFF ALLEN: That was the only fright we ever had at home; when the Rangers fans ran on. But football-wise we were fantastic and we'd grown in confidence – I could see it in the dressing room and in Joe as well. I think he knew we weren't going to be beaten here.

RON GUTHRIE: I was out by that point too, having had a cartilage operation back in February. One thing I remember is that after the match, the apprentices collected stacks of whisky bottles and beer bottles, took them back to the shops and got a lot of money for them.

BENNY ARENTOFT: The feeling in the dressing room after was top, top, top. The atmosphere outside was a nightmare – it's difficult to explain how it was, but inside it was happiness at beating Rangers, and then the next day, when you start training, you start thinking of the final. If I remember rightly, Újpest beat Leeds in the quarter-final, and Leeds were top of the English league at that time. That Újpest could beat Leeds was unbelievable. It showed the calibre of the competition.

IN NEWCASTLE TOWN CENTRE

Newcastle City Police sergeants Ashwell and Parsons are out on the beat. Tuesdays are normally quiet in the town centre, especially on warm summer evenings and this one, as they

near the bottom end of Northumberland Street, is no exception. Suddenly, they hear a commotion coming around the corner from the direction of Grey's Monument.
It's Spow, Bill Gibbs, Harry Watson, the two Peters and others. They are still chatting loudly as they make their way up towards their various bus stops.

HARRY WATSON: Rangers at home was just electric, mind. It was buzzing. It felt almost like, if someone would touch you, you'd get an electric shock. Both sets of fans were so passionate. Bill, where were you?
BILL GIBBS: In my favourite spot, the centre of the Leazes End. I'll always remember when they came on to the pitch, the chant went around the ground: *'ANIMALS! Ch, ch, ch; ANIMALS! Ch, ch, ch!'*
HARRY WATSON: Aye, it started off in one section and then went right around the stadium.

They all join in as they turn to go up Northumberland Street.

'ANIMALS! Ch, ch, ch; ANIMALS! CH, CH, CH!'

Mid-chant, they round the corner and bump straight into the young, puzzled policemen.

SERGEANT ASHWELL: Good evening, gentlemen. What's happening here then?
SPOW: Cripes! Nowt, Sir.
SERGEANT PARSONS: Bit noisy, aren't we, for a midweek stroll around town?
TONY RODGERS: Sorry, Sir. We've just been down to supporters club at the Bridge. Signing up for next season.
SERGEANT PARSONS: I see. Let's hope 'Animals' isn't the latest terrace chant.

HARRY WATSON (politely chuckling): No, it's not. We've all been talking about the Fairs Cup this evening. We were just remembering how this was the chant going round the ground when the Rangers fans invaded the pitch in the semi-final.

SERGEANT PARSONS: Ah yes. The infamous date with Rangers. I was on the desk at the station that evening but weren't you there, Sergeant Ashwell?

SERGEANT ASHWELL: I certainly was. I started early at about 10 o' clock and our job was to try to control the Rangers supporters.

BILL GIBBS: A big job then?

SERGEANT ASHWELL: At that time, they weren't bad. They just came and sat on the pavement and asked: *'See, Jimmy, where can we get a drink?'*

So everything in my area was fine. But when the match kicked off, the atmosphere was electric. The overwhelming desire was to beat the Jocks.

MALCOLM DIX, another fan who'd gone to the Bridge Hotel earlier to meet his friend Peter Ratcliffe: It was. It really was. You must have had a rare view of the riot. What happened?

SERGEANT ASHWELL: Well, the Rangers crowd weren't happy about something which led up to the second goal. I wasn't up that end – I was by the Popular Side. It was possible they wanted to get the game abandoned because otherwise, why would you cause a disturbance? Bottles went everywhere. One of our colleagues – an inspector – was hit on the head by a bottle and I don't know how many others were too.

HARRY WATSON: Really? I didn't know that. What were you actually meant to do at the match?

SERGEANT ASHWELL: Ah, you see, there were certain of us who are employed on special duty to work in the ground – be around the pitch, at the back of the crowd and one or two might be in the crowd too.

Your job is to catch anyone that runs onto the pitch to disturb the game. So it may have been that some supporters thought if we riot, they'll abandon the match and we'll have another chance. They basically got on the pitch and then wondered: *'What do we do now?'*
BILL GIBBS: But then you still have to get them off the pitch.
SERGEANT ASHWELL: Yes. We have a drill to deal with pitch invasions so initially we run towards them. Then you get aligned, so you get in a line across and sweep them back so once that happens you can clear the pitch. When it kicked off, the bobbies initially ran to stop the Scots getting to the Leazes End and then they formed a line and just gradually moved them backwards and got them off the pitch. Policemen with dogs were also there. At the start, I stayed on the terrace on the Popular Side but after a few minutes I went down to support.
We had mounted police outside the ground and they were asked to come in. They don't walk towards you but the horses turn to one side and they side step. It took quite a few minutes, about a quarter of an hour, for things to settle down and it was decided they might as well finish the match because if you abandon it, what's going to happen? It might happen again.
TONY RODGERS: That's true. But how did you stop them doing it again, right there and then?
SERGEANT ASHWELL: Once we'd shepherded them off the pitch and into the Gallowgate End, we just stayed there and watched them to stop them coming on again. The Scots were kept back in the Gallowgate for a little while because you've got an explosive mixture – if you let them out, there could be fighting in the streets but if you kept them penned in for a long while, there might be fighting in the ground.
Quite a lot was made of the Rangers match in the Press – naturally too, because it was a riot. But fortunately the bobbies were able to contain it without too many people being injured. I don't think there were actually many injuries despite the bottles being thrown.

I remember when the bottles had been flying onto the pitch, Newcastle's goalkeeper Willie McFaul was off like a shot and quite rightly too.

Anyway, enough of me gassing. Sergeant Parsons, shall we get on?

SERGEANT PARSONS: Yes, definitely. Good night, gentlemen, and just be aware of your noise please.

HARRY WATSON: We definitely will be. All the best. **(to his friends)** What nice blokes.

SPOW: They were. What a cracking job, working at the match – although maybe not that exact one. I won't forget that afterwards, I walked down this street and got my bus from Worswick Street out towards Gateshead. There'd been 12,000 Rangers fans inside the ground and nearly the same outside without tickets, so we all knew there were 20,000 plus Scots in the toon. My bus driver told me it was already kicking off and I found out next day that a few mates had been filled in by away fans when they'd headed down towards The Bridge.

Just at that moment, the group comprising Bill Gibbs, Harry Watson, Spow, Tony and Mick Rodgers, Malcolm Dix, Peter Ratcliffe, Peter Donaghy and a Newcastle United fan of Greek origin, Vassilis Koukoulis, hear a shout as they walk past Fenwick's department store on their way towards Haymarket bus station.

'Peter! Malcolm!'

It's Arthur Noutch, the head of Newcastle United Development Association, the club's promotional and fundraising arm, who has just given Peter Ratcliffe his first job working in United's marketing department. Peter is due to start the very next week but hasn't told his friends yet. It's through Peter that Arthur knows Malcolm Dix, whose family have held shares in Newcastle United for several generations.

Now that the celebratory meal upstairs in Michael's Club has all but finished, Arthur, a larger-than-life character who's never short of a new scheme to raise money for the club, has asked Newcastle United captain Bob Moncur for a quick word about a new idea involving the players. He's taking in some fresh air at the entrance while waiting for Bob to pop down.

PETER RATCLIFFE: Ah, hello! How are you, Mr Noutch?

Peter's group move across the street towards Michael's Club.

ARTHUR NOUTCH: Peter, just call me Arthur. I'm very well, thank you. Are you ready and raring to go next Monday? There's plenty of work to be done.

PETER RATCLIFFE: Oh absolutely! Please meet my friends. We've been at the Supporters Club at the Bridge reminiscing about the Fairs Cup.

ARTHUR NOUTCH: Nice to meet you all, gentlemen. What a coincidence. The club's just been holding its official celebratory banquet, so we've been doing the same. The top brass will probably leave soon but the players might stay around, as there's a dance to follow.

Just at this moment, Bob Moncur sticks his head around the door and sees Arthur chatting.

BOB MONCUR: Arthur, can we just have a chat inside now? Now that the food's finished they're taking the tables away before the dance **(notices Peter Donaghy, the team's interpreter at the Real Zaragoza matches)** Hello Peter, nice to see you again. Are you keeping well?

PETER DONAGHY: I am, Bob, yes, thanks. And you?

BOB MONCUR (with a smile; he's clearly enjoying himself): Just champion. Look, I'd like to go back in now but there's plenty of space by the bar. If you gentlemen can keep a low profile, you can sit and have a drink there if you like while we're with our wives on the other

side of the room. Gibbo tells me our two barmen are Fairs Cup encyclopaedias, so I'm sure you can entertain each other. OK?
ARTHUR NOUTCH: Very good of you, Bob. **(turning to the others, who thankfully are fairly well presented this time)** Anyone?
EVERYONE SIMULTANEOUSLY: Hmm, Oh yes. Yes. Oh aye. Definitely.
SPOW (under his breath): Thank God it's too warm for my usual Doc Martens and combat jacket...

AT THE BAR IN MICHAEL'S CLUB

BAR MANAGER: This all just becomes more and more enthralling. And I remember those visiting fans all too well. We'd closed for the day because of the warnings but they still tried to pull down our big neon sign, up a height outside.
Anyway, let's move on. After, the quarter-final performances, I guess there were no surprises in the other semi-final, were there?
BARMAN 2: None at all. Újpest Dózsa brushed aside the plucky Turks, it seems. George's match reports and interviews are here:

BENE AND DUNAI AT THE DOUBLE AS DÓZSA TRIUMPH IN TURKEY 23RD APRIL 1969

Újpest Dózsa's deadly striking duo of Ferenc Bene and Antal Dunai helped themselves to two goals each in Izmir, as Hungary's only representatives in Europe this season defeated Göztepe 4-1 in the first leg of their Fairs Cup semi-final on Wednesday.

In front of a fiery home crowd, Lajos Baróti's men took control from the start, overwhelming their enthusiastic but technically inferior opponents and taking a 12th-minute lead through Bene's firm close-range strike after neat interplay with Antal Dunai.

Moments later, there was a temporary setback when centre-back Ernő Solymosi handled in his own box and Çağlayan Derebaşı restored parity from the spot. But normal service was resumed just after the half-hour when Bene bagged his second courtesy of a tremendous, swerving free-kick from 20 yards, which beat keeper Ali Artuner all ends up.

The bookies' favourites to win the competition continued to press and were rewarded with a third goal on 63 minutes when Bene slalomed past two defenders and set up his striking partner in crime, Antal Dunai, for a shot at goal, a chance the angular attacker took with ruthless ferocity.

A second goal for the hosts in the remaining time could have left the tie finely balanced at the half-way stage and they certainly pressed forward in search of it. However, Szentmihályi saved well on more than one occasion and instead it was Dózsa who took a huge stride towards their first European final with a fourth goal nine minutes from time.

Winger László Fazekas released Bene in space and when he drew the Göztepe defence's attention, Dunai was left alone to convert the pass.

Four-one was the way it stayed and with the home leg still to come, Újpest fans must surely be confident that a final spot is all but assured.

CENAP ÖZTEZEL, Göztepe FC forward: Hungarian football is very strong these days. We were very excited when it became clear that we were going to play with Újpest.
The pitch in our stadium isn't grass, more like earth and dried mud. At the very beginning, their winger László Fazekas, controlled the ball on his foot and pulled it back so sweetly that me and my teammates Ertan and Mehmet crashed into each other almost head-on. In that second, Ertan said: '*Oh guys, they'll beat us very badly today.*' And they did; we've lost 4-1.
On the one hand, naturally, we're very sad and unhappy, but on the other hand we're very proud that such a great team has come to our country and to our city and that Göztepe fans have been given a chance to watch them play.

ERTAN ÖZNUR, Göztepe FC midfielder: You might think we played very badly but it's not true. The truth is that they are really very much stronger than us – not physically, but mentally and technically. I can admit that we were very stressed and nervous.

ADNAN SUVARI, Göztepe head coach: Their physical strength was great. Technically and tactically they stand tall above us. Göröcs is a born leader who sends scampering devils in on the opponents' goal.

ISTANBUL RADIO REPORTER: On the basis of this 90-minute performance, the Ankara Great Opera wishes to sign Göröcs as its lead ballet dancer.

BENE HAT-TRICK SEALS GREATEST EUROPEAN ACHIEVEMENT 30TH APRIL 1969

Ferenc Bene's marvellous hat-trick sealed a 4-0 victory for Újpest Dózsa over Turkish club Göztepe and ensured Lajos Baróti's side will reach a major pan-European final this season for the first time.
Újpest, of course, are former Mitropa Cup winners but their best record in post-war European competition is a Cup Winners' Cup semi-final loss to Fiorentina in 1962. That's history now though and this team will surely fancy its chances against either Rangers or Newcastle United in the final.
Brave Göztepe, already trailing 4-1 from the first leg in Izmir a week ago, never really stood much of a chance, especially once Bene latched onto Çağlayan Derebaşı's short pass back to the keeper, tricked goalkeeper Güngör Çelikçiler and slotted the ball into an empty net to open the scoring in the 24th minute.
Both teams had chosen to change their goalkeepers for the second leg and Dózsa's László Borbely proved he's a more-than-capable understudy for Antal Szentmihályi when he did superbly to reach Fevzi's thunderous effort from 22 metres. Güngör also impressed with two saves before half-time but he couldn't do anything to stop the hosts doubling their lead in the 55th minute, Antal Dunai turning and running from right to left before slipping a pass through for Bene, who made no mistake from ten metres out.
This served to open the floodgates for a short time, Ernő Noskó setting up László Nagy a minute later for a crisp finish into the bottom left-hand corner of the net eight metres from goal. Bene completed his hat-trick from a rebound on the hour, after his own shot had been blocked by Güngör. Further opportunities came and went for both teams but nothing was going to change the destination of this tie, Újpest confirming a 4-0 success and an 8-1 aggregate victory, which puts them into the two-legged final.

LAJOS BARÓTI, Újpest Dózsa coach: I'm very happy because 64 teams started this Fairs Cup tournament and we have reached the final without suffering defeat.

ERTAN ÖZNUR, Göztepe FC midfielder: Ahead of this second leg, we were thinking that we didn't have much to lose. We were very relaxed and at the end of the day, we can be proud of finishing fourth in such an important competition. Actually during both matches, Újpest's players allowed us to keep the ball and play with the ball. We made many more passes than them but when they had the ball, they were very organised and fast and they used their chances much more clinically than we did.
I have to admit one important thing; we simply couldn't stop Ferenc Bene; he scored five goals in two games. He scored a really fantastic goal here when he played around with our goalkeeper Ali like a cat plays with a mouse. He put our goalkeeper down on his backside three or four times by feinting to kick the ball but then stopping at the last second, before finally, he put the ball in the back of the net. We've all been kidding our goalkeeper about this goal. Bene was very important to them here.

NEVZAT GÜZELIRMAK, Göztepe FC midfielder: It was a very big honour for me to play against an Hungarian team because I had a special interest in Hungarian football starting when I was 12 years old. The Hungarian national team led by Puskás was very strong at that time.
I've also been very positively influenced by our experiences in Budapest. The city is nice, the people are very kind, the stadium and the pitch are fantastic. We've lost the matches but we have a lot of good memories. In both matches there were really good atmospheres but they played much better than us both times.

CENAP ÖZTEZEL, Göztepe FC forward: We all agreed Budapest is one of the best cities in Europe and it's clear Hungarians have a deep

love for football. We've been positively influenced by the sporting infrastructure in Budapest.
Our guide has taken us to many places, including Margaret Island, the Citadella, the Castle district and Gül Baba's Tomb. Gül Baba was a Turkish dervish. A member of a Muslim – specifically Sufi – religious order who has taken vows of poverty and austerity. He lived in the 16th century in Budapest during the days of the Ottoman Empire and we prayed at his tomb and made many wishes.
During the match, I don't think we were actually worse than Újpest, but we lost 4-0. Perhaps the game would have been different if the referee had not disallowed a goal scored by my teammate Halil at the very beginning. After this though, Újpest created several opportunities and used them very well, hitting four goals. Ferenc Bene scored three times… we just couldn't control him. He's a very strong, quick and technical player. The stadium was fantastic and held 20,000 raucous Újpest fans. The pitch was excellent and their players were all true sportsmen and gentlemen with us.

MICHAEL'S CLUB, NEWCASTLE UPON TYNE

Bob Moncur and the group of fans come back in the room and Bob gestures for them to sit down in the corner, near the bar.

BARMAN 1: So that was that. Újpest Dózsa, the *only* club out of 128 in the three major continental competitions last season to survive and remain undefeated until the last week of May, would play Newcastle United for the right to be crowned 1969 Inter-Cities Fairs Cup winners. Should we find out what happened?
BAR MANAGER: You're dead right we should. I can't wait!

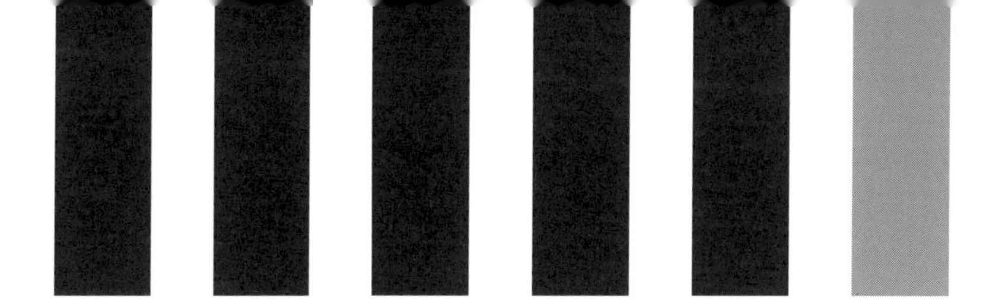

FAIRS CUP FINAL

NEWCASTLE UNITED

v

ÚJPESTI DÓZSA

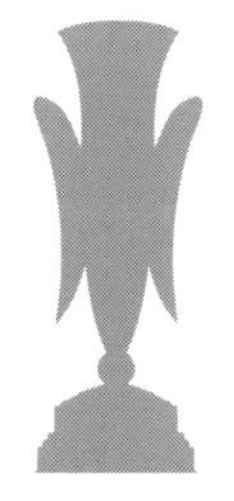

ÚJPESTI DÓZSA AT HOME...

INTER-CITIES FAIRS CUP FINAL 1ST LEG

NEWCASTLE UNITED 3
ÚJPESTI DÓZSA 0

Kick-off: 19:30, Thursday 29th May 1969
Venue: St James' Park, Newcastle upon Tyne, England
Attendance: 59,234
Referee: Joseph Hannet (Belgium)

Newcastle United: Willie McFaul; David Craig, Bob Moncur (c), Ollie Burton, Frank Clark; Preben Arentoft; Tommy Gibb; Jim Scott, Wyn Davies, Bryan Robson, Jackie Sinclair (Alan Foggon 70)
Substitutes not used: John Hope (GK), John Craggs

Újpesti Dózsa: Antal Szentmihályi; Benő Káposzta, Ernő Solymosi, Ernő Noskó, István Bánkuti; Ede Dunai, János Göröcs (c); László Fazekas, Antal Dunai, Ferenc Bene, Sándor Zámbó
Substitutes not used: László Borbely (GK), József Szini, István Nyírő, László Nagy

Goalscorers:
1-0: Bob Moncur (63)
2-0: Bob Moncur (71)
3-0: Jim Scott (84)

MICHAEL'S CLUB, NEWCASTLE UPON TYNE

Newcastle United's Fairs Cup celebration banquet is nearing its end and becoming an altogether more relaxed affair now that the meal is finished.

ANNOUNCEMENT: Ladies and Gentlemen: 'Coffee a la Ujpest Dozsa Hungarian' is now served!

Strong, black coffee in small, espresso-sized cups is served at each of the high tables near the bar as the rest of the room is prepared for live music and dancing. Some order more drinks at the bar. The players, their partners and the Press pack – all friends after many foreign trips together in the last year – continue entertaining each other with their best stories of the Fairs Cup. Now, it's time for the big one. The final.

LORD WESTWOOD (who has just been introduced to Tony Boullemier's fiancee Marie Pinkham while passing the couple on the fringes of the big group): It's very nice to meet you, Marie. I must tell you that I regard your young Tony here as being the team's lucky mascot for our Fairs Cup games.
GIBBO (within earshot): And a spot of good luck is always important on the way to a major final! **(Lord Westwood smiles politely and continues on his way)** Craigy, since you're stood next to me now, was there any difference in the way these fans were treating you by the time of the final?
DAVID CRAIG: No, not really. We were reasonably confident that we would perform well and the fans just got behind us. Obviously they wanted us to win it but as a player you're trying to keep that out of your mind and take every game as it comes, but there was a great atmosphere in the city and everyone was on a high. I'm sure everybody's work ethic was a lot better than it would have been if

we hadn't been in it. When the team wins, it lifts everybody and the place is brilliant to be around.

FRANK CLARK: Some things never change, mind. The bookies still had us down as hot favourites to lose and based on the fact that Újpest had beaten Leeeds home and away, I suppose it was hardly surprising. Anyway, we liked being underdogs. It spurred us on and providing our magnificent fans played their part, we fancied our chances against anyone at home.

TONY BOULLEMIER: You could tell this was different though. It was as big as it could possibly get. There was a stampede for tickets at St James' Park the previous Sunday afternoon, which saw five people taken to hospital and 30 youngsters treated by ambulancemen after they'd been crushed against iron gates and trampled underfoot.

A total of 25,000 tickets had already been allocated and all 35,000 tickets on offer to the public were sold within 90 minutes. A further 10,000 people left disappointed, some of whom had queued for more than four hours. There were well-founded fears that touts had got their hands on a considerable numbers of tickets and Members of Parliament such as Wallsend's Ted Garrett and Edward Milne of Blyth even waded into the controversy.

GIBBO: That's right. One exiled fan, 18-year-old John McNaughton, arrived from Stoke on Trent the day before and waited 36 hours in the rain and cold for his ticket. Lord Westwood was apologetic afterwards, saying: '*I'm terribly sorry but we just could not do the impossible. We could have sold 100,000 tickets.*'

A day later, on Bank Holiday Monday, United's players reported bright and early for their first training session since beating Rangers.

(Gibbo to Dave Smith, United's first-team coach) Dave, I remember overnight rain killed your hopes of using the St James' Park pitch, so you had to settle for kicking the ball around in the car park, isn't that right?

DAVE SMITH: That's right, Gibbo. We had another hard session the next day and then tapered off before the final on the Thursday.

Bryan Pop Robson shoots at goal during the Rangers v Newcastle United Fairs Cup semi-final 1st leg at Ibrox in 1969 (photo courtesy of Bryan Pop Robson)

United defender John McNamee revelled in the challenge of marking Rangers striker Colin Stein at Ibrox (Mirrorpix)

Referee John Adair points to the penalty spot after Newcastle goalkeeper Willie McFaul had fouled Rangers winger Örjan Persson (Mirrorpix)

Willie McFaul dives to his right to save Andy Penman's fiercely-struck penalty (Gordon Amory, Daily Express, Express Syndication)

Jubilation in the Newcastle goalmouth as Andy Penman of Rangers (No. 8) walks away dejected after seeing his penalty kick saved by Willie McFaul, who is congratulated by Tommy Gibb, John Craggs and Frank Clark (Mirrorpix)

Frank Clark and Jackie Sinclair seek to ward off a Rangers raid in the second leg in Newcastle (Mirrorpix)

A Rangers players fires a shot towards the Newcastle goal at St James' Park. Note the visiting fans who have scaled one of the Gallowgate floodlight pylons to find space to watch (photo courtesy of Newcastle United FC)

Jim Scott opens the scoring for hosts Newcastle United against Rangers (photo with kind permission of Newcastle United FC)

Tempers fray on the St James' Park pitch between Newcastle and Rangers players. Note the fans watching on rooftops in the background (photo with kind permission of Newcastle United FC)

United goalkeeper Willie McFaul claims a cross during the semi-final 2nd leg against Rangers (photo with kind permission of Newcastle United FC)

Newcastle winger Jackie Sinclair slams in his team's second goal against Rangers at St James' Park (photo with kind permission of Newcastle United FC)

The extent of the pitch invasion which stopped the Newcastle United vs Rangers semi-final 2nd leg (photo with kind permission of Newcastle United FC)

The players wait for play to restart at St James' Park (PA/PA Images)

Police with dogs seek to quell the disturbances after fans invade the pitch (Gordon Amory-Daily Express-Express Syndication)

Newcastle City Police restore order and supporters return to the terraces (photo with kind permission of Newcastle United FC)

Újpesti Dózsa's squad for the 1968-69 season (photo: László Almási)

Joe Harvey (2nd from left) with the referee
for the first leg of the final, Joseph Hannet (2nd from right)
(photo courtesy of referees' interpreter Austin Fagan)

Bryan Pop Robson shoots at goal during the Newcastle United v Újpest Dózsa Fairs Cup final first leg (Mirrorpix)

Newcastle United on the attack in the second half of the final's first match in Newcastle (Gordon Amory, Daily Express, Express Syndication)

Hungarian goalkeeper Antal Szentmihályi thwarts another United attack in the final's first leg at St James' Park (photo with kind permission of Newcastle United FC)

Antal Dunai evades the attentions of Tommy Gibb and Ollie Burton in the Newcastle penalty area in the first leg of the final (photo with kind permission of Newcastle United FC)

Bob Moncur scores his first goal of the final at home against Újpest Dózsa (PA/PA Images)

The Mighty Wyn bravely shrugs off the attentions of two Újpesti Dózsa defenders at St James' Park (photo with kind permission of Newcastle United FC)

Bob Moncur celebrates his second goal of the final's first leg against Újpest Dózsa at St James' Park (Mirrorpix)

Jim Scott surges through to score United's third goal against Újpest Dózsa at St James' Park (Mirrorpix)

Tony Rodgers (on the right) and his brother Mick (centre) relaxing outside a bar near the Danube river on the day of the final in Budapest (photo courtesy of Tony Rodgers)

Joe Harvey and his team of Pressmen line up for a team photo on the Megyeri út pitch on the day of the final's second leg (photo courtesy of Doug Weatherall)

Bob Moncur clears the ball from under the nose of Újpest Dózsa and Hungary striker Antal Dunai (photo courtesy of Gusztáv Mravik)

László Fazekas crosses the ball despite the efforts of Jackie Sinclair and Frank Clark during the second leg in Budapest (photo courtesy of Gusztáv Mravik)

János Göröcs tries to shake off the attentions of Benny Arentoft (photo courtesy of the author)

Újpesti Dózsa midfielder Ede Dunai tries to equalise on the night with a low shot late in the second leg in Budapest (photo courtesy of Gusztáv Mravik)

Antal Dunai tries to surge past Bob Moncur in the second leg of the final in Újpest's Megyeri úti stadium (photo courtesy of Gusztáv Mravik)

Bob Moncur shows off the Fairs Cup trophy whilst sitting on the shoulders of John McNamee and surrounded by jubilant players and fans (photo courtesy of the author)

BENNY ARENTOFT: Everybody knew Újpest had beaten Leeds and that more than half the team were Hungarian national team players. That they had good footballers, very technical, playing lovely football on the ground. So that's what we were trying to be prepared for – the one-twos. We played small-side football in the car park in front of the main stand. It was one-two, one-two… especially for Újpest. That was good preparation.
DAVID CRAIG: There hadn't been much time between the semi and the final because we'd had the Home Nations internationals in May and then the Rangers semi-final straight after. Then we were straight into the final at the end of May and start of June. The Football League gives out the Manager of the Month award and Joe pointed out we were the only team to play in June, but he still didn't win it **(much laughter amongst those listening)**.
JOE HARVEY (smiling): Now then, son, you mention Rangers. Everyone had said the matches against Rangers were just to decide the beaten finalists, but we had no inferiority complex *at all*, did we? People had us out in every round but we were still there. The thought of playing against Újpest didn't worry me or the players.
GIBBO: I hear you, Joe, but if you don't mind me saying, I'm not entirely sure your right-hand man felt the same way, isn't that right, Dave? You'd said after watching Újpest beat the Fairs Cup holders Leeds at Elland Road: '*If we draw Újpest, I wouldn't know how to stop them. They are the greatest team I've seen in a long time.*' How were you feeling now that we had to play them?
DAVE SMITH: I knew that if we were to have a chance of winning, we needed to get a good result at home. Újpest were brilliant but certainly not unbeatable. They'd played some great stuff at Leeds. Their forwards can juggle about with the ball around the edge of the penalty area, then, ping… in goes a shot. In Scottie, Jackie Sinclair and Alan Foggon though, we had the players to get past their full-backs and I thought we could cause their defence a lot of trouble.

FRANK CLARK: The only concession we really made to preparing for foreign opposition was through Dave. You're a shrewd coach, I reckon. Without being too technical, most of the continental teams, especially Újpest, played good, passing football, pass, pass... until they were through on goal. As Benny says, we worked and worked on stopping the one-twos, so that if someone came at you with the ball and they played inside, you wouldn't turn and follow that ball, but you'd stick with him when he made his run. Then, when he got it back he wouldn't get in behind you.

So we worked very, very hard at that and that was never more important than in the first leg at our place. We were able to frustrate Újpest for a good hour before we scored one. Dave hasn't had a lot of credit yet but he should get loads for that because we worked incessantly on it and it was very, very useful. In fact, I'd say it was as important as Big Wyn, because he was what they'd never met before and this was what we'd never met before. But we learnt to deal with it.

DAVID CRAIG: I think we were all totally clear that we needed a lead to take to Hungary. I think we preferred it the other way around – to play away first so we knew what we had to do with the crowd behind us, roaring us on. It's more difficult to play your home games first because there's more pressure on you to score goals, but we knew we needed a good lead, obviously. Again, it was just one of those nights when everything went for us – we were just meant to win this competition, it's as simple as that. I'm a great believer in fate and that it's either meant to be or not meant to be sometimes, and we were meant to win it.

By the way, Hungary was almost unknown to me. My only connection was through Ferenc Puskás because of Jackie Milburn's testimonial, when I was on the subs' bench. I actually came on for Puskás with about 10 minutes to go!

TONY BOULLEMIER: Well, you only have to remember what some of the game's great managers, who remember the likes of Puskás in his heyday, said about these Hungarians to realise the size of the task. Don Revie said: *'Újpest have the greatest players in the world. This is a great side – the best Leeds United have met in eight years. Újpest have such fantastic control of the ball. They play it around. You think you have them under control, then, bang, bang bang. Before you realise what's happened, they are shooting at your goal. Newcastle have had a remarkable run, but if they play on a firm ground, they are going into the toughest match of the club's history.'*

GIBBO: Liverpool's Bill Shankly weighed in, saying: *'Újpest are the greatest team in the whole of Europe. They have scored 129 goals in 30 league games.'*

TONY BOULLEMIER: And Jock Stein didn't fancy our chances either: *'As much as I would like to see Joe Harvey and the Anglo-Scots win the Fairs Cup, I cannot see it over two legs,'* he said. *'A Hungarian contact tells me that this is the most accomplished side his country has known for many years.'*

GIBBO: A modicum of hope came with news of an injury to centre-back Ernő Noskó in a World Cup qualifier for Hungary against Czechoslovakia the previous Saturday. His 19th-minute substitution put his participation at Newcastle in severe doubt. But in the end, Noskó trained the day before the match and took his place in the starting lineup.

DAVID CRAIG: Újpest Dózsa beat Leeds in the quarter-final and Leeds were probably the best team in England that year. I knew what beating them meant because I grew up with most of the Leeds lads and played against them in the juniors – the likes of Gary Sprake, Paul Reaney, Peter Lorimer and Terry Cooper. They were in the same junior league as I was, plus there was Giles, Bremner and Big Jack Charlton. Revie liked them to get stuck in physically so I can understand how they lost to a team like Újpest; they were different.

DAVE SMITH: I was sure it would be the best match we'd seen yet in the competition. Újpest would be a treat to watch if we'd allow them to settle down and play football. We'd go all out for goals in the home match, try to keep a clean sheet at the back and then it'd be backs to the wall over there. We thought we could do it.

The fans near the other end of the bar near the entrance of Michael's Club

BILL GIBBS: The bad part was queuing for the bloody tickets. Me mam made me a blanket which I could turn into a sleeping bag. Ten of us went out there and we queued from 8pm on Saturday night and got wor tickets at 1pm on the Sunday. I'd queued 17 hours but then got thrown out of the queue. What happened was some idiot was throwing apples at the coppers. It wasn't me but one copper thought it was, so he says: *'Right you – out!'*
I says: *'What the heck? I only want one ticket, just for me, but I've got my brother's money too.'*
So they allowed me to go back over and I said to my mate John: *'Here, get me my ticket, will yer? Here's the money.'*
So I got it in the end. Seventeen hours though and I nearly missed oot. I had to go back over the road and wait. Then, on the night, once you were in the ground, you had to hand your ticket over – there were no tear-offs unless you were in the Paddock.

KISBOJTÁR BAR, BUDAPEST, 15TH JULY

It's mid-July and the Újpesti Dózsa players have been on their summer break since scoring 15 goals in winning three rearranged league fixtures at the end of June. The chance to relax is coming to an end all too soon though. Nine of the players have been called up to a Hungarian national team training camp starting in two days' time.
Remarkably, around half the team have had their birthdays in the last few weeks, so after some time away on holiday, most of the players and their wives have come together one warm

evening to mark the happy occasions with a few drinks before the hard work starts again.
They're at a small, almost-deserted, garden bar in Pest, close to the Danube riverside. It's called *Kisbojtár* – 'The Little Shepherd' – and they're watching a young acoustic guitarist play a mix of Western and Hungarian covers. The chords of *Oly jó lenne veled* – 'It would be so good to be with you' – by the Tolcsvay Trió, fill the air as the group arrives. They sit at two white, decorative iron tables, next to each other.
Meanwhile, a young English woman, Elizabeth, who's been living in Budapest for a few months, is watching her friend Ernő play guitar in front of a small audience. She gets talking to Újpest defender Benö Káposzta's wife Gyöngyi at the bar and with their different backgrounds and friendly dispositions, they get on well. Eventually, Elizabeth is invited to come over and sit with their group.

BENŐ: Guys, this is Gyöngyi's friend, Elizabeth. She's with the guitarist.
ELIZABETH (appreciatively): Thank you for your kind invitation.

The girls find a couple of free chairs just as the opening chords of the guitarist's latest cover song, *Paperback Writer* by the Beatles, can be heard.

GYÖNGYI: Tell me, Elizabeth, what did you think when you first arrived here?
ELIZABETH: Well, firstly, it was a relief that my friend Margit and her father were there to meet me off the train from Vienna. I was several hours late after missing the first one.
I was curious, definitely. One of the first things I noticed in Mártonvásár was that the main roads were tarmacked but most other roads were

dirt tracks. There were lots of horses and carts and basically I felt like I'd entered my father's childhood. There were water pumps in the streets because there wasn't running water in the houses.
However, I've also noticed that some people already have automatic washing machines, whereas in the West these are very new. The few people who have them don't have the drainage systems they're designed for, so they use them in their back gardens. But still, in a few ways, they seem to have skipped forward a couple of stages in terms of technology.
Of course, I'm the only foreigner in the village so everyone knows who I am and where I'm from, but at the start I couldn't really communicate with them.
And what about you all? You all seem to know each other so well.
GYÖNGYI: Well, nominally we have jobs at the Interior Ministry but really I play volleyball and Benő's a footballer. These are his teammates. We're all from a club called Újpest Dózsa.
ELIZABETH: Oh, wow! I've heard of them. I like football, although I don't know much about it outside Britain. Didn't your team play Leeds this season? That's where I was at university.
JÁNOS GÖRÖCS: Yes, we did. They were hard matches against Leeds. We managed to beat them and knock them out though.
SÁNDOR ZÁMBÓ: It's interesting you're from England and like football. I like English football. For example, I really like Bobby Charlton. He's my favourite player – a determined player who can go past defenders.
ELIZABETH: Oh yes, everyone loves him at home. He was one of our favourites at the World Cup last time. As were Hungary, when your team beat Brazil of course. We all marvelled at Mr Bene's great individual goal on television.
BENŐ KÁPOSZTA: Both Feri and Charlton scored brilliant goals that weekend. Bobby Charlton's the next day from 25 metres against Mexico – a wonderful strike. Bobby is from Manchester but his

older brother Jack played for Leeds against us, didn't he?
ELIZABETH: They play in those cities but actually they were both born further north just above Newcastle.
BENŐ KÁPOSZTA: Ah well, Newcastle.
ELIZABETH: Yes, I know. You played that team in the Fairs Cup final. I'm sorry you lost, but you should know the English football world was already very impressed with you. The Leeds and Liverpool managers have both said you are the best team in Europe nowadays.
LÁSZLÓ FAZEKAS: Really? I didn't know that. This is the first time I've heard this. I don't know if the quotes made their way into our papers but if they did I think I'd have remembered them. However, beating Leeds the way we did – 1-0 there and 2-0 here – well, that should command respect.
ELIZABETH: No goals conceded means your goalkeeper and defence must be good, but in England we have rather heard about Újpest Dózsa because of the forward line.
LÁSZLÓ NAGY: Yes, it goes Fazekas, Göröcs, Bene, Antal Dunai and Zámbó upfront who produce so many goals. Last year, in my debut season, the team scored 102 goals but still only came second.
LÁSZLÓ FAZEKAS: I don't know if you remember this, skipper, but before the Newcastle match, you turned round to 'Pixi' Solymosi and told him: *'Pixi, listen here because finally, we've got a game from which we can earn some real money.'*
The thing is, Newcastle had won every one of their matches at home in the Fairs Cup, and against four or five big-name teams too. That gives you confidence and if the crowds come, the fans become the 12th man, so maybe we should have paid more attention to their impressive home record.
ELIZABETH: You have a really experienced coach though, right?
ANTAL DUNAI: We have a fantastic coach. Lajos Baróti matched up all our capabilities and created the system where our captain János

Göröcs dominates the pitch and says how we'll play. Previously Göröcs had always been a right-sided forward but Baróti brought him deeper so he could run the game. Baróti is very intelligent, a very nice man.

ANDRÁS TÓTH (young squad player): Baróti had previously been the national-team coach and hadn't selected János for the 1966 World Cup squad. That's what led the Újpest leadership to approach János to ask if they should appoint Baróti or not. To his credit, Göröcs put aside any personal differences and said: *'Yes, bring him here because he's a good coach.'*

SÁNDOR ZÁMBÓ: The truth is we look up a lot to Lajos Baróti.

ANTAL SZENTMIHÁLYI: We knew it was going to be very tough over in Newcastle because they are a very good team. We tried to prepare for them but physically I felt there was a difference between the two teams; that sooner or later they would find a way through and that we would tire or make mistakes.

ANDRÁS TÓTH: Yes, they were a bigger, stronger team and physically, we just ended up not coping with them.

MICHAEL'S CLUB, NEWCASTLE UPON TYNE

The group of fans are at one end of the bar, delighted and obviously in shock at their good luck at being invited inside to share a room for a short time with their heroes, even if it was only until the dancing got underway. Over come Frank Clark and Bryan Pop Robson, the latter of whom has spotted one of his friends, fellow table-tennis enthusiast Peter Ratcliffe, who is also pals with Pop's new wife Maureen.

BRYAN POP ROBSON (smiling): Hello, Peter, what are you doing here? Popped into say hello to a few new colleagues?

PETER RATCLIFFE: Hello Pop. Me and my pals saw Arthur outside and then Bob Moncur stuck his head out, recognised Peter Donaghy here from when he was the interpreter in Zaragoza **(Pop clocks him now and shakes his hand)** and asked did we fancy a drink inside while things get set up for your dancing. So of course we said yes.
BRYAN POP ROBSON: See, that's Captain Bob, always looking out for everyone.

He glances around at them.

Listen, there's not too many of you – what? Six or seven? So just come down the bar a bit and meet the rest of the lads while they turn the room around. The lasses are enjoying themselves over there and most of the players and journos are just here talking about Újpest. Hey, Peter, you can tell us about your dodgy midnight trip to Budapest in a bit!
PETER RATCLIFFE: Right you are, Pop.
SPOW: Bloody hell. This is great!

The lads shuffle down, nervously at first, but Pop puts them at ease.
Everyone is gathered around the bar which runs down the left side of the room. There must be about 30 people there in smaller groups but all are pretty much within earshot of each other – Joe, Dave, the players and the journalists.

BRYAN POP ROBSON: Lads, a couple of us have pals amongst these lads here so Bob's let them have a quick drink with us. You'll all remember Peter, who was our interpreter in Zaragoza, and this other Peter is coming to work for the club next week.
FRANK CLARK: Aye, and this lot were all at the final too, so they can tell us how many times they think Bob's second shot bounced before it hit the net! **(chuckles all round)**

▌FINAL 1ST LEG ▌

After a momentary lull.

GIBBO: So gents, don't be shy with us. Who's got a story from the first leg of the final?
PETER DONAGHY: Ok, a fellow teacher at my school, Austin Fagan, was actually the interpreter for the referees prior to the Real Zaragoza and Újpest Dózsa home games. He took Monsieur Hannet and his two linesmen from Belgium shopping down Northumberland Street on the morning of the final while they were in their official blazers. where they kept being stopped for autographs by well-wishers. Also, apparently Joe Harvey was keen to know how hard the challenges could be, so certainly on the morning of the Real Zaragoza home match he asked the referee to describe a good, fair tackle to him. I imagine he asked the same of Monsieur Hannet too.
BILL GIBBS (a bit hesitantly at first): Well, erm, on the night, I got into the first part of the Leazes but I couldn't get any further because it was absolutely chocca. You couldn't move, even if we'd normally be in there at a quarter to seven for a 7.30 pm kick-off.
HARRY WATSON: You never get the feeling that it's dangerous with that many people because of the cameraderie, you know. The feeling is it's all fine and that when we'd move and sway, we'd all move together. Also, I don't think we knew enough about any of their players to actually be concerned about them. They were a mystery so because you didn't know anything, you had no fear of them really. It was more about your own side.
TONY BOULLEMIER: And with that, Newcastle started by swarming all over the mighty Magyars in the first 15 minutes. Goals looked ready to come at any time. Újpest were steadily settling though and I remember writing in the Journal that Wyn Davies was wearing three shirts – his own and those of Dózsa defenders Ede Dunai and Noskó, who never left him.
BRYAN POP ROBSON: It was nearly June – playing in June was so

weird. The other Fairs Cup games had been played under floodlights but this was played under bright skies, so it didn't quite have the same atmosphere. It was a very nervous atmosphere – not the same as the others.

And I still never thought we'd win the Cup. I didn't think we could win at any stage... even getting to the the final. You start thinking about it but then the match starts and you realise you're up against some excellent players who can really pass the ball.

Maybe they weren't so good at defending from setplays. Maybe Wyn bothered them at setpieces and Bob was lucky enough to get a goal from a setplay. Obviously from Újpest's point of view, that disturbs you when you've got most of the play and the ball but you're not really going anywhere. They didn't seem to have a lot of efforts on target in the first leg.

GIBBO: Saying that, for a brief period before half time, Újpest looked like a good team. They were pushing the ball around well, giving us a preview of what to expect in Budapest.

WILLIE McFAUL: I had a quiet start but a 'bender' from Solymosi just before half-time almost squeezed into the corner and I never thought I'd reach a backpass from Ollie a little earlier.

GIBBO: Skipper Göröcs, although at walking pace, looked precise in midfield and big Antal Dunai showed glimpses of his striking ability, but it all vanished into the night air when United turned it on again. Big Wyn here, battered from start to finish, tortured Újpest in the air.

BRYAN POP ROBSON: I didn't score in either of the finals but Wyn certainly took a lot of pressure off me. Sometimes two men were marking him, so that was giving me a bit more space and at least a chance to occupy other players.

GIBBO: There were performances all over the pitch. Ollie Burton turned in one of his best games for United against an under-par Ferenc Bene.

BRYAN POP ROBSON: Obviously we were aware of past Hungarian players like Puskás and Hidegkuti and the like, but Ferenc Bene is a really good player, you know.
GIBBO: Oh, aye, absolutely. There's no denying that.
BRYAN POP ROBSON: He isn't much bigger than me but he's stocky with so much energy and so much control. He was probably quicker than me and his is a name you look out for afterwards and you think: 'Wow, how did we win that against the likes of him?' He's very experienced and he scored against Brazil in the World Cup so we knew we always had to be alert.
DOUG WEATHERALL: I certainly didn't think the fairytale was going to end here. What I really think helped them win the match was the fans. They set up a chant which went on and on and on – NEW-CASS-EL, NEW-CASS-EL! – and the players responded magnificently.
BOB MONCUR: I think it's fair to say it was the biggest match of our lives. In all these big games, Willie used to go to the loo half an hour before the game and you could hear him being sick. Most of the big matches. That's just his way. If I can, my way of getting half-ready is to just put my head against the wall and just try and doze for a little bit just to calm me down.
FRANK CLARK: We hadn't lost a game at St James' all season in Europe, so we're pretty formidable at home and have a really good back five – Willie and the back four – with two real grafters in midfield, Tommy Gibb and Benny. For this first hour at home though, we were really pushed all the way and for a while it was touch and go. Then Bob here got the goal and obviously that knocked them a bit because goals change football matches.
One of the beauties of football is that it creates platforms for people to emerge as heroes – and this time it couldn't have happened to a nicer bloke.
IVOR BROADIS: They had ample warning of Bob's intent – a run into the gap for a 58th-minute clipped free-kick from Gibb that slid off his

head and ran perilously near. Up he came again for another free-kick in the 63rd minute and it was Gibb again, flighting the ball in, this time for Wyn to kill it 10 yards from the far post and hammer it at Szentmihályi as he flung himself forward to try and smother the ball.

WYN DAVIES: Aye, I'd actually fallen over in the process and the ball hit the keeper before coming back out.

GIBBO: And Bob, like a swooping hawk, was onto the rebound to lash home a left-footer low inside the near left post.

TONY BOULLEMIER: This goal was a total inspiration. Nine minutes later Bob got another, bringing the ball out of defence and playing a smart one-two with Benny Arentoft before lashing in what was only the second goal of his senior competitive career. It was like he'd been a striker all his life.

BENNY ARENTOFT: You see, Dave Smith had earlier explained that Újpest, like many European teams, played a lot of one-twos. I knew this from Denmark, having played Italian teams in friendly matches. It was always one-twos, one-twos, and this is what I used in the final with Bob. He made a one-two with me, between the box and the halfway line and he went on to score from just outside the box.

BOB MONCUR: I'd actually controlled a long kick, not very well, but the ball was in front of me so I thought: 'Well, OK, I'll keep going.' I got well over the halfway line before I started to think 'What am I going to do now?' Benny was inside so I gave it to him and I sort of half kept on running.

He returned it, so I played another pass which came back and bounced just in front of me just outside the box. I thought 'I'll just hit this, 'cos I don't know what else to do with it now.'

So I hit it, not spectacularly well but I kept it down and I remember thinking: 'Don't miss the target!'

It bounced across the keeper with just enough force and into the corner of the net. Clarky said: *'It bounced about 20 times.'* But I said: *'I don't care!'* **(laughter all round).**

JACKIE SINCLAIR: I have to say the Fairs Cup hadn't been a bed of roses for me but the boss was very good and kept giving me another chance to show I was the answer. When I came off for Alan Foggon midway through the the second half against Újpest at St James', I felt I'd played my part in a team effort.

TONY BOULLEMIER: Yes, Jackie, I did write that it was a little hard on you to be brought off. Bob's opener had rocked Ujpest back on their heels and they then tried to keep it to two. But Jim Scott, who kept popping up with important Fairs Cup goals, slotted in the third from Benny's pass. And that was the cue for pure delirium from the fans.

BENNY ARENTOFT: Yes, we did it again. I played a one-two with Jim Scott and his goal was priceless.

JIM SCOTT: We'd actually practised one-twos like this all week and they'd usually worked better than this one. I thought the ball was too far ahead of me and the keeper was going to get it, but I stuck out my foot and pushed it over his head just in time. I think they'd have been quite happy getting beat 1-0 or maybe 2-0, but three...

BILL GIBBS: And you'll never guess what happened to me. A lass collapsed in front of us so I carried her down to the First Aid area, made sure she was alright and made my way back to my place, just in time to see Scottie score the third. I was lucky. And then the roars. It was great on the film like but I don't believe there were just 60,000 there – 66,000 more like!

DAVID CRAIG: Aye, it's possible the atmosphere and the crowd got to them a bit.

GIBBO: Tommy, right at the end, I remember you frantically asking the referee in sign language whether Solymosi's goal from a free-kick on the dot of time had counted or not.

TOMMY GIBB: Well, I wasnae sure whether he was pointing to the centre circle to start play again or whether it was time, but when he indicated 3-0, I thought: *'Great, three goals – that must be it.'*

DAVE SMITH: I hadn't heard the final whistle go and thought for a moment that it was a goal. I tell you, I was ready to do my nut at the way the defensive wall opened up to let that ball through.

WILLIE McFAUL: There was no need to worry though, Dave. Most of us heard the referee blow for time as Solymosi ran up to kick the ball and the lads in the wall just walked away. It was all over. If the game had stayed in progress, Újpest wouldn't have scored because the shot wouldn't have beaten the wall.

JIM SCOTT: Újpest were a smashing team, a first-class team, but the goal at St James' Park in the last ten minutes was the goal that beat them eventually. And not only the third one that I scored but also their strike on the final whistle which was disallowed.

I honestly think when you play in cups, if your name's on the cup, it's on. It doesn't matter in life what you do, if you don't have that bit of luck, you'll not win anything. You can be the best team in the world but at times you've still got to have that wee bit of luck – it plays a big part. When things go your way like that, you've got to use it. If you don't, things will go against you.

So the scoreline was 3-0 by the end, which I'd say over the 90 minutes flattered us a wee bit, but we scored goals and that's it – goals win games. Bobby Moncur... I wouldn't say they were classics but they're two of the best goals he's scored in his life!

DAVE SMITH: The best team we faced was in the final – Újpest Dózsa, over there – but we went over with a 3-0 lead. It was the way football was played then. Feyenoord, Setúbal, Újpest… had they come over here and really gone forward, I think the football would have been far different. I mean, they came over to our place and sat back, Újpest included; they just sat back. Fine. That was how we liked it.

DOUG WEATHERALL: It was a wonderful win. 3-0. So convincing.

FRANK CLARK: I thought we dealt with the occasion very well. By this point, we had quite an experienced team even though I'm only 25, Craigy's 25, Willie's 25. Jimmy's a little bit older, Ollie's a bit older, John

Mac, Jackie Sinclair, big Wyn are all a little bit older, so we've got a lot of experience in the team and I think everyone dealt with it very well.

WYN DAVIES: At one point I was standing way outside the box and Bob was by the goal line when a corner came in. Pop centred it and I went in to try and meet it and who was coming out as well, but Bob! We both went up for it and boom! He smashed my cheekbone in. We came off and we went to the dressing room. I was under the shower when Bob came in and asked: *'Are you alright there, Wyn?'* I just said: *'Get lost!'* The thing is I might not have been able to play in the second leg. So I went to see club director Fenton Braithwaite who was also the club surgeon and he said he wasn't sure I was well enough to play. I said: *'I'm not having this,'* so I went and played.

DAVE SMITH: I've never known anyone with more courage than Wyn.

GIBBO: Meanwhile, Bob didn't go crazy in celebrating his goals – he dashed away from the scene of his triumph to present a darts trophy at a dance. And another story of courage came out too when Pop told me: *'I'd hurt my knee laying tiles at our new house before we got married and I was under treatment before the game. I just couldn't let the secret out. The knee was full of fluid and very painful but I was desperate to play.'*

BRYAN POP ROBSON: It was a double-wedding as well. We said we'd get married in May. Then Kathleen, Maureen's sister, said she wanted to get married in the summer as well, so we decided on a double wedding. They were getting more and more annoyed though, because we kept having to shift the dates as we progressed through the rounds. So we got married on June 4th in St Mary's church in Hexham, instead of what we'd planned on June 11th – the day of the final in Budapest! It was a good day, eh, Frank?

FRANK CLARK: Aye, for one day at least it gave us something else to think about. At least it did for me as your best man.

GIBBO: And don't forget the golf! We hacks were all searching for stories to satisfy the huge demand on Tyneside for news about you lads.

Bob, Pop, Craigy and Willie were out for a round of golf at Tyneside Golf Club on the Saturday before the second leg. Perhaps to celebrate Bob's fitness declaration after a groin strain in a full-scale practice match the previous Monday threatened to send our Cup bid spinning. With Wyn declared fit too, despite his fractured cheekbone, the lads were in good spirits as they made up a delegation of 30 players and officials and 16 Press men on the flight out to Budapest on Monday June 9th.

CHARLIE SUMMERBELL: The plane got a big send-off from banner-waving Geordie fans when it left and easily the most precious possession on it was the Fairs Cup trophy. Holders Leeds United had handed it over before the first leg so it could be ready for the winners in Hungary's capital city.

TONY BOULLEMIER: Mind, Lord Westwood had been a little cavalier when he said it seemed a waste of time to carry the Cup all the way there, just to have to bring it back again.

CHARLIE SUMMERBELL: Joe had a glass of champagne on the flight over but it was probably more an attempt to calm nerves than anything else. He said: *'I would like 24 hours off from football to collect my thoughts. It's driving me crazy. We are so near to winning the Fairs Cup that I dare not think about losing. I don't want a silver medal. Only gold will do.'*

ÚJPESTI DÓZSA AWAY...

INTER-CITIES FAIRS CUP FINAL 2ND LEG

ÚJPESTI DÓZSA 2
NEWCASTLE UNITED 3

Kick-off: 20:00, Wednesday 11th June 1969
Venue: Megyeri úti stadion, Budapest, Hungary
Attendance: 37,000
Referee: Joseph Heymann (SUI)

Newcastle United: Willie McFaul; David Craig, Bob Moncur (c), Ollie Burton, Frank Clark; Preben Arentoft, Tommy Gibb; Jim Scott (Alan Foggon 68), Bryan Robson, Wyn Davies, Jackie Sinclair. Substitutes not used: John Hope (GK), John McNamee. Travelling reserves: John Craggs, Eric Ross.

Újpesti Dózsa: Antal Szentmihályi; Benő Káposzta, Ernő Solymosi, Ernő Noskó, István Bánkuti; Ede Dunai, János Göröcs (c); László Fazekas, Antal Dunai, Ferenc Bene, Sándor Zámbó. Substitutes not used: László Borbely (GK), József Szini, Péter Juhász, László Nagy.

Goalscorers:
1-0: Ferenc Bene (31)
2-0: János Göröcs (42)
2-1: Bob Moncur (46)
2-2: Preben Arentoft (52)
2-3: Alan Foggon (75)

Newcastle United win the final 6-2 on aggregate.

IN A CAR ON THE A1 (M) NORTHBOUND TO NEWCASTLE UPON TYNE, 15TH JULY 1969

Leeds United's Glaswegian winger Eddie Gray is driving his younger brother, budding footballer Frank, home after a short visit to Yorkshire. As a favour, he also agrees to drop off his two Geordie teammates, Norman Hunter and Jackie Charlton on the way so they can see family for a few days before pre-season training starts.
They've just passed Durham, around 19 miles from Newcastle.

EDDIE GRAY: Getting back to the Fairs Cup, these Hungarians had knocked us out and then we had to watch them come and play the final against the Geordies, who we'd done the double over in the league!
JACKIE CHARLTON: Aye, my goal beat them in the first game up here.
NORMAN HUNTER (smiling): Trust you to remember that, Jack.
JACKIE CHARLTON (grinning too): Well, it's true. I'm only telling the truth.
NORMAN HUNTER: You know, I never play particularly well up here. I remember the first time I came back and I went out before the game. I had a look at the Gallowgate End, because that's where I used to stand. I sometimes wonder to myself why I don't play well when all my family come to watch me. I never play well at Newcastle.
I always look for their results though. I would have crawled on my hands and knees to play for Newcastle, but nobody came in for me because back then, so many people wanted to play for Newcastle. It's no accident that the saying goes: '*You shout down the mines and two or three footballers come up.*' I was just playing locally for Birtley – I was coming back after I'd broken an ankle – without realising there was a Leeds scout there. And then the next thing I got was: '*Would you like a trial?*' And that was it.

EDDIE GRAY: Same with me. The only team I wanted to play for was Celtic; I used to train at Celtic Park and I'd been to a few of the big clubs in England, but I didn't have any intention of going there; I was going to go to Celtic. Then a scout called John Barr approached my dad and asked if I'd go down to Leeds United.

NORMAN HUNTER: Funnily enough, if it hadn't have been for my mum I might not have stayed in the game. I didn't know my dad because he died of a heart attack playing in a charity football match before I was born, so I was told. But my mum knew I'd always wanted to play football. When the letter from Leeds arrived, I said to her I didn't want to leave home; it was too far away, but she said: *'Go on, try it and if it doesn't work out, come back.'*

Luckily I went into digs and little Billy Bremner was there. The lady who ran the house was Mrs Leyton – she was the mother figure who looked after us and I've got her to thank too, because without her, I can tell you, I might have gone home. You stick it out though, don't you?

EDDIE GRAY: You do. Funnily enough, I look at it and think Newcastle's victory in the Fairs Cup was meant to be. I'm a great believer that you make that happen yourself. It's not all luck you know, circumstances have a lot to do with it. But you have to give Newcastle a lot of credit.

FRANK GRAY: Surely you'd have been backing the team that knocked you out though, no?

EDDIE GRAY: I thought Újpest would beat them, yeah. I think they're just reaching their peak now. This is them at their best; they beat us and apparently they're well on their way to winning the league and cup in Hungary this season too. That's why I thought they would beat Newcastle. Also, Újpest play the game as if they think they'll beat every other team. Like the great Celtic team you've been watching, Frank – the one that won the European Cup a couple of years ago. Celtic are used to winning games and Újpesti Dózsa run over the top of teams, just like Celtic do.

It doesn't make a difference who they're playing, they're expected to win – a bit like our team; we expect to win nearly every game we play. It doesn't happen all the time and it obviously didn't happen for Újpest against Newcastle, but in general, if you have that confidence in the players you're playing with, you'll be successful. That's why, and no disrespect to the Geordies, but in the football world it was a bit of a surprise they won.

FRANK GRAY: I don't know Newcastle much, to be honest, but they seem to be a bit of a local rival to you...

EDDIE GRAY: Well, it's definitely always a tough game for us. There's always that North v South divide, but because we're now up there with the top teams in the North-West, Newcastle and Sunderland resent that. Until recently, Newcastle were traditionally a bigger club than Leeds – going back to all their cup finals and all their great players that played in them – so they always thought they were top dogs up here. To me, Newcastle's a right tough place to go, especially in cup football, in one-off games. Leeds going to Newcastle is always played like a cup final because they're right up for the game. Although I thought Újpest would beat them, I suppose it shouldn't be a great surprise that Newcastle won in the end.

FRANK GRAY: So how did they do it? What are they good at?

EDDIE GRAY: Well, Joe Harvey's got some good players. Bobby Moncur's a proper defender. He knows what he can do, what he's good at, what his limitations are and he makes the best of his ability. I think Bobby epitomises what Newcastle are about. He's got that bulldog spirit.

NORMAN HUNTER: Jimmy Scott gets a few goals – he's a bit silky, isn't he? You know what I mean – a ball player. He isn't physical like Wyn, more of a silky sort of player. And Big John McNamee rolls his sleeves up – he's a man mountain.

JACKIE CHARLTON (exclaiming): Oh aye, Big Mac. We have our battles.

NORMAN HUNTER: And then there's Wyn the Leap. He's very honest, very tough, not one to be a bully or anything. Honest and strong, and he *can* jump. If he gets a run at it, not many people can stay with him. I can't. Jack can, mind.

JACKIE CHARLTON: Thank you, Norm. Very nice of you to say.

EDDIE GRAY (smiling): Aye, true, there's big Wyn Davies and Pop Robson playing off him; they're a good partnership. Obviously Wyn's great in the air but he's also a good footballer. Pop's a top player. He's right up there with the top finishers.

I'd also mention Willie McFaul here, Newcastle's keeper, because he put the shutters up that night a month ago. The game should have been dead and buried in the first half over in Hungary. Before the Fairs Cup final I remember thinking to myself: 'They'll get murdered.' When I looked at it, I saw the Újpest Dózsa side and thought: 'This is the national team they're playing.' Hungary's national team is good and that's basically who Newcastle were playing against.

Do I think they've the same quality of player that Újpesti Dózsa have? No, I don't; I've got to be honest. But that's all credit to the Newcastle players and fans – they also played a part in that run, because they were really up for it. I think they thought: *'Right, this is our chance of winning a European trophy.'* It was a tremendous victory for Newcastle.

Right, nearly there, lads. Where am I dropping you?

JACKIE CHARLTON: Anywhere in town, bonny lad. A pal's picking me up at Grey's Monument at 11pm.

NORMAN HUNTER: That'll do for me. I'll keep my head down on the bus to Gateshead, it's easy to get there and then I'll get a taxi to Eighton Banks, where I'm from.

EDDIE GRAY: Right you are. It's Tuesday today so how about I see you right here at 3pm on Thursday.

JACKIE CHARLTON: Champion, Eddie.

NORMAN HUNTER: Aye, that's fine. Cheerio, Frank. Keep on training!

MICHAEL'S CLUB, NEWCASTLE UPON TYNE

Newcastle United's Fairs Cup celebration banquet is nearing its end and has become a more relaxed affair now that the meal is finished.
Some of the players, journalists and a small group of lucky fans are at the high tables near the bar as the rest of the room is prepared for live music and dancing. Some move between here and their wives who are enjoying themselves a few yards away, but the group continues to entertain each other with their best stories of the Fairs Cup. Now it's time for the away leg, beyond the Iron Curtain.

BAR MANAGER TO THE GROUP: Would anyone like any more coffee?
GIBBO: Thank you, but I don't think we need more coffee. How about something more Hungarian? How about that schnapps over there?
TONY BOULLEMIER: I don't suppose they have Doug's favourite red wine from Budapest, the Bull's Blood?
DOUG WEATHERALL: Oh, it's good that. I was drinking Bull's Blood after we left the stadium.
GIBBO: Well, I doubt we'll get much more than French Merlot here, so get ready for a peach schnapps, everyone.
We were drinking something like this at that party the Press lads went to the night before the game. Do you remember, boys? We'd been for drinks and nibbles at the British Embassy before piling into a couple of official cars and speeding off to a house party.
When we got out though, a pretty slip of a lass pulled us to one side and said:
'Just to let you know, it might be a good idea if we didn't discuss anything political or about the 1956 Uprising once we're inside.'

'*Why?*' we asked.

'*Well, we know the house is bugged, which means the Soviets will be listening in. We don't want to give them anything to latch on to, do we?*'

'*Bugged? Is that why we're talking in the street now, not in the car?*'

'*Oh, we know everything is bugged,*' came the reply, matter-of-factly. '*We sweep the place periodically, find the hidden recorders and get rid of them. Then they come along shortly afterwards and place listening devices somewhere different. It's a bit of a game really.*'

We could hardly drink our spirits for wondering what was behind the big pictures on the walls and at one stage, I discovered one of our lads staring wide-eyed at a huge mirror while bragging loud and clear about how Newcastle were going to stuff the Hungarians the next night. I bet that worried Moscow! **(chuckles all around)**

MALCOLM DIX: Well, back at home, it had been impossible to see Newcastle in the Fairs Cup when I was working down south, so I made it my business to get in touch with the BBC and speak to the producer of 'Sportsnight with Coleman', which went out on a Wednesday night. I asked him: '*Are you considering going across to cover the final 2nd leg in Hungary?*' to which he replied: '*Ummm, no, we'll probably just pick up the local stuff.*' I said: '*You do realise this is probably the only opportunity to cover the possibility of a British club winning something in Europe?*'

He hadn't, of course, but it got through to him and he assured me if they were going to do anything, they'd get back in touch.

A week before the game I was contacted by a very nice lady who said to me:

'*Mr Dix, I am ringing you in strict confidence to tell you that the highlights of the game will be broadcast on Wednesday 11th June but you mustn't tell anybody because that's the deal.*'

So I was straight on the phone to my mates in the North-East to tell them the match would be on!

I don't think the Press were even told until the day of the game. It was nice to know in advance it was going to happen.

VASSILIS KOUKOULIS: Good evening, everyone. I'm Vassilis from Athens and I'm studying Marine Engineering at Newcastle University. I captain the university team so I've played you guys in pre-season friendlies in the past couple of years. I'm a huge Newcastle fan so some friends and I hired a knackered minibus and found someone to drive it. We all piled into this old rustbucket and off we went to Hungary. It took us several days and it was as basic as it gets, I can tell you.

BOB MONCUR: Wait a minute. You did what? You went to Budapest in a minibus to watch us?

VASSILIS: Yes, Bob.

GIBBO: Crikey, I've heard everything now. That's superb.

BOB MONCUR: Let me shake your hand, young man. Incredible.

BENNY ARENTOFT: Wow! The things our fans'll do for us. Mind, I don't blame you actually. I hate flying.

PETER RATCLIFFE: Well, I can't quite match that, but here's my midnight story that Pop mentioned earlier. I flew with Pop's father-in-law Lennie and my pal David Macbeth.

FRANK CLARK: Oh, you mean David the singer? Local lad? I thought I recognised you, Peter. You were with us after the match in Budapest, weren't you? Yes, David's here tonight, by the way. He's going to do a turn later on, up on stage.

PETER RATCLIFFE: I did wonder if anyone would recognise me after all those drinks we had!

Yes, so David, Lennie and I went on this flight which took off from Newcastle after midnight. The interesting thing was that the chap who organised it was a Hungarian expatriate who was stuck in this country and wanted to go back home. He organised the plane and everything. Somehow, he had a connection with the people who had the planes, so the one we flew on turned out to be the first Russian jet ever to fly into Newcastle.

So this chap, probably in his 30s, came to Budapest with us and just stayed there – he wasn't on the return flight. I remember he even organised a very good exchange rate. The whole trip cost us around £41 but it was very word-of-mouth, you know. It wasn't well-advertised but there *was* a little bit in the paper.

GIBBO: I remember that being in the Chronicle, actually, because my neighbour and his daughter were thinking about going. The gentleman's name was something like a Mr D Bosnak and the company was called the Universal Travel Bureau in Gateshead.

PETER RATCLIFFE: That could be right. We were introduced to goulash and strudel before the match in some sort of hostelry. It was great. The locals were very hospitable. I was with Lennie and Dave and we got a special bus to the ground. You didn't want to go on too early but you certainly didn't want to miss the players coming out and giving them a cheer.

FRANK CLARK: The hotel was wonderful. I think it was on an island, Margaret Island. There were no distractions on the trip and everything went very smoothly, which it didn't always do for us. So organisation-wise, we'd have had no excuses had we lost. We didn't see much of the town though, did we?

DAVID CRAIG (smiling): Well I didn't see much. Even if I'd wanted to, you wouldn't have let me.

FRANK CLARK: We were fine where we were. We'd train and then we'd rest and then we'd eat and then we'd rest. I'm never one for doing any sightseeing if I'm there to play football. We went on a riverboat though. It was a very pleasant cruise down the Danube and a nice way to fill up an afternoon a day before the game. Occasionally I take my guitar on away trips but I certainly didn't on this one.

TONY RODGERS: As for Mick and I, as soon as we reached the final, we decided to go to the away leg in Budapest whatever the result of the home match. We'd booked to travel on the Official Newcastle United Supporters' Club trip and set about getting the necessary paperwork, because Hungary is very much part of the Communist Bloc and behind the Iron Curtain.

After the 3-0 victory in the first leg there was a big rush for tickets, but the Hungarian/Russian authorities would only grant us one British Caledonian charter flight. Following pressure from Newcastle United and the travel company Hunting Lambert, a second plane from the Russian airline Aeroflot was allowed, which is the one Peter and David were on. This second plane was arranged at such short notice that most of the fans travelling on it arrived in Budapest without visas, which led to much fun and games at the airport.

PETER RATCLIFFE: Ah, so this organiser who was returning to Hungary might have been 'persona non grata' after defecting earlier, so he may have seen a chance to capitalise on all the visa chaos by blending into the crowd while the airport staff were trying to set them on their way as soon as possible.

TONY RODGERS: You could be right there, Peter. Anyway, the itinerary for our trip consisted of a match ticket, all airport and match transfers, a city sight-seeing tour and two meals in the Hotel Astoria, one of the best in Budapest. The total cost including the return rail fare from London was £35. And my wages are only around £24 a week before deductions.

BOB MONCUR: So yours was a big effort to get there too.

TONY RODGERS: I suppose you could say that, Bob. On arrival in Budapest we checked in at the hotel and went for a stroll downtown to the 'Grey' Danube, then back for a meal and out for a few pre-match beers. We quickly discovered a huge difference in the prices of drinks. In a local bar with waitress service, a round of five draught beers cost less than one bottle in the hotel.

SPOW: We arrived in Budapest at around 2pm on matchday and in the lead-up I'd had to find some money to spend over there. So I visited some relations. My gran gave me a couple of quid, my sister too. And me mam.

I remember getting off that plane. My, it was hot. I had a combat jacket, scarves all over the place and a standard cine-camera.

Of course, we were in Eastern Europe now and you had these huge security people. There was this woman, six foot tall and she must have weighed 20 stone. She and a couple of the guards pinned me against the wall and I thought: 'Oh God! Here we go.' But soon I got the OK and we were off to the Astoria.

We had a couple of hours of free time so we walked towards the river. I remember on every corner there were guys in military uniform carrying guns. They were keeping an eye on us. We'd never seen anything like it. You'd move along a bit and then there was someone else looking at you. We were thinking: 'Bloody hell, you can get away with nowt round here.'

One of the lads was a bit concerned. *'Do you think they're gunning for us?'* So I replied: *'Let's sup up then and not stay to find out.'* So we returned to the Astoria for a drink and some goulash before the bus to the ground.

TONY RODGERS: When we boarded the coaches, everyone was in high spirits after the first leg and the beers we'd just had.

PETER RATCLIFFE: I remember we were driving parallel with a public service bus that came alongside ours, which had all the windows down because it was really warm. They were all giving the thumbs down saying we were going to lose and we were doing the opposite, obviously. It was all good-natured.

SPOW: Aye, but none of their fans ever came over to talk to us and I never saw any home fans in the city centre. We arrived there and someone asked: *'How many programmes are you gonna get, Spow?'*

I said: *'Well, I've got to get as many as I can.'*

I only got one in the end though. There were only these two or three kids selling them and they only had about 20 each, but there were 150 of us – three busloads.

One lad shouted: *'This guy's got one!'* so I bought it, but this other lad, he'd gone a bit further down the road and asked a seller for ten of them. He was handed a bundle, paid and came back but I said: *'What's all that underneath?'*

The seller had given this lad one official programme on top but a load of some kind of circulars underneath and then buggered off. The next thing you know, the lad's shouting:

*'F******, robbing b*****d! I've only got one programme but I paid for bloody ten!'*

I remember going in and sitting in the stand. There was only our plane run by the supporters club and another plane, so about 300 of us in total – 150 of us down one side of the stadium and another 150 behind the goal. We were undercover in the main stand, but all the way round the rest of the ground it was open to the elements.

A lad wondered what the score would be, to which I answered: *'Well, we're 3-0 up from the first leg so let's just keep it like that – I'll be happy with that.'*

JOHN McNAMEE: It was my birthday and the boss's birthday on matchday, don't forget. He was turning 51 and I was 28. The lads organised a birthday cake, so before we set off from the hotel for the match we lit the candles and the boss and I blew them out. That was the last we saw of the cake. When we got back intending to eat it, we found somebody had nicked it.

BOB MONCUR: It was June 11th; a hot, sweaty, balmy evening. I had to toss the coin in the dressing room with the other captain and the one who won the toss had the choice of going out and warming up first, because the teams didn't warm up together at the same time. I won the toss so we went out first, but we'd only been out there a few minutes when the sweat started pouring down us because it was so humid.

I thought: 'Stuff this. This is a waste of time', so I said: *'Right, lads, let's go back in.'* We go back in and Joe asks: *'What are you doing here?'*

I said: *'I've brought the lads back in because it's a waste of time going out there when we'll be knackered 'cos it's so hot and balmy.'*

So he says: *'Right, OK, fine. I'll go and have a look at the enemy then.'*
So out goes Joe, only to come back five minutes later:
*'F****** hell!'* he says.
'You want to see that lot out there. They're like rabbits. They're pinging balls and chasing things around at full speed. By, they've got some pace. Anyway, get stuck in, lads. Good luck.'
And off he went. We were like: *'Oh, thanks, gaffer!'*
One of the first things I used to do as the skipper was to run onto the pitch with the ball and make sure we all actually ran out. Not walk out but run, and the same after half-time. It was just my way of saying: *'Right, let's show a bit of intent here'* and I think the crowd liked it too because it showed we were up for the battle.
DAVID CRAIG: Újpest had been out on the pitch half an hour before the kick-off – we never did that; we just ran out ten minutes beforehand. They were out getting warmed up and I remember as we were coming out they were coming off to change their tops to their match jerseys and they were completely lathered in sweat. I'm not sure if their warm-up meant they were absolutely knackered later on but they blitzed us from the start. The captain, Göröcs... what a good player. And the left winger Zámbó too.
DOUG WEATHERALL: That first half of the return match had Újpest Dózsa playing some of the finest football I've ever seen. I was watching through my fingers as wave after wave of attacks took place and these names which hadn't stood out at St James' Park... God, they looked brilliant – especially Antal Dunai and Bene.
IVOR BROADIS: The match started at a feverish pace with every United player except Davies back inside the box to repel the opening Újpest attack. On ten minutes, Bánkuti hit a swerving left-footer that McFaul tipped around the post and a Bene-Göröcs-Ede Dunai move on the quarter-hour ended with Ede Dunai flashing in a 25-yarder that McFaul only just managed to tip onto the corner of the goalframe.

KISBOJTÁR BAR, BUDAPEST, 15TH JULY

It's mid-July and the Újpest Dózsa players and partners have come together to celebrate some recent birthdays amongst the squad.
They're at a small, almost-deserted, garden bar called Kisbojtár – 'The Little Shepherd' – where a young acoustic guitarist plays a mix of Western and Hungarian covers. Újpest defender Benö Káposzta's wife Gyöngyi befriends at the bar a young English woman, Elizabeth Hooper, who's been living in Budapest for a few months and is watching her friend Ernő Harasztos play the music. Gyöngyi invites her to come and sit with their group.
When it becomes apparent that most of the Újpest Dózsa squad is here, the conversation with football-loving Elizabeth soon turns to the team's recent European matches with English clubs Leeds United and now Newcastle United. During the interval, guitarist Ernő introduces himself and joins them. They're discussing the lead-up to the return leg of the final in Budapest.

FERENC 'FERI' BENE: The Hungarian national team had beaten Czechoslovakia and Ireland in World Cup qualifiers four days before each of the two legs of the final, but I felt the team wasn't together. The unease was neverending. We players from Újpest were resentful that others wouldn't accept that we're obviously now the best Hungarian club side.
Flórián Albert didn't really feel in tune with my game, nor me with his. The worst thing was the tension between us and Vasas striker János Farkas's clique, caused by the league title which we lost the previous year.
ERNŐ: Oh yes. When that a controversial end-of-season draw between Fradi and Vasas ensured Fradi won the championship instead of Dózsa. So this was the atmosphere in which you guys had to approach the second leg of the final against the English?

FERENC BENE: Yes. Nevertheless, our national squad members were actually there, sitting on benches placed on the running track because the stadium was so packed. And amongst these supporters were Fradi fans who cheered as much as they could for us to wipe out the three-goal deficit.

ZSOLT ZSENGELLÉR: It wasn't just a full house that evening. They put benches and chairs all around the pitch. I couldn't get to my normal place so I stood by the scoreboard in the standing sector because that was the only space I could find.

LÁSZLÓ FAZEKAS: It was packed again, just as it had been against Leeds. The truth is no one wants to play against English teams. We're not comfortable with the style of football they play. We like a technical, spectacular game, whereas they go in like crazy people. Even in the 89th minute, you can't tell if they're in a winning or losing position – they just play the same way all the time and that's totally different to the Eastern Europeans.

Leeds had been the title-holders and tournament favourites, a big name, but we coped with them and the fact we didn't concede any goals was a rarity for us in these kind of games.

Going into the second leg against Newcastle, having already shut out the English champions gave us some confidence. We started well and Feri here scored the first after about half an hour.

BENŐ KÁPOSZTA: Yes, some nice interplay and Feri did what Feri does. Even from a tight angle, he fired the ball low into the net at the near post.

LÁSZLÓ FAZEKAS: Then came our captain's goal a few minutes before the break. Two-nil.

JÁNOS GÖRÖCS (smiling): Yes, that was mine.

ERNŐ: Ah, I read that this one was really good. A slaloming run into the left side of the penalty box, outpacing defenders and then driving the ball low inside the post from close range. Is this one up there with your best ever goals?

JÁNOS GÖRÖCS (nodding appreciatively): I think so, yes. I scored the winner for Hungary against East Germany a few years ago which hit both posts on its way in. Perhaps that was my best goal.
LÁSZLÓ FAZEKAS: We'd just have needed Anti (Antal Dunai) to join in and score too…
PÉTER JUHÁSZ (one of Újpest's unused substitutes): We could have scored four in the first half, but we missed many chances. Just before half time, Anti looped a header from Sanyi Zámbó's cross towards an empty goal after the goalkeeper had come to challenge for it, but it bounced onto the crossbar and over. It was a huge chance.
EDE DUNAI: Yes, Anti did well to reach the ball before the keeper but he could only head it up and onto the woodwork.
JÁNOS GÖRÖCS: If that had gone in, it'd have been 3-3 on aggregate.
PÉTER JUHÁSZ: So there we were. Two-nil up at half-time. Stanley Rous brought the trophy to the dressing-room corridor. It was there, in my hands.
FERENC BENE: At half-time, we pleaded with the defence: *'Please really take care in front of our goal. Let's play in relaxed fashion because there's plenty of time to score another goal.'*
EDE DUNAI: Our coach Lajos Baróti never really said much: *'Kids, sit down, get your breath back.'*
PÉTER JUHÁSZ: This time though, he said we didn't need to panic – there will be more chances, there will be more chances.

MICHAEL'S CLUB, NEWCASTLE UPON TYNE, 15TH JULY 1969

BRYAN POP ROBSON: We were just chasing the ball around and the lads at the back had a job to contain things. Willie McFaul was having to deal with a lot of efforts on goal and we weren't getting

many touches. We were just chasing defenders and trying to stop them playing forward passes. They were moving the ball quickly though and their movement was fantastic.
They were using little angles which made it difficult to stop them – they weren't playing direct passes straight forward but little angled balls in. Bene always struck me as having good movement and good control. You could see these white shirts darting all over the place. How are you gonna stop it?
DAVID CRAIG: We learnt a lot from playing against European sides such as Újpest in this first half; if you dive in, you play into their hands. Frank and I at full-back have different ways of defending. He's tremendous at sticking his foot in and taking the ball from between a winger's feet. I can't do that. I try to keep my man going down the touchline, I wait until he starts to go past me, then I put in the tackle.
DOUG WEATHERALL: In the 29th minute, Ollie Burton was pulled up for one of the 20 fouls Newcastle gave away in the first half. They took a short free-kick and with some dazzling short passing engineered a break for their centre forward. He was at a difficult angle but he slotted the ball in well at the near post.
BENNY ARENTOFT: The second goal was from the guy I was playing against in midfield, Göröcs. He got the ball and he was bloody fast. I couldn't catch him. I thought I had him but he got the ball and he was going for goal. He ran inside and Craigy daren't touch him because he was already inside the penalty box, so he shot low and scored from six metres out.
SPOW: When they got the first, an old Újpest fan not far away from us was giving it some – kissing the tips of his fingers all together, then opening his hand into the air. I was thinking: 'Here we go.' And then they scored again just before half-time, at which point the old man turned around and offered us a lolly. Well, I told him: '*You can stick that up your arse, mate.*' The cheeky sod.

DAVID CRAIG: We got battered that first half, didn't we? Really hammered until half-time. It was 2-0 but it could easily have been five.
OLLIE BURTON: We were really having to defend but Willie was excellent. If it hadn't been for him, I think we'd have gone in more than a few down.
DOUG WEATHERALL: They were brilliant but so was Willie. Two down at half-time. The last thing imaginable at that stage was a Newcastle goal.
BRYAN POP ROBSON: We went in at half time at a loss as to how we were going to stop them. Joe doesn't have any great ideas tactically but he comes out with the statements. We were exhausted after chasing the ball without having any control or touches.
BOB MONCUR: So we'd come in and the sweat's dripping off us. I remembered when we trudged into the dressing room at home having gone 3-0 up in the first leg. The fans thought we were going to win it because there was no way we'd let three goals in. However, most of them weren't there – we were though – and I thought: 'Jesus, the punters will be amazed that we're going to give up a three-goal lead. We're gonna get beat here 'cos it's half-time and we're already 2-0 down.'
I was sat with a pool of sweat below me on the floor, it was dripping off me and my shirt and everyone else was the same. Absolutely sodden. Sat there. Silence. I remember saying to Clarky: *'If ever there's a time we need the gaffer to give us a lift, this is the hour.'*
But there was no sign of Joe. He was still trying to find our dressing room! The doors were like saloon doors in a cowboy film. Ker-bang! They finally burst open and in he comes. It was like John Wayne had entered with a cigarette in his hand. He looks around the room and asks:
'What's the problem?'
Nobody lifts their head.
'C'mon, what's the problem?'
I whisper to Clarky:

'Is he for real?'
For the third time:
'What's the problem?'
I snapped.
'I'll tell you the problem, boss. We're getting battered here and we don't know what to do about it. Craigy's getting screwed down the right, there are all sorts of things wrong – THAT'S the problem!'
He took the cigarette out of his mouth and replied:
'There is no problem.'
Some of the lads went *'Eh?'* 'cos they were like me. Thinking, the gaffer's gone a bit...
'There is no problem.' And a few of the heads looked up.
'What do you mean there's no problem?'
'All you've got to do is...'
'What's that, gaffer?'
'All you've got to do is go out there in the second half and score a goal.'
*'Score a f****** goal?'* I retorted. *'We've never been over the halfway line, never mind score a goal!'*
*'I'm telling you! That's all you've got to do. Score a goal and these foreigners'll collapse like a pack of f****** cards!*
*'Score a goal and these foreigners'll collapse like a pack of f****** cards!'*
*'Score a goal and these foreigners'll collapse like a pack of f****** cards!'*
He'd repeated it, probably twice more. *'And that's all you've got to do – now get out!'* So he left us and off he went. That was his teamtalk for half-time.
FRANK CLARK: I'm sure it made one or two think, who hadn't really thought about it, because we then had a brief discussion and one of the lads asked: *'What did he mean?'* because some of them didn't really understand the new away goals rule. So one of us said: *'Well, it's 'cos if we get one, they'll need to get another three, so five in total.'*

GIBBO: Meanwhile, Benny changed his boots. What made you do that, Benny?
BENNY: I just wasn't feeling right in them. But those boots I had in the second half, they were the golden boots. It was the best decision of my life!
TONY BOULLEMIER: Meanwhile, in the stands, 21-year-old Bill McLeod of West Denton couldn't stand the tension and went to listen to the second half radio commentary in a local bar.
And Bobby Cowell, who'd won the FA Cup three times with us in the 1950s, was also urged by certain fans to leave, because he kept saying he was a bad-luck charm. This time he plucked up the courage to stay put and what a great decision that was.
BOB MONCUR: So we go out again and what happens? We score a goal and they collapse like a pack of cards.
DAVID CRAIG: Absolutely prophetic from Joe.
SPOW: As soon as we scored, it became deafening where we were – we were jumping up and doon and then I was trying to work oot what we needed – it was now 4-2 but we had the away goal so they needed three more.
GIBBO: Go on, Bob. Indulge yourself. Tell us how you managed to hit that ball as sweetly as any striker in the world ever has. I mean, even the great Puskás would've been proud of that one.
BOB MONCUR: Ahh, go on then **(smiling).** Wyn forced a corner out on the left which Jackie Sinclair took. I'd just started to go up for deadball situations, hence the first goal against Újpest at St James' Park. Even so, going into that penalty area just after half-time in Budapest, I wasn't thinking 'Right, I'm going to hit this and score the goal which'll destroy them.' I didn't think anything like that at the time.
Anyway, the corner came over and was cleared to Jackie who swung it back in. I'd often practised volleying in the past so I'm pretty good with both left and right-foot volleys.

The ball came in and it was just slightly behind me but I thought: 'I can hit this – but I've got to keep it low.' I hit it beautifully and it rocketed in. There was a full-back on the line who tried to stop it but he couldn't 'cos I'd hit it like a rocket.

I look back now and think how all that training had suddenly paid off. I'm right-footed but I scored all three goals over the two legs with my left foot, so now everyone thinks I'm left-footed! **(chuckles all round)**.

TONY BOULLEMIER: Bob's goal in Budapest was the most crucial scored in Newcastle colours since the 1955 FA Cup final. It stopped Újpest dead in their tracks.

BOB MONCUR: Even when we'd got that goal and then we got another one fairly quickly, I remember running back to Clarky and asking: *'Frank, how many have they got to score to beat us?'* And him replying: *'I wouldn't worry about that now, Bob. We'll be fine.'*

TONY BOULLEMIER: I'm not just saying this because he's here next to me now, but in my opinion, Bob's the biggest single reason why we've won the Fairs Cup. He's a superb game reader with great positioning and marshalling of the defence and very impressive captaincy. Not to mention the small matter of those three goals in the final.

ALAN FOGGON: I don't know where he got these goals from. I still don't know!

JOHN CRAGGS: Bob's no-nonsense, with a never-say-die attitude that rubs off on the rest of us. The players always want to give 100 per cent but when they aren't playing well, Bob's able to stop them going into their shells. He's able to ensure they keep giving 100 per cent and he's able to keep everyone together.

JACKIE SINCLAIR: Aye, once Bob had belted in my cross just after half-time, I knew we were on our way to the victory lap.

FRANK CLARK: Bob's goal changed the whole context because they knew they had to score another three times and I could see it on their faces. It was as if someone had pricked a balloon – all the zest just drained out of them. You could sense it, you could see it.

They may also have run out of steam because they did so much running in the first half on a really hot night. I know they're more acclimatised to it than we were, but they'd put so much into that first half that when they found themselves, within a minute of the second period, at 2-1, it must have been a massive blow.

BRYAN POP ROBSON: They collapsed and we had total control. Once they'd conceded they knew the consequences. They'd put a massive press on from the start but it was really warm and we were gasping for breath. We were just chasing shadows but what happened at half-time and at the start of the second half totally changed the game.

GIBBO: Benny – it's your turn to tell us all how you scored. That was one mighty volley, wasn't it?

BENNY ARENTOFT (laughing): Gibbo, it was the golden boots. It started with their full-back slipping over and Jackie Sinclair taking the ball. Jackie played a high ball in, which was headed out to Jimmy Scott here. He took the ball down, dribbled towards the box on the right and shot.

Now when Jackie had stolen the ball, I'd come running out to him to play a one-two, so I was well outside the penalty area when I thought 'bloody hell, here comes a chance'. So as Jim Scott takes the ball inside and shoots against the back of one of their defenders, I run into the box. The ball loops up high in the air and it takes an age to come down, down, down. Every time I see it again in my mind, I'm sure I'm going to hit it over the bar.

But I didn't. I hit it just right. And from my new left boot, it arcs past the goalkeeper's left hand and slams into the right corner of the net. Every time I see it, I think: 'How could you score?' Because every time I see other players try it, they hit it high over the bar. I ran from the goal, shaking my arm like I was ringing a bell, all the way to the touchline. Everyone was off the bench... it was unbelievable.

It's the most important goal I've ever scored and it meant so much for the game. We were now level at 2-2 and 5-2 on aggregate. We felt we could play now and we had more space. Újpest had lost the feeling and didn't believe in themselves anymore.

SPOW: It's true. Benny got us the equaliser and that was it – we didn't need to work out the away goals anymore!

BRYAN POP ROBSON: They *were* finished by this point. They were dead on their feet because they'd worked their b*****ks off – even in the warm-up. It was so hot you didn't want to do too much because it felt like there wasn't much air around. They had started off absolutely flying and it had been scary, but now they were perhaps paying the price for their fast start.

FRANK CLARK: I have to say the last 20 minutes were among the most comfortable I've ever had on a football pitch. I love the lifestyle, the training and the camaradarie of being a footballer but I don't actually enjoy the 90 minutes of a match – it's too important.

I remember Foggon's goal more than anyone else's, when the game was virtually over.

WYN DAVIES: That's right. Willie kicked it long and I flicked it on. The idea was simple – I was there and the other two were running on to my knockdowns.

ALAN FOGGON: Joe probably said what he always says as I'm about to come on as a substitute, which is: *'Get the ball and run at them,'* so I did.

I've been on around ten minutes when Willie launches a goal-kick to Wyn who flicks it on, and it goes between two of their defenders. I get there first, head it down towards their goal and just keep on running. A defender tries to kick me but he misses, so I shoot.

The keeper does well. He knocks it high but only onto the bar and when it drops down, I'm there.

I stab it into the net on the half-volley with my left foot, get back on my feet and raise my arms just as Sinky jumps on me. Then the rest arrive. We'd won. Now it was just about waiting until the 90 minutes were up.

FRANK CLARK: It was typical Foggon galloping through like that, people trying to bring him down but him being very strong, hitting the bar and it coming down before he whacked it in. So yeah, I really enjoyed that last part. I knew the game was over and they couldn't possibly come back from that.

HARRY WATSON: And they knew as well?

FRANK CLARK: Yes, you could see it in their eyes.

BOB MONCUR: My wife Camille was there in the crowd that night with Willie's wife Eileen and a few others. She was sitting in front of a priest who accidentally hit her over the head with an umbrella. **(everyone winces but with a smile too, knowing it hadn't been serious)**

VASSILIS KOUKOULIS, who had travelled by minibus to Budapest: There were great moments at the end of the match but sadly we had to leave straight afterwards because of our tight schedule. We were rushed back to the bus – which we'd been sleeping in as well, by the way – and we set off. But the driver took a wrong turning and drove us all the way up to the Polish border.

There was all sorts of trouble there because we didn't have the necessary paperwork to take that route back home. And we missed all the celebrations back in Newcastle because we were still travelling across Europe.

WYN DAVIES comes back from the bar with a beer in his hand: Never mind though, eh? At least you could all talk about how this Újpest team had been full of Hungarian internationals, yet they became the only team we beat away from home. We hadn't won an away game. We'd only drawn or lost our away legs.

VASSILIS: That's all true, Wyn. By the way, how were you with your fractured cheekbone?

WYN DAVIES: OK, thanks. Obviously I'd had this cheekbone problem so I never got involved with the goalkeeper over there or anything like I'd normally have done. I suppose I got away with it in a way. Personally, I'd like to say it's been an honour to play with you lads this season. I did get a bit emotional at the final whistle, I can tell you.

Singer David Macbeth strolls up to everyone, having finished preparations for his short performance that evening.

DAVID MACBETH: I can personally vouch for that, Wyn!
FRANK CLARK: Hello, Dave. Nice to see you.

The singer shakes the hands of Peter Ratcliffe, Pop, Wyn and a few others he knows well there.

DAVID MACBETH: You too, gentlemen. So, Peter, Lennie and I actually got onto the pitch at the end. How did we we do that again, Peter?
PETER RATCLIFFE: Well, it was a long night but I remember the three of us clambered over this fence while soldiers with Kalashnikovs shouted at us: *'Don't come! No! No!'*
We just shouted: *'We're coming!'* and jumped down onto the pitch.
DAVID MACBETH: That's right. So I went over to where Wyn, Bob and Craigy were. You all looked at each other and with your arms around me, Wyn, you shouted at the top of your voice: *'We've done it! WE'VE EFF-ING DONE IT!'* **(Everyone laughs).**
PETER RATCLIFFE: I made a beeline to Pop and we really did jump for joy. Then we started running around the pitch and waving to everybody on the lap of honour. Suddenly, Pop and I slipped and we both fell into a long-jump pit. We were just so happy at winning that we hadn't been looking where we were going.
BOB MONCUR: I remember doing the lap of honour and the Hungarians were great. They were actually applauding us and the

stadium was still quite full. They hadn't all deserted it. As we were going around, someone jumped on my back. I said: *'F****** hell! Get off!'* And it was Camille!

Eventually we got back into the dressing room but Joe wasn't there as he was still making his way through the crowds. Eventually, in he walks like John Wayne again. The doors crack open and he says:

'What did I tell you?'

True story. Brilliant man-management. A bluff... call it what you like, but he was spot on. He must have known that it was a bluff as well because it seemed there was no way we were going to score a goal. We did though and he was proved right. They collapsed like a pack of cards.

PETER RATCLIFFE: We went to the dressing room and a side room where David started a sing-song and we opened the box of champagne Lord Westwood had brought from England – just in case. Benny Arentoft and myself were next to each other and we ended up sitting on the floor under this high table sipping the chairman's champagne.

The champagne was probably an afterthought by the chairman but we certainly sorted it out – it flowed quite nicely.

FRANK CLARK: We'd won 6-2 on aggregate against a team which by common consent was the best team in Europe. It was a battering but really it bore no resemblance to the relative quality of the two teams.

GIBBO: Knowing that the Hungary national team, which was full of Újpest Dózsa players, had played tough World Cup qualifers against Czechoslovakia and Ireland four days before both legs, do you reckon this could have helped them to stay in the match groove and start so quickly? Or do you think this may it have counted against them towards the ends of the matches?

FRANK CLARK: That's a hard one, Gibbo. Only they will know. It could have gone either way, but only they'll know.

KISBOJTÁR BAR, BUDAPEST, 15TH JULY

GEBAY (a Dózsa fan who knows the players well): I stayed right until the very end. I waited and cried as the Newcastle players ran past me with the Cup. Their fans had constantly been twirling their black and white scarves and chanting loudly. Mind, we'd been loud too.

ANTAL 'MISI' SZENTMIHÁLYI: It was very unlucky. We made mistakes which you simply can't make. We had a great opportunity to wipe out the deficit after the first leg but Anti's header just before half time didn't go in.

ERNŐ: A couple of weeks ago I read that Lajos Baróti said: *'Newcastle beat us in the air. Whoever paid attention to them will have seen that they don't just head the ball but they link up together in the air.'* Was there more to it though, especially in the second period?

JÁNOS GÖRÖCS: Unfortunately we were out of it in the second half. We conceded such stupid goals. They weren't even chances which they *created*. They came from deflections and the like.

ANTAL DUNAI: We started the second half with the referee mistakenly thinking Solymosi had kicked the ball out for a corner, when in fact it came off their player. Misi then came out for the corner and it ended up in the net.

ANTAL SZENTMIHÁLYI: Pixi was arguing with the referee about the corner though. OK, it was debatable, but these can be given.

PÉTER JUHÁSZ: I know he's not here tonight but honestly Pixi's slow. He was a great defender in the past and he has a fearsome free-kick, but if he's the last man nowadays…

FERENC BENE: I'm convinced that we'd achieve even more on the international stage if the authorities would simply allow Lajos Szűcs or Miklós Pancsics to sign for us from Ferencváros.

ANDRÁS TÓTH: If they'd sign, it's almost certain that we'd reach two or three European Cup finals, at least.

ANTAL SZENTMIHÁLYI: We'd win one of them too.
ELIZABETH: Sorry, I don't understand. Why can't you sign them?
ERNŐ: There's no transfer market allowed here under Communism. If a player is to move clubs, both clubs need to agree he can leave. If a player wants to leave but his current club refuses him permission, he must serve a one-year suspension from all football-related activities. Therefore, hardly any players change clubs nowadays and it's almost impossible for a team to add top-class Hungarian talent to its ranks, because no club wants to allow their best players to leave or strengthen their rivals.
SÁNDOR ZÁMBÓ: I'm very sorry that we haven't won a European trophy so far, because it's within the team's capablities to do it. We have the materials to do it because we've a forward line that could play for foreign clubs.
ERNŐ: You mean if they'd be allowed to play abroad by the authorities? Yes, it's fair to say there'd be plenty of top-class suitors for you guys.
FERENC BENE: The English took that wonderful trophy out from under our noses and away from Megyeri út. I don't know if we'll ever be as close again to European success as we were on that evening.
JÁNOS GÖRÖCS: Me neither. The Fairs Cup final loss to Newcastle is in the top three most painful memories of my career.
FERENC BENE: However, it's no accident that under your captaincy we've reached the final of the Fairs Cup and the Central-European Cup. The Fairs Cup silver medal I've got still means a lot to me because I really think the field of teams was strongest in this competition.

MICHAEL'S CLUB, NEWCASTLE UPON TYNE

BOB MONCUR: One thing I do remember about the Hungarians after the game is that there was no antipathy. They just said that they'd given it a good go but the best team had won on the night.

TONY RODGERS: The Újpest fans were generous in their applause and accepted that the better team had won. Although the home fans were friendly, one did run off with my scarf. I gave chase and persuaded him to give it back, which he did with a smile and a handshake.
JIM SCOTT: As fans, what was your best moment in the whole Cup run?
SPOW: Seeing you lift the trophy. Without a doubt.
GIBBO: After the match, Sir Stanley Rous said: *'It was a great match and at 2-0 I wasn't counting on this, but Newcaste have been a revolution for football. I can't quite believe that I've handed Moncur the Cup.'*
FRANK CLARK: The celebrations were amazing. We were running around the pitch with the Cup and all of a sudden Bob's wife Camille and some friends appeared on the track beside us. They were running around with us, together with lots of other supporters.
It was obviously absolute bedlam in the dressing room. David Macbeth was in, Gibbo was in, Bob Cass was in, Dougie Weatherall and the other Press lads. We were very close with the Press lads by then because they all went on the trips and we have a good relationship with them. It was quite possible that the entire North-East Press contingent was in that dressing room.
GIBBO: On my way down I turned the corner and there was Benny on the phone, still in his full strip with sweat pouring down his face. He nodded, looking a bit sheepish as I disappeared through the door and a short while later, Benny came back in. It turns out he was working for a Danish newspaper and filing a report on the final!
BENNY ARENTOFT: Actually, Gibbo, I was on the phone to my good friend Flemming Nielsen, the former Denmark and Atalanta player who is now Sports Editor at the 'Politiken' newspaper. Denmark were playing Hungary in a World Cup qualifier less than four days later so I was giving him my report on the many Újpest players who would play in Copenhagen and how best to try and stop them. I said: 'Don't fear them, because they aren't as good as they think they are'. It might have helped, because Denmark won 3-2.

DOUG WEATHERALL: I got into the dressing room and I remember Joe Harvey gave me the biggest bearhug ever – to this day, I can almost feel it. It was a joyful, wonderful place to be.

FRANK CLARK: The Press were enjoying it every bit as much as we were because it was good for them as well, of course. It'd have been a long time since they'd experienced anything like that. I'm not much of a drinker, but I had a glass or two.

BOB MONCUR: So then we went back to a hotel and the Fairs Cup committee was there and we were given champagne and something to eat. Then we had to get our trophies 'cos you didn't get them at the stadium. You got the Cup but you had to get your little trophies later. Someone said *you've* got to go and get them. I said '*What about the lads?*' I was told I had to get them all. So off I went, got a trayful of trophies and handed them out. Then, we went back to our own hotel where the Press boys were.

FRANK CLARK: Back in the hotel Bob Cass and I did some mean rock and roll medleys. He was actually on the bench during the match. Typical Bob. When he got to the stadium he didn't have a ticket or pass for the Press box. Joe saw him wandering about outside and so he brought him in and let him sit on the subs' bench. That's one of Bob's biggest claims to fame.

SPOW: We got the supporters' bus back to the hotel and then a couple of busloads of us went up to the Citadella where there was organised entertainment and a few drinks – wine I think, although I'm not a wine drinker.

PETER RATCLIFFE: When we heard where the team was staying some of us decided to go over in a taxi.

TONY RODGERS: After the game, Mick and I joined Bill McEwan and Alan Robinson, the chairman and secretary of the supporters' club and a couple of others and we took taxis to the players' hotel, hoping to see them arrive with the trophy.

A few other fans were there and about 12-15 of us sat round a table and beers were ordered. A waitress arrived with the drinks and put down the bill. A fat chap in an expensive-looking leather jacket picked it up and said: '*That comes to about £5 – that's not bad.*' And he paid it. Now £5 was a lot of money in those days. A pint of beer in England cost about 2 shillings (10 pence).

There was no way any of us could afford a round so we sat sipping our drinks wondering what to do next. I asked Alan Robinson who our fat friend was. '*He's a flash b*****d – he's a season ticket holder,*' I was told. News then came through that the players had gone to an official reception so we decided to go back into town and ordered two taxis. Just as the taxis arrived, so did our coach party. They'd been to a winetasting. We told them the players weren't coming and were about to board the coaches when a member of the hotel staff said we had to pay for the taxis. Quick as a flash, Alan Robinson told them the fat man in the leather jacket, now at the bar on his own, had ordered them and that he would pay.

Back in town we ended up in a nightclub. We were shown to a table on which were placed two bowls of peanuts. We ordered beers but the manager insisted we should have champagne to celebrate the Newcastle victory. An argument took place – we wanted beer but the manager said champagne only. Fearing we would be conned we decided to leave, but they wouldn't let us out until we'd paid the cloakroom attendant for the peanuts!

By now it was getting late and we found a basement bar where a small band was playing. More Geordies arrived and we soon had the band accompanying us to the Blaydon Races, other North East tunes and various football songs. '*No-el No-el, No-el No-el, Wyn is the King of New-cassell.*' And '*He's here, he's there, he's every f****** where, McNamee, McNamee*'. Plus '*Frank Clark knew my father*' and a few others.

As always when alcohol takes effect, people who can sing and some who only think they can sing take the microphone. One lady, after giving a rousing performance, suddenly turned round and was sick

The Newcastle United delegation celebrate with the Fairs Cup on the banks of the Danube (photo courtesy of Wyn Davies)

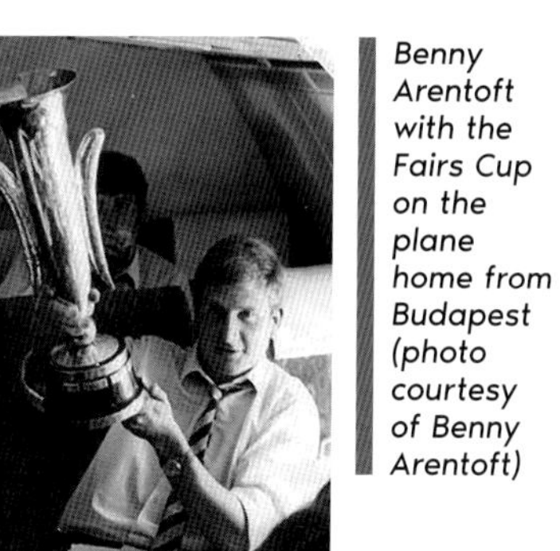

Benny Arentoft with the Fairs Cup on the plane home from Budapest (photo courtesy of Benny Arentoft)

Newcastle United captain Bob Moncur (left), manager Joe Harvey (right) and director Stan Seymour show off the Fairs Cup the morning after the final in Budapest (photo by Gyula Kovács)

Club captain Bob Moncur celebrates Fairs Cup victory with manager Joe Harvey and the Newcastle United directors on the plane home (Mirrorpix)

Newcastle United players display the Fairs Cup on their open-top bus from the airport to St James' Park (Mirrorpix)

Fans at St James' Park greet the bus carrying the trophy and the Newcastle United players from the airport (Peter Robinson/PA Images)

Bob Moncur holds aloft the Fairs Cup outside St James' Park (Peter Robinson/PA Images)

A fan holds up a huge Newcastle United rosette at the trophy parade (Peter Robinson/PA Images)

Bob Moncur shows off the Fairs Cup on the pitch at a packed St James' Park (photo with kind permission of Newcastle United FC)

Fans applaud the players as they greet
the St James' Park crowd after Fairs Cup victory
(Peter Robinson/PA Images)

It's Jim Scott's turn to hold the Fairs Cup as the United manager and players do a lap of honour at a packed St James' Park (photo with kind permission of Newcastle United FC)

Wyn Davies surrounded by fans on the pitch at a packed St James' Park (photo with kind permission of Newcastle United FC)

Willie McFaul holds up the Fairs Cup as the players walk around the St James' Park pitch in front of their adoring fans (photo with kind permission of Newcastle United FC)

Wyn Davies is hugged by a joyful fan as a policeman watches on (Mirrorpix)

Alan Foggon and Tommy Gibb parading the Cup (Mirrorpix)

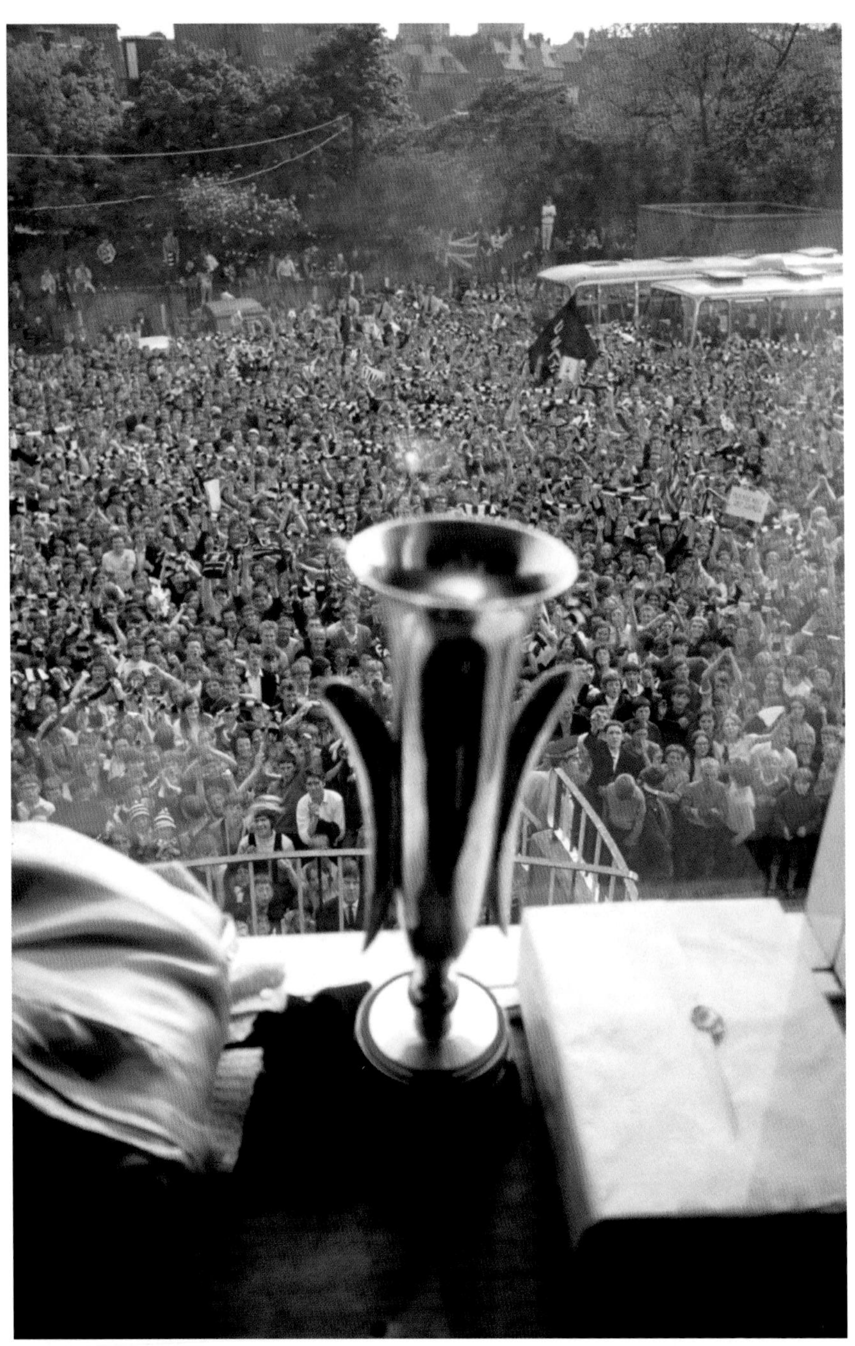

The crowd which Wyn Davies was looking out on from a St James' Park boardroom window (Peter Robinson/PA Images)

Wyn Davies thanks the Newcastle fans from the St James' Park boardroom window with the Fairs Cup trohy in his arms (Peter Robinson/PA Images)

Newcastle United team photo on the St James' Park pitch after the Fairs Cup trophy parade (Peter Robinson/PA Images)

Spow kisses the Fairs Cup at the Mayfair Club in Newcastle Upon Tyne. Above the trophies are the official match pennants given by Newcastle United's opponents

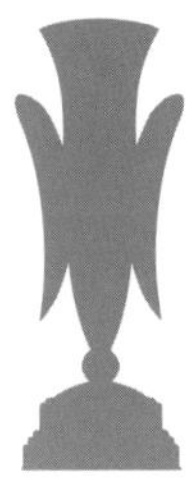

into the ice bucket at an adjoining table. I think that got a bigger cheer than the song.

We finally stepped outside as dawn was breaking. We thought about taking a stroll but decided enough was enough. BED was calling.

Later that morning after the beer, the duty-free spirits from our rooms and about 25 cigarettes, my mouth was like the bottom of a bird cage. I felt severely dehydrated and drank about 10 glasses of fruit juice and three pots of tea with breakfast. There was no way I could face a two-hour sightseeing tour of the city so after some packing, we went down to the banks of the Danube for a few beers before setting off to the airport.

The only disappointment was that the team had left on an earlier flight so by the time we arrived back, we'd missed the victory parade and presentation of the Fairs Cup to a packed St James' Park.

SPOW: After the game, we went to the Citadella until about 1am, where there was gypsy music and big bottles of wine. One lad said: *'Howay, Spow, we've been invited to the players' hotel. It's on an island in the middle of the Danube.'* So off we went. But when we got there, they said we couldn't come in so we went back at our hotel.

I still had my combat jacket on and all my scarves and there was nightclub downstairs. Everyone got in but me. The lad on the door said: *'Nah, not with that stuff on.'* I was like: *'Ah come on, all my mates are in there!'* but he wasn't having it. That's all I had with me so I was going back upstairs when I saw another guy heading up. So I asked: *'Can I borrow your jacket and give it back in the morning? They won't let me in with me combat jacket.'*

He said: *'Aye, go on then,'* so I went back downstairs and got through, didn't I? Of course, as soon as I was in, I just took this coat off. There were a couple of supporters' club members in there, Bill McEwan and Alan Robinson.

Now, I used to like Black Velvet, which was Mackeson or Guinness with cider. And a lad said: *'Do you like champagne, Spow?'*
'You must be joking,' I replied. *'I've never touched the stuff.'*
Well, it turns out a real Black Velvet is Guinness or Mackies with champagne. The next thing you know, there's a bottle of champagne in front of us and luckily the bar had a couple of bottles of Mackeson too. So I had two Black Velvets made with the real recipe and we eventually got to bed about 6 o'clock in the morning.
BOB MONCUR: So we went to the evening event back at our hotel but the directors didn't come. On the way out they said: *'Get the boys some champagne and put it on the bill – but not the French champagne; the Hungarian stuff.'*
Oh. Cheers!
So we had a great night. All the Press boys were back. There was a big, long table and we had a bite to eat. Then Dougie Weatherall says: *'Let's have a sing-song.'*
David Macbeth was there. He got up on the table and started us off and he was absolutely brilliant.
He got us all going and then we said we've got to have a singer from the Press and a singer from the players. The first person to get up from the Press was Tony Boullemier here. I was sitting next to Bob Cass who said: *'You'll like this, you'll have a laugh.'* So we're all like, *'OK, what's all this then? Is he a great singer?'*
So he gets up, giving it the big licks, singing 'House of the Rising Sun'. And he was absolutely dreadful! What we didn't know is that Tony's tone-deaf but he was singing this song in front of the Press boys and the lads and their wives – 'cos they were invited back too – and we were all in tears. But he was actually serious! Tony's a nice lad and he's famous for that now. His singing is hopeless but it was ever so funny.
JOHN CRAGGS: I roomed with Benny Arentoft on that trip and afterwards, because of all the champagne, Benny had to help me into our room.

JIM SCOTT: I don't think we ever got to our beds that night. It was certainly something to remember.
GIBBO: Dave, this is a bit of a leftfield question but your tasks are often only serious, so personally, what was your funniest moment of the campaign?
DAVE SMITH: Oh, there were so many. I remember our second match against Feyenoord. We had a player go down and they thought people were dropping down injured and that we'd told them to do it to waste time. But we never did anything like that. One of our players went down, away over on the far side.
Because I was the trainer and coach, I did the treatment of injuries as well so I picked up my bag and was running on when two of their players saw me. They thought we were wasting time so they picked me up by the arms, turned me round and ran off with me back to the touchline. So when Frank Clark got injured and Jim Iley had to come on, I got carried off by two of their players **(everyone laughs)**.
On Joe, I think he just has that knack, I don't know how – of getting players to a higher level. I suppose it's no surprise that I think of winning the Fairs Cup as my biggest achievement.
TONY BOULLEMIER: Dave, coaches aren't often recognised enough but I'd like to take this opportunity in front of everyone before the dancing starts to say you're a lovely fellow and an absolutely vital part of the team. As coach and tactician, you slot in very well with Joe, whose big strengths are spotting good players and motivating them. You're very chirpy and your nickname of 'The Mynah Bird' because you hardly ever stop talking, is one of my favourites. Your banter keeps everyone smiling and I expect, behind the scenes, this and your shrewd tactics have been priceless.
DAVE SMITH: Thank you, Tony. That's really nice of you.
BOB MONCUR: The Fairs Cup side of 1968/69 is a great *team* without any great superstars. There are good players like Wyn and

Pop, good wingers, a good back five and we all play for each other. We've no cliques. A few of the lads like Wyn and Tommy Gibb like to go to the races while me, Clarky, Craigy, Pop and Willie, go golfing. But on the pitch it's all for one and one for all. Absolutely no doubt about that. It was a fantastic team spirit this year, lads. So, a toast, everyone! To winning the Fairs Cup! **(there's a huge cheer)**.

The celebratory banquet's original guests head to the bar for more drinks and start to move onto the dance floor. Arthur Noutch gathers the fans who've been lucky enough to spend a while with their heroes, reminiscing about the epic final. Now it's time for them to head home.

ARTHUR NOUTCH: Well, gentlemen, did you enjoy that?

PETER RATCLIFFE: I'm sure I speak for everyone when I say we're extremely grateful. It was wonderful.

Bill Gibbs, Harry Watson, Peter Donaghy, Spow, Vassilis, Mick and Tony Rodgers and Malcolm Dix all nod in agreement.

ARTHUR NOUTCH: Very good, I'm glad to hear it. Have a safe journey home and see you at the football soon!

ON NORTHUMBERLAND STREET

HARRY WATSON: Wow. I've absolutely no words to describe what just happened there.

PETER DONAGHY: We're not going to forget that in a hurry, that's for sure.

MALCOLM DIX: I think we all owe Peter Ratcliffe a drink or two the next time we're out, eh? Right. I'm off to the Haymarket to get my bus.

SPOW: My last one from Haymarket will have gone so I'll walk down and get the bus from Worswick Street instead.
BILL GIBBS: Alreet, Spow. Mind how you go. Canny night, mind, eh? See you for the Hull game on August 2nd. Morden Street for the bus at 08:30, reet?
SPOW (still buzzing): Aye, that'll dee. Cheerio, lads.

Spow strolls down to the dimly-lit Worswick Street bus station. The bus is also dark and quite full. He sits next to a tall, burly chap in his mid-20s in a zipped-up coat with a peaked cap pulled down to partially conceal his face, and a white duffle bag on his lap.

SPOW: Evening.
YOUNG CHAP: Evening.

The bus driver starts the engine and it pulls out of the station.

SPOW (bursting to talk to someone about his good luck): You'll never guess what an evening I've had.
YOUNG CHAP (from under his cap, smiling to himself and ready to humour this young lad): Oh aye? How's that then?
SPOW: I was with me mates and a couple of them have contacts at the football club so we ended up with all the Newcastle United players celebrating the Fairs Cup.
YOUNG CHAP: That must have made you happy.
SPOW (looking ahead, still a bit in his own world): Oh aye, well, it was just such a surprise. I'm Arthur, by the way, but me mates call me Spow. What's yours?
YOUNG CHAP: Norman. Nice to meet you.
SPOW: Do you follow the lads then?

YOUNG CHAP: Oh aye. I'm a Geordie and Newcastle's my team. I went there a couple of times but I didn't like being amongst the big crowds. The crowds were huge then. If we kids were late getting there, we'd have to tie our money in a handkerchief and stick it in our pocket for our bus fare. Then the crowd would pick you up and pass you over their heads all the way down and put you right at the front.
SPOW: When was that, like?
YOUNG CHAP: The days of Jackie Milburn and Jimmy Scoular. What I remember about Jimmy was the size of his legs. A good player, mind you. Bobby Mitchell, Ronnie Simpson in goal, Bob Stokoe, George Hannah, the Robledo brothers, Len White at centre-forward – he was a good player. Little guy, quick, scored a lot of goals.
SPOW: Well, we've got Pop now who scores a lot too. What do you think of him?
NORMAN: Pop's a good player – a good goalscorer, doesn't make a fuss. Very quiet lad.
SPOW: Oh aye, do you know him like?
NORMAN: Oh, just in passing. Did you see him tonight?
SPOW: Aye, one of my mates is his pal. Crackin' night. Mind I was in Budapest yer knaa, for the final as well. Best night of me life. We beat the best team in Europe that night, you know.
NORMAN: Aye, maybe. I know a few who'd disagree with that, but either way, when you look at it, the Fairs Cup is as hard a competition as the European Cup. It's good.

The bus pulls into Gateshead bus station.

SPOW: You really think so? Have you been to many matches, like?
NORMAN: Aye, a few. I work down in Leeds now so I go to the match there. This where I get off, Spow. Nice to have met you.
SPOW: Alreet, Norm. You too. Mind how you go.

Norman stands upright, steps off the dark bus and heads to the taxi rank. Spow ponders over the Leeds United crest on Norman's duffle bag as it disappears into the distance.

'Naaahhh. It can't be...'

Shaking his head, Spow settles back in his seat.

CELEBRATION DAY

THE NEWCASTLE-SOUTH SHIELDS BUS, 15TH JULY 1969

Spow lies back in his seat on the darkened bus taking him home to South Shields after a fabulous evening of nostalgia with his pals and his heroes. Now he remembers how the day after the match began to unfold.

I woke up in the Astoria at about 8am. I'd only just crashed into bed a couple of hours previous, so I might even still have been in my clothes from the night before. I took a shower and headed down for breakfast. There, they tell me: *'Mind, you look rough, Spow.'* To which I reply: *'I'm not surprised – I drank everything there was, including champagne in Black Velvet.'*

Anyway, we had a sightseeing tour arranged so off we went to the national stadium, the Népstadion, at around 10am. We returned for 1pm, grabbed something to eat and then went to the airport. We missed the parade and all that because the players had arrived back before we'd even taken off.

MICHAEL'S CLUB, NEWCASTLE UPON TYNE, 15TH JULY 1969

Some of the players and journalists take a break from dancing to finish off the Fairs Cup story. It's Celebration Day on Tyneside as the heroes return home.

BENNY ARENTOFT: We went to bed late, or should I say early in the morning. We'd had a lot to drink. I can't even remember breakfast. I was sure we stayed in the hotel until leaving for the airport but there's a photo taken somewhere where we all look merry. There's also one of us on the banks of the Danube with the trophy, all in suits.

DOUG WEATHERALL: It was great fun on the plane – more drink and more fun.

GIBBO: And a mile high up, we remembered that fan, Jim Bowden from Winlaton, whom Rupert Morters had written about in the Daily Mirror. At the start of last season Jim put half a crown on Newcastle to win the Fairs Cup at odds of 1,000-1. Now he's £125 richer.

DAVE SMITH: I remember coming down to land and there was fog and the plane kept on going lower and lower. We thought, bloody hell, until we broke through the cloud at what seemed a hundred feet off the ground. And of course, crowds were lining the road back to St James' Park and we had a wonderful reception. It was a lovely time.

JIM SCOTT: It was eight miles from the airport to St James' Park and there were people lined up all the way. It was a red hot day, a lovely day, and the reception we got was unbelievable. We never really thought about it until we stepped off the plane. We were expecting maybe two or three hundred people but there were thousands. I think there were about 20 or 30,000 in St James' Park. You don't realise how important the game of football is until you're here. Newcastle is a footballing city.

BOB MONCUR: We flew back with a few sore heads and there's a picture somewhere of me on the plane – it wasn't a Dakota but an

Elizabethan or something like that – with the Cup and Joe Harvey, Fenton Braithwaite and Stan Seymour. Now, when we got back we're still thinking – or at least I am anyway – that yes, we've done well in winning this Cup. But I hadn't realised just how significant it is.

We were coming back on a Thursday afternoon so there'd be no one at the airport – they'd all be at work. We're about to land when Joe comes up to me and says: *'You've got to go out first with the Cup.'* I said: *'You're kidding, aren't you?'* He says: *'No, you've got to go out with the Cup first.'*

I said, all embarrassed: *'I'm not doing that.'* Then Lord Westwood intervened: *'Well, we think it's a good idea you should go out first,'* to which I replied: *'Aye, OK, alright then.'*

So, I've got the trophy and they open the door... and the *ROARRR!* There were hundreds of people there. And I was thinking: 'Just don't fall down the steps!'

The road was lined with people and when we got on the bus it was a single-decker because the road from Newcastle to Woolsington has a low bridge at Kenton Bank Foot. It couldn't take a double-decker, when really you'd want one with an open-top, wouldn't you?

So we're going through Woolsington with people waving on the streets and we come to this bridge. What they'd done on the bus was they'd opened the big sunroof and put a table on the seats so we could stand and show the trophy outside. Suddenly, there was a bang...

ZAPP!

What was that???

We'd hit an overhead electric wire! There was a black burn mark on the Cup because of it and I'd been standing on that wooden table, which may have saved me.

Then, we drove down Barrack Road and you could see there were 40,000 people inside the Leazes End and the Main Stand on a Thursday afternoon! There were no tickets or anything. It was just *'the boys are coming back'* and they piled in. It was fantastic!

When the bus parked, there's a great photograph in the car park with me, John McNamee and Willie McFaul holding the Cup, coming into the stadium through the gate. Then we had to get out and go up the steps. Joe gave a short speech and sang the Blaydon Races while we were in the stand and after that, we were on the pitch singing songs. I can't remember how long it lasted but quite a while. Then I went for a television interview with Mike Neville.

BENNY ARENTOFT: It was hectic, unbelievably hectic. It's funny when I think about sleeping on the flight home, I only remember the bus coming out of the airport and there being lots of people the whole way into town. Everybody so very happy. It was fantastic at the stadium. The whole pitch was full of people and the stands were full of people. You wouldn't believe the welcome we got. I feel, thinking back, that it went too quickly.

I have a photo of when I come walking onto the pitch and Wyn Davies follows me on. And some photos in the stand with Joe Harvey.

GIBBO: That young lad Bill, who was one of the fans with us just now, said he'd been in the Leazes End one minute and was then swept across the field right underneath where the players came out to hold up the trophy. Before that, when you lads were coming around in front of the terraces to hold up the Cup, apparently you could hear a chant of: '*What about the Leazes?*' So whoever was holding the Cup at that point held it up towards the Leazes and there was an almighty roar.

BENNY ARENTOFT: I was supposed to go home because I had tickets to go on holiday to Denmark and we were late. We only had three weeks' holiday and had to return by the middle of July for pre-season training, so there wasn't much time.

However, we did go to the boardroom to have a drink and finish it in the right way. It wasn't like today when there are celebrations and everything is arranged. This was all purely spontaneous. Fans just saying to themselves: '*When the players come home, we'll be there.*'

It was just a great feeling. The club was going to invite us and our wives to a celebration dinner straightaway but I think that was postponed until tonight because everybody was going on holiday.

JOHN McNAMEE: I have very happy memories of the Fairs Cup, not least that fantastic welcome from thousands of Geordies.

JACKIE SINCLAIR: Aye, John, I was really knocked out by the welcome when we came home from Budapest. It was a fitting climax to a quite extraordinary season.

GEOFF ALLEN: It was an absolutely fantastic experience because this was what the Geordie public wanted. People in Newcastle were saying: *'We've won a European competition? Bloody hell! Marvellous!'* When we put those jerseys on, you could see no one was going to let the fans down and that's how we all felt. And we didn't. We frightened the rest to death.

JOHN CRAGGS: It was unbelievable. The roads from the airport were lined with people and the ground was choc-a-bloc.

BRYAN POP ROBSON: You want to win things but you want the fans to enjoy what you're doing and they certainly supported us home and away. It is a fantastic time to be in Newcastle.

BOB MONCUR: Coming down Barrack Road and seeing all the fans celebrating was fantastic. OK, we'd walked into the competition through the back door, but we sure walked out of the front door with the Cup in our hands.

GIBBO: You certainly did that, Bob. **(turning to Frank Clark)** Frank, what does the Fairs Cup mean to you?

FRANK CLARK: A hell of a lot, really. It's fantastic in its own right. An incredible achievement and a real thrill for me. I'd like to think I've never been cowed by the occasion. I always tried to play the game and not the occasion.

WYN DAVIES: It was tremendous, you know. Even in my wallet now, I've got a photo of us going around St James' Park with the trophy. Mind you, straight after that, I was into hospital for an operation on the cheekbone that was fractured here in the first leg of the final.

FRANK CLARK: It's a massive boost for the club, the city and the area and obviously for the players it was a fantastic experience. It's put me in the running for the World Cup next year in Mexico, although I won't be surprised if I don't get into the provisional squad of 40 because there are one or two very good left-backs around. Still, it's put a few of us into the spotlight a bit more.

GIBBO: My next door neighbour took his daughter Angie to the trophy parade, which of course she absolutely loved. On the way, she asked: '*Will we win a trophy every year, Daddy?*' He told her that unfortunately, it doesn't quite work like that.

JOHN CRAGGS: The fans and the players get on well, as we've seen tonight. They treat you as a normal person, so it's great for the fans that the club has won this trophy. The players love the supporters and the fans know we give 100 per cent. Winning the trophy is a present for them because they really deserve it. Of course, the players wanted to win it for personal pride but definitely for the fans too.

GIBBO: Now lads, you may be wondering who this young man is here next to me. This is Peter Robinson, who's a rising star in the photography world. He's photographed many famous rock and pop bands around today and he worked at the Mexico Olympics last year. Peter was actually one of the few photographers present on the St James' Park pitch for your parade of the Fairs Cup trophy.

FRANK: Ah, interesting. I'm sorry if we weren't at our prettiest at that point. It had been a long couple of days. **(smiles all round)**

GIBBO: Peter, firstly, here's another beer, to top you up. Secondly, what was it like working on that day up here, during one of our biggest moments?

PETER ROBINSON: Thanks John, and thanks for the invitation too. I work for the *Football League Review* magazine and when I drove across from Lancashire that morning there were already plenty of fans milling around outside St James'. There was no actual plan to the shots – maybe there should have been. Some were shot in black and white and some in colour, but what made me make those decisions, I don't know.

The *Football League Review* performs a different function to newspapers or *Shoot* or *Match* magazine, so my job as one of their photographers is be intimate with the players and get images to make the magazine stand out.

There's a picture of Wyn with the trophy looking out onto the crowd. That's the kind of picture I enjoyed taking – it has an intimacy. It's the sort of picture a newspaper wouldn't bother with because they wouldn't want any ambiguity. They'd want one of him with the Cup on his head pulling a funny expression.

I took that picture without really knowing what I was doing. I was almost working from understanding the moment without being conscious of it. I just took a picture that worked but I didn't know its significance.

There is another thing though as a photographer, I like the look of Wyn physically. He doesn't look like a normal player. And I like shooting players in a context which is not necessarily the one you expect.

To the average fan, he's on the field playing and that's it. Anything else is irrelevant. They only see the player on the field in his shirt. Well, on this day, none of the Newcastle fottball players are in their shirts, that's for sure. They're in a context which is not normal and I'm having to give the pictures a connection to football.

In terms of arranging the team photo, I would have gone to someone I knew like Joe Harvey and asked permission to get the picture. There's no other way of doing it – I have to ask someone who can tell the rest what to do.

It was never mentioned about taking off their suits and putting on a strip – I was just happy to get any picture at all!

I walked over and told them where I wanted them to stand. Had I been more careful, I'd have removed that hosepipe lying to the right of them. I just took what I could with the time I had and took the photos on a five inch by four inch positive transparency on a quaintly-named Press Camera. They only took two pictures. Picture 1 is the one that you've seen that's been published but the other one is of the squad not looking as happy.

I'm always very welcome here and it's always a fabulous drive here, which puts you in a good frame of mind to go to Newcastle, this amazing city with great people. My father was a football fan. His heart was with Bishop Auckland, where was from, but he liked football in general, preferably played by teams from the North East and especially Newcastle United. And as soon as I got back home I rang my father and told him all about it. Anything that touches on his region, I always pick up the phone and tell him.

I'm a big fan of the Animals and I shoot that band a hell of a lot. They're great to be around, particularly Chas. There's a lot of positivity about Newcastle and I like the fact it's out on a limb and making its own way.

Another thing that's positive is this being a victory abroad, against foreign opposition. Last year I was working at the Olympic Games in Mexico and next year I'll be going to the World Cup there too – I'll be FIFA's official photographer.

Whether there's any relevance in this or not, I don't know, but Hungary is a fantastic country and has tremendous depth in terms of its visually creative people, photographers, film directors and cameramen. Some of the greatest film directors and photographers in the world are Hungarian.

I've always had quite an interesting feeling about Hungary too, so for the team to have gone to Budapest to play a Hungarian team and to have lifted the Cup there is amazing. Also, like everyone, I used to be interested in the Hungary team of 1954.

I suppose the biggest football match I've covered until this point is the 1968 Olympic final last year, which Hungary actually won. Four of those players I photographed then were ones that Newcastle have just beaten now – László Fazekas, Antal Dunai, Ernő Noskó and substitute László Nagy.

I have a real affinity with Newcastle. It gives me a big buzz when I walk down from the town centre towards the river and the road drops dramatically and there's a road overhead. Amazing!

The city centre has far more energy than London has ever had for me. This past decade has seen all these bands emerge from northern cities like Newcastle, Liverpool and Manchester.

So photographing the parade wasn't just another job. I didn't just get in the car, drive there and go 'flash, bang, wallop', as I would have done if I'd been going to, say, Manchester. This was Newcastle.

It was a very positive job I had to do on that day and it wouldn't have been treated with the same reverence if it had been in a different city. I know it wouldn't.

It was Newcastle. I like Newcastle, love Newcastle and that was it. I didn't have to think about it. This was something special.

GIBBO: Thank you, Peter.

FRANK CLARK: Fascinating that, Peter. A really unique insight. And if it's Wyn Davies you like, then this is your moment:

Frank turns to some of his teammates a few yards away

Hey, lads, look at this! Wyn's getting up to sing!

(turning back) He never normally sings, Peter. That's why I'm so surprised.

The resident backing band start to play Buddy Holly's 'It Doesn't Matter Anymore' and Wyn absolutely brings the house down with his performance.

'There you go and baby, here am I
Well, you left me here so I could sit and cry
Well golly gee, what have you done to me
Well I guess it doesn't matter anymore'

Wyn's comes off to great applause and heads over to his date for the evening, Angela, the nurse who looked after him in hospital recently.
Later, Frank asks him what persuaded him to get up on stage.

WYN DAVIES: Well, there was a competition to come up to the stage and sing a song, you see, with a teddy bear as a prize. So I said to Angela – and I don't know why I said it – but I said: *'I'll win this for you.'* And damn me, I went up and they gave me this mic, so I started singing. And sure enough, I won it and I gave it to her!
GIBBO: It's Wyn by name, Win by nature for you these days, isn't it?
(everyone smiles).

SOUTH SHIELDS, 15TH JULY 1969

Spow has just got off the last bus and is reminiscing to himself about his return from Budapest after the famous final. He's walking the short walk home.

I remember, when we got back I went down the Magpie Club for a few drinks and then we decided to come down to the Bridge. And I asked: *'You haven't got a bottle of champagne, have you? I'd like to share it with these lads.'*
'You're joking though, aren't you, Spow? Have you got the money?' I held out my hands and said:
'I've got this much left.'

'Give us it here, Spow.'

I don't know how much it was, maybe a couple of quid, but the lads are good. They said: *'Hey, don't worry, we'll have a whipround.'*

I think I got the last bus home and I remember walking up the darkened street. I was exhausted. And me mam was waiting outside the house – just as she always is when I'm not home before the last bus. She sees me coming and she's halfway down the path to meet me. We have a cat called Topsy and she's dressed it up in black and white – it has black and white ribbons all over it!

When I was almost within touching distance she broke into a smile – you know, that special relieved one a parent always has when their child comes home from a big adventure:

'How are you?'

'Bloody brilliant, Mam!'

'That's good, pet. You must be really pleased for them winning the Cup.'

'I am, but I'm knackered too, like.'

'You must be, love. Come on. Let's get you inside.'

And with that, the door clicked shut.

EPILOGUE

This epilogue is simply designed as a home for some of the stories I heard during the making of this book, which I was unable to find a place for in earlier chapters. They're interesting nonetheless and I hope you enjoy them. And we finish with a few words from our Fairs Cup-winning captain.

A CONVERSATION WITH WYN DAVIES ABOUT HIS REAL NAME BOLTON, 30TH OCTOBER 2018

ME: Wyn, is it true your first name is actually Ronald?
WYN: Look at this. Have a read – it's my birth certificate.
ME: It says Roland! It's not even Ronald!
WYN: My Dad wanted to call me Donald but my Mum said: *'No, we're not having that – they'll be calling him Donald Duck!'* I didn't know that until 12 months ago. With Roland, you can put an 's' at the end and it would sound Welsh, see?
Even though it was thought then that my first name was Ronald, I was always just Wyn. My song wouldn't have worked as well either, would it? *You've not seen nothing like the Mighty Ron!*

Interestingly, the first name of Wyn's clubmate and fellow Wales international Ollie Burton, isn't Ollie or even Oliver, but Alwyn. Burton was Newcastle United's first-ever substitute in a competitive match and the first-ever Magpie to score a competitive goal as a substitute.

Újpest Dózsa central defender Ernő Solymosi had a interesting change of career after giving up football. He became the personal bodyguard of János Kádár, the Communist leader of Hungary from 1956 to 1988.

Antal Dunai's brother János (also known as Dunai I in the Hungarian sports media) gained a modicum of revenge for their family when he came on as a late substitute and scored the fourth penalty for Pécsi Dózsa in the penalty shootout, which knocked Newcastle United out of the 1970/71 European Fairs Cup at the second-round stage.

Eddie Gray's 15-year-old brother Frank, who featured in chapters 4 and 6, signed for Leeds in 1972 and was the team's left back in the 1975 European Cup final loss against Bayern Munich.
In 1979, one of our Fairs Cup heroes, Frank Clark, won the European Cup in his final appearance in professional football before being replaced that summer by Frank Gray on the left side of Nottingham Forest's defence. Gray helped Forest to retain the European Cup in 1980 by beating Kevin Keegan's Hamburg 1-0.

In the Fairs Cup first round first leg against Newcastle in September 1968, Feyenoord found Wyn Davies' heading ability and his flick-ons for teammates caused their flat four-man defence untold problems. So Rinus Isräel and Wim van Hanegem decided that Rinus would step back into a sweeper role, to be the libero, and the team would play more of a 1-3-3-3 formation.

This is how it was in the 2nd leg in Rotterdam, where Feyenoord won 2-0, and for the rest of the season they only lost one more match in winning the Dutch league and cup. The following year, still using Rinus as a sweeper, Feyenoord swept all before them in winning the European Cup.

Soon, the Netherlands national team started to use Rinus in the same way, often as a sweeper in some of the more physically-demanding matches (Arie Haan would often fill this role in other games). This formed part of the overall strategy that took the Netherlands all the way to the final of the 1974 World Cup.

In the 1970s, the Dutch national team and Dutch club Ajax became known as pioneers of Total Football, an attractive, fluid style of play developed by head coach Rinus Michels and star forward Johan Cruyff, in which adaptable players would quickly switch positions according to the match situation.

Real Zaragoza's goalkeeper in the Fairs Cup 3rd round first leg and the first half-an-hour of the second leg, Nieves, was later on the same Spanish coaching course in Albacete as Newcastle United manager Rafael Benítez.

One of the dangers of the 1960s was a career-ending knee injury. Geoff Allen's career was ended prematurely by a cruciate ligament injury just weeks after his match-winning display against Feyenoord.

Similarly, Real Zaragoza's Miguel Ángel Bustillo impressed many Geordies during their Fairs Cup 3rd round tie, but his time at the top level was cruelly ended when he suffered broken ligaments in his knee, meniscus damage and a rupture to his anterior cruciate ligament. This happened during his Barcelona debut against Real Madrid in 'El Clasico', in the opening match of the 1969/70 season. The Catalans had gone 2-0 up inside seven minutes, Bustillo scoring both goals.

Furthermore, the legendary captain of Újpest Dózsa, János Göröcs, was also to find that the end of his elite-level career was unexpectedly near. A serious knee injury playing for Hungary against Austria in September 1970 was the start of 18 months on the sidelines and after just five more games in the lilac-and-white shirt, the midfield maestro moved to provincial club Tatabánya, where he made 23 more league appearances and won two Central-European Cups before retiring at the age of 35.

Who said being knocked out by Newcastle United wasn't terminal? Apart from Újpest Dózsa, every other opponent of Newcastle during the 1968/69 Fairs Cup experienced a change of manager at the end of the season.

So just how resilient were Joe Harvey's men? Well, of the 13 goals conceded in 12 games, only five came in the second half and only two in the last 20 minutes of matches.

Moreover, every one of Newcastle United's six opponents found themselves at a point in the second half of their second leg when they simply needed to score one or two more goals without conceding to force extra-time or knock out United. None of them managed to do it.

And just how strong was this tournament? The following year's European Cup quarter-final lineup featured FIVE teams from the 1968/69 Fairs Cup. Three of these reached the semi-finals and the winner of the European Cup in 1970 was Feyenoord, whom Newcastle United had knocked out in the first round.

In 2006, one of the fans featured in this book, Bill Gibbs, founded The Fairs Club, an organisation which initially included some of those fans lucky enough to follow Newcastle United's first season in Europe and which, via reunions and personal visits, pays tribute to United's heroes of the past, especially those who played in the Fairs Cup. Others involved at the start included David Gibbs, Bill McNaughton, Arthur 'Spow' Spowart, Paddy Donaghue, Brian Wilkinson, Dave Thompson, David Nicholson Dave Johnson and Eddie Hedley. Nowadays, Bill Gibbs and Harry Watson run the club's events and the Evening Chronicle's John Gibson is the club's president.

THE IMPORTANCE OF THE FAIRS CUP REFLECTIONS BY BOB MONCUR

I didn't realise how important winning the Fairs Cup was. I didn't know how it was for the fans because I was still a player, doing my job, going out and playing. I'd say the right things to the camera about how great it was for the fans but I didn't really know. It's only since I've sat in the stands and watched the passion for the last 20 years or more that I've begun to understand.

It was a massive adventure and as it's turned out it's now a historical thing 50 years on. Who would ever have thought that we wouldn't win anything else since then?

The club should have moved on from there. They had the base of a good side. They should have built on that but as it so happens, they didn't. It was a good team that won the Fairs Cup and then we got Jimmy Smith too. Maybe they should have invested a bit more to make the team even better.

I don't know if anyone can teach the Newcastle fans very much because they know so much. I suppose in fairness to the directors we were in the Fairs Cup the following year and then again the year after that, so I suppose they were trying to build. The problem's always been that it's very difficult to keep all your best players at Newcastle because sadly there are other places people want to go and there are bigger teams than Newcastle United.

Not bigger-supported teams, by the way, but just ones like certain London teams and the Manchester clubs, which are just a bit bigger and where any good player would want to play. That's why you lose your Gascoignes and your Waddles. They all want to play at the top level, myself included. I suppose in our day it was a bit different. I just didn't want to leave the North-East.

I could have gone to Derby when Cloughie was there. He wanted me. At one time Arsenal were interested, but I wasn't interested in leaving the North-East because I had my family here.

Nowadays it's bit different with travel being easier. It was a nightmare going abroad in the old days. Now you can just jump on a plane and you're there so you could easily play abroad, couldn't you?

'The last man to pick up a trophy for Newcastle United.' If I hear that one more time, I'll swing for someone! But sadly it's a fact. I don't like it when they say it in front of younger players. I don't think it inspires them.

Modern players and their agents have their own agendas now and to be fair, when we won the Fairs Cup we didn't know how important it was to the fans. It's only after all these years that we've realised.

The fact that we were getting full houses at St James' Park should have told me that at the time. I mean the fans were queuing up to buy tickets. It was these fans that made me, that made me famous and I never get fed up of talking with them – they paid our wages and made us what we are.

Mind you, I'd never have thought the memory of the Fairs Cup would last this long. Who knows how long it will go on for?

NEWCASTLE UNITED APPEARANCES-MAKERS IN THE 1968/69 INTER-CITIES FAIRS CUP

(number of substitute appearances in brackets)
Twelve (12) : Bryan 'Pop' Robson, Wyn Davies, Frank Clark, Jim Scott, Tommy Gibb, Willie McFaul
Eleven (11): Ollie Burton
Ten: (10): Bob Moncur
Nine (9): David Craig
Eight (8): Alan Foggon: 6 (2)
Six (6): Jackie Sinclair: 4 (2)
Four (4): Preben Arentoft, John McNamee 3 (1), Keith Dyson: 3 (1)
Three (3): Dave Elliott, John Craggs
Two (2): Geoff Allen
One (1): Tot Winstanley, Arthur Horsfield
One substitute appearance: Ron Guthrie, Jim Iley, Albert Bennett

NEWCASTLE UNITED GOALSCORERS IN THE 1968/69 INTER-CITIES FAIRS CUP

Six: Bryan 'Pop' Robson
Four: Wyn Davies, Jim Scott
Three: Bob Moncur, Tommy Gibb
Two: Alan Foggon
One: Jackie Sinclair, Preben Arentoft

NEWCASTLE UNITED'S ASSISTS IN THE 1968/69 INTER-CITIES FAIRS CUP*

Five: Wyn Davies – Feyenoord (h), Sporting (h), Rangers (h), Újpest Dózsa (h+a)
Four: Bryan 'Pop' Robson – Sporting (a), Real Zaragoza (h), Vitória Setubal x2 (h)
Three: Jim Scott – Feyenoord x2 (h), Újpest Dózsa (a); Tommy Gibb – Real Zaragoza x2 (a), Rangers (h)
Two: Frank Clark – Vitória Setubal (h+a); Preben Arentoft – Újpest Dózsa x2 (h)
One: Jackie Sinclair – Újpest Dózsa (a); Alan Foggon – Real Zaragoza (h); Geoff Allen – Feyenoord (h); John Craggs – Vitória Setubal (h);
No assist – Vitória Setubal (h)

**Working out assists has been contentious over the years. Here, an assist is given to the last Newcastle United player to have touched the ball before the goalscorer. The only exception to this is if an opponent makes a significant and intentional touch on the ball, which changes the likelihood of who would score.*
Therefore, Jim Scott's shot in Budapest was accidentally deflected far away to Benny Arentoft who scored, so Scott still gets the assist. Alan Foggon followed up his own shot to score in Budapest after the keeper saved it, so the assist remains with Wyn Davies after his earlier flick-on.
However, Bryan Pop Robson's first goal against Vitória Setubal came from an intended clearance by Vitoria defender Carrico, so this is the only instance where there is no assist. I know it's debatable but at least you know how I've worked it out.

RECOMMENDED READING

In addition to those books noted in the bibliography, for Newcastle United, you'll never go wrong if you pick up a book by club's perceptive and thorough historian Paul Joannou; I particularly liked 'Pioneers of the North' on the early days of football in the region and have recently been reading his latest work, 'To the Glory of God', on Newcastle United during the First World War. I enjoyed Martin Hardy's book on Kevin Keegan's Entertainers, 'Touching Distance' and if I look further back on a regional level, Arthur Appleton's 'Hotbed of Soccer' was one of my early favourites.

Looking beyond the North-East, almost anything by Jonathan Wilson is going to be worthwhile reading. 'Inverting the Pyramid', a history of tactics, is, in its own way, a modern football classic; 'Behind the Curtain' introduced me to fabulous stories from outside Hungary but still in Eastern Europe; and his latest project may be his best yet, a book chronicling the extraordinary feats of Hungary's footballing pioneers in the early and mid 20th century, some of whom genuinely revolutionised the game around the world until or despite harrowing experiences and personal tragedy.

Another writer whose work you may also enjoy is Rory Smith, 'Mister' being one book I learnt a lot from, specifically on how English coaches once exported football around the world. Finally, I'd be silly not to mention another book I've worked on, György Szöllősi's biography on Hungarian legend Ferenc Puskás, published in 2015 by Back Page Press. A prolific goalscorer with Honvéd, Real Madrid and Hungary, Puskás has an incredible story and there's lots to be learnt from his 23-year career as an elite footballer about life and reinvention.

BIBLIOGRAPHY

ONLINE SOURCES:

www.mlsz.hu; www.uefa.com; www.nufc.co.uk; www.nufc.com; www.zerozero.pt; www.worldfootball.net; www.nso.hu; www.puskas.com; www.magyarfutball.hu; www.ujpestfc.hu; www.toon1892.com; www.11v11.com; www.mightyleeds.co.uk; www.arcanum.hu

The Animals – lyrics to 'The House of the Rising Sun' on page 12 courtesy of: Lyrics0007, https://www.lyrics007.com/the+animals+Lyrics/the+house+of+the+rising+sun+Lyrics.html
Buddy Holly – lyrics to 'It Doesn't Matter Anymore' written by Paul Anka on page 258 courtesy of AZ Lyrics:
https://www.azlyrics.com/lyrics/buddyholly/itdoesntmatteranymore.html

BOOKS:

The Grand Tour –Newcastle United's Adventures in Europe, Paul Joannou, 2006
The Complete Results and Line-ups of the European Fairs Cup 1955-1971 – Romeo Ionescu, 2003
Black & White and Red All Over – Frank Clark, The Autobiography, 2018
The Newcastle United Story – John Gibson, 1969
The Newcastle United Story 2 – John Gibson, 1970
The Gibbo Files – John Gibson, 2014
United We Stand – Bob Moncur with John Gibson, 1970
Cult Heroes – Dylan Younger, 2006
The Damned United – David Peace, 2006
Newcastle United, The 1968/69 Fairs Cup Story – Jim Jeffrey, 2009 (I was particularly indebted to this book for how it gave me a platform to try something different rather than just repeat the largely excellent work done already by Jim)

Ferike, a Góleádor – István Zsiday, 1984
Újpest futballtörténete 1885-125-2010 – Tibor Kocsis, 2010
11 Újpesti Legenda – Ede Dunai Junior, 2017
Baróti – Attila Tóth-Szenesi, 2004
Kapitányságom Története… Baróti Lajos – György Lepies, 1984
A Magyar Labdarúgás Története IV – Szocialista Profizmus (1967-1986): Tamás Dénes, Mihály Sándor, Éva B. Bába, 2015
Az Újpesti Aranycsapat – László Hetyei, 2015
Titi – Göröcs János, a varázsló – Károly Lakat T., 2017

NEWSPAPERS AND PUBLICATIONS:

Our Fabulous Fairs Cup – by the Newcastle players who won it, 1969
Newcastle United FC Official Brochure, 1969
The six official Newcastle United programmes from the 1968/69 Fairs Cup home matches
In terms of background reading and reporters' quotes, I'd like to thank British national newspapers such as The Daily Telegraph, The Times, The Daily Express, The Sunday Express, The Sun, The Daily Mirror, The Scotsman, the News of the World and the Daily Mail, as well as local newspapers: Newcastle Evening Chronicle, The Newcastle Journal, The Sunday Sun, The Northern Echo, The Sunderland Echo, the Glasgow Evening Times, the Yorkshire Evening Post, the Shields Gazette and The Pink. I'd also like to thank foreign newspapers such as the De Telegraaf, Rotterdamsch Nieuwsblad, Algemeen Dagblad, Nieuwe Rotterdamsche Courant, Heraldo de Aragon, Népszava, Népsport (now Nemzeti Sport), Képes Sport, Labdarúgás, Népszabadság and Magyar Nemzet.

ACKNOWLEDGEMENTS

I'd like to thank all the many interviewees I've had the pleasure of meeting during my research for this book, including almost every surviving member of the Newcastle United and Újpest Dózsa squads, United first-team coach Dave Smith and many former players from their opponents en route to the final.
In addition, I am indebted to the following kind people:

My wife, my parents and all my family

The clubs featured in this book including: Newcastle United, Újpest Dózsa, Vitória Setúbal, Real Zaragoza, Sporting Clube de Portugal, Göztepe and Hamburger SV.

John Gibson
Tony Boullemier
Doug Weatherall
Bill Gibbs
Harry Watson
Angie Stanger-Leathes
Arthur Spowart
The Fairs Club
Peter Robinson
György Szöllősi
Márton Dinnyés
Ken Harvey
Urs Meier
Mustafa Kalkandelen
Mark Hannen
Paul Joannou
Mike Bolam
John Helm
Roger Tames
Barbara Hooper
Daniel Harasztos
István Harasztos
Emil Lindegaard
Niels Bøving
Ilias Faratzis
Austin Fagan

Peter Donaghy
Paul Donaghy
Frank Starforth
Ken Roddam
John Allan
Peter Ratcliffe
Tony Rodgers
Harry Lambert
Will Walshe
Mark Rogers
Sgt Ashwell
Chris & Michael Dobson
Ian Dart
John Derrick
Jesse van de Woestijne
Mikos Gouka
Heike Bult
Joel Meijer
Mark Vullings
Vasco B. Campos
Henrique Albuquerque
Canário
Miguel Gay
Luis Fando
Fran Diaz
Miguel Laporte

Mapi Rodríguez Molina
João Roque
Andrew Clark
Mark Tansey
James Koukoulis
Lyn Koukoulis
Anthony Britton
István Zámbó
Gusztáv Mravik
József Bazsánt
János Váczi & parents
Gergely Kovács
Zsolt Zsengellér
Gyula Márton
Gábor Borsche
Imre Lelkes
Ernő Bostyán
Andrea Mayer
Dénes Eglesz
Tamás Dénes
Ede Dunai junior
Chris Emmerson of
Toon Legends Club
Newcastle United
Supporters' Club
(London)

THE AUTHOR IS A KEEN COLLECTOR OF VINTAGE FOOTBALL MEMORABILIA RELATING TO NEWCASTLE UNITED AND HUNGARIAN FOOTBALL.

If you might have any such items from this period or earlier, such as early photographs, programmes or Fairs Cup match ticket stubs, please send an email to **amazingfairscup@gmail.com** and Matthew will be delighted to discuss them with you.